Improving The Outside Of Your Home

Improving The Outside Of Your Home

Joseph F. Schram

Structures Publishing Co. 1978
Farmington, Mich. 48024

Manufactured in the United States of America

Book edited by Shirley Horowitz

Cover photo courtesy of Western Wood Products Assn.

Book Design by Carey Ferchland, Typographic Insight, Ltd.

Current Printing (last digit)
10 9 8 7 6 5 4 3 2 1

Structures Publishing Co.
Box 423
Farmington, Mich. 48024

The remarkable setting on the cover of this book was created by Alex Pierce, AIA, Portland, who relied heavily on the use of western woods for all home surfaces and the deck-firepit constructed of 2 x 4 Douglas fir. (Photo: Western Wood Products Association.)

Library of Congress Cataloging in Publication Data

Schram, Joseph F
    Improving the outside of your home.

    Includes index.
    1. Dwellings—Remodeling.   I. Title.
TH4816.S283   643'.7   77-28008
ISBN 0-912336-64-1
ISBN 0-912336-65-X pbk.

CONTENTS

Decorative entry doors such as these insulated steel units by Jim Walter Corporation help embellish the front of a home. Note how both in-ground and hanging plants are used to soften the brick expanse.

1. Entryways

A home's front door can say a lot about the family living there. The entrance may be cold and forbidding, or it can offer a welcome even before the door is opened.

If your home entrance doesn't have the desired personality, you can change it. But first consider the entranceway, the approach, the planting, the lighting, the walkways, the overhang or porch setting, sidelights, columns and other decorative elements. They should blend together as one setting, of course, in keeping with the overall architectural design of your home.

Doors

Few remodeling projects can make as dramatic an impact as the relatively simple job of hanging a new panel door in the frame of an existing entranceway.

Designers suggest that the best way to decorate with doors is to let the front entry "key" the door design. This also is known as "architectural continuity" and it often may make or break the effect sought by the homeowner.

Homeowners who admire the uncluttered look of Colonial or Federal architecture can now duplicate the classic design with either wood or metal-clad door assemblies that are factory-made yet contain the look of fine hand-crafted detailing.

Stock panel doors sold by local retail lumber dealers have anywhere from 2 to 32 panels, glazed for light and visibility, or solid construction for complete privacy. Among the most popular designs now being used for both new construction and remodeling are:

- Colonial six-panel Cross-and-Bible, in which four upper panels form a cross and the two lower panels depict an open book
- St. Andrew's Cross, with wood panels or glass panes set above an X-shaped cross. This design is often used for Dutch doors which, though rarely used inside a house, make a handsome back or side entrance. In Dutch doors, the top and bottom halves operate separately
- Eight-panel Florentine doors
- Fifteen-panel Tudor doors
- Three-panel contemporary; the panels are large squares, deeply-grooved, and set vertically down the center of the door
- Mediterranean, multi-paneled, often with elaborate carving, rich embossing and exotic-looking grillwork

This protected entry features a classic Cross-and-Bible design for stile-and-rail doors with stock fluted surround and two matching design columns. (Photo: Western Wood Products Assn.)

7

All of these doors can be purchased for single—or double-door entries that provide the popular wide opening for modern entry halls. Companion sidelights (fixed or opening), columns, fanlights, pediments and other decorative accessories also are offered. The sidelights range from plain glass and straight-angle surrounds, to elaborate Early American fanlights with massive pediment heads and reeded pilasters.

Today's doors are among the finest ever made. Wood units can be solid, hand-carved models or manufactured units offering the same fine detailing. They are treated at the factory with a chemical preservative to provide long-lasting protection against the elements and can easily be weatherstripped to keep out drafts. Since wood does not readily conduct heat, these entryways are also good insulators. Sidelights can be obtained with double-pane insulating glass.

Highly engineered steel entry doors greatly resemble wood designs and feature a core of insulating polystyrene foam. The doors are guaranteed not to warp, twist, swell or shrink and can be finish-painted at the factory in a choice of several hundred colors or painted any color at the job. Several brands of steel entry doors boast 2½ times better insulating value than solid-core wood doors, thus eliminating the need for storm doors in cold climates.

Wood and steel entry doors come in standard 6 ft. 8 in. and 7 ft. heights and in single door widths of 2 ft. 4 in., 2 ft. 6 in., 2 ft. 8 in., 3 ft., 3 ft. 6 in., and 3 ft. 8 in. Double-door widths are 5 ft., 5 ft. 4 in., and 6 ft. Door thicknesses generally are 1⅜ or 1¾ in. Special sizes may be ordered both from local millwork firms and national manufacturers.

Installation

Replacement of existing entrance doors usually permits usage of the existing door frame, but if this is weathered or damaged, you may wish to select a complete pre-hung package with steel or wood frame that replaces the entire assembly. Such packaged units are fully weatherstripped, predrilled for entry lockset and relatively simple to set in place.

Quality wood-panel doors of ponderosa pine also are easy to install. These doors, when supplied unfinished, come with untrimmed side rails which stick out about a half-inch beyond the top and bottom rails. Trim these first to achieve a flush and

Changing an entry door oftentimes can be a simple matter of removing the existing unit, frame and all, and replacing it with a fully-packaged unit. This steel entrance system by Steelcraft Manufacturing Company even has the lockset in place.

Homeowners can choose from a wide variety of richly carved wood doors and raised panel doors in patterns that blend with the architectural styling of the home. These Chateau doors by Simpson Timber Co. are 1¾ in. thick, with stiles, rails and mullions of select vertical grain, kiln-dried hemlock.

A Different
Entry Look

These specially designed replacement doors for home entrances are Perma-Door units by Steelcraft. The doors are designed to fit into existing wood frames and utilize existing interior trim. Applied wood stops are supplied with factory-installed weatherstripping, and are attached to the frame after the door is hung; they are then adjusted to the door to assure a complete seal.

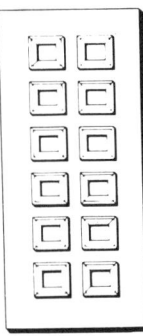

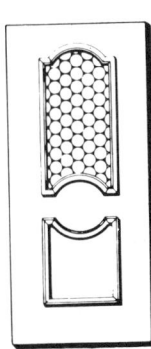

Installing a Pre-hung Entry Door

1. Remove Old Door

A. Carefully remove interior trim.
B. Remove old door.
C. Remove old hinges, strike plate and sill.
D. Clean floor of all dirt and caulking.

NOTE:
Be careful not to damage interior trim. It must be re-installed after installation is complete (See Step #9).

2. Install Unit

A. Do not remove retainer straps at this time.
B. Place door unit into existing opening.
C. If threshold of unit hits existing frame, notch existing frame so that the entire unit fits into opening.

Notch stop of existing frame for threshold as required.

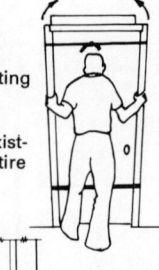

3. Secure Unit

A. Secure door unit into opening by nailing with 6 underlay nails, frame is pre-drilled for nailing.
B. Remove retainer straps and open door.
C. If a deadlock is being used, chisel or drill out area behind deadlock strike to allow maximum penetration of latch. This can be done with unit in place.

4. Secure Jambs

A. Attach strike plate with (2) jamb anchor screws use 1½" long screws securing jamb to stud behind existing frame. Repeat procedure for deadlock strike plate.

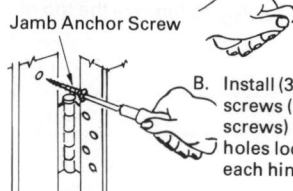

Jamb Anchor Screw

B. Install (3) jamb anchor screws (1½" long screws) in hinge jamb holes located above each hinge.

NOTE:
Do not overtighten screws—this could cause jambs to bow.

5. Install Hardware

A. Replacement door unit is prepared for a Gov't. 160 lock with 2¾" bracket. Install lock per manufacturers instructions.

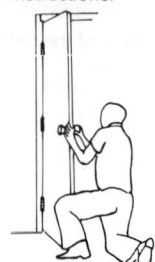

B. If applicable, install deadlock per manufacturers instructions.

6. Install Weatherstrip

A. Cut wood stops with factory-installed weatherstrip to length as required and attach to existing frame.

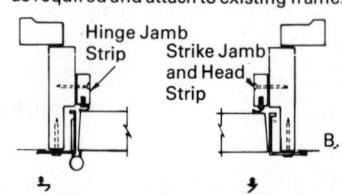

Hinge Jamb Strip

Strike Jamb and Head Strip

Hinge Jamb Weatherstrip

Strike Jamb & Head Weatherstrip

Dead Latch
Extended when door is in open position

B. Attach wood stop with door in closed position.
C. Do not set stop too tight against door. Make a good seal.
D. Trim hinge and strike jamb weatherstrip to fit flush with top of vinyl threshold cap.

CAUTION:
Make sure latch bolt engages in strike and dead latching device depressed while door is in closed position before nailing stop to frame.

7. Secure Threshold

A. Caulk outside of sill and bottom edge of wood stops.
B. For wood floor install (2) anchor down screws into the counter sunk holes in the threshold.

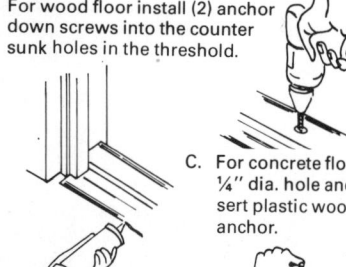

C. For concrete floor drill ¼" dia. hole and insert plastic wood screw anchor.

NOTE:
Start screws into plastic anchors before installation through holes in threshold.

8. Install Pile Corner Seals

A. Remove paper backing

B. Install corner seal snugly against threshold and butt corner seal against jamb weatherstrip.

9. Re-attach Interior Trim

A. Use existing holes if possible. It may be necessary to drill ³/₃₂" dia. holes through steel frame in order to nail trim into place.

PAINTING INSTRUCTIONS
A. Sand lightly with #100-120 emery paper and wipe clean.
B. Paint door in open position.
C. If latex paints are used, be sure to use high-quality exterior type.
D. Do not paint weatherstrip.
E. Do not close door until paint is completely dry.

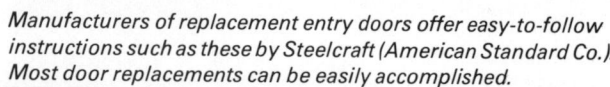

Manufacturers of replacement entry doors offer easy-to-follow instructions such as these by Steelcraft (American Standard Co.). Most door replacements can be easily accomplished.

Additional Installation Instructions for Special Conditions

he Replacement Door Unit is designed to fit into the existing oor opening requiring little or o modification; provided the pening height and width are vithin the limits of our uggested minimum and maximum dimensions.

If the door opening does not meet these dimension requirements, or if there is a special condition, it may be possible to modify the opening to accept the Replacement Door Unit by using one of the methods shown below.

One or more of these methods may enable the installation of a Replacement Door Unit. For example, an opening with a one piece oak sill/threshold that exceeds the recommended maximum width could possibly be modified by using two of the methods shown below.

nstallation of Replacement Door Unit on Oak Sill/Threshold Combination

n some instances, you may encounter a one piece oak sill/threshold combination in the existing opening. Since this is an integral art of the opening, it would be very difficult to remove. The methods shown below allows the installation of a new door unit without removing the oak sill/threshold.

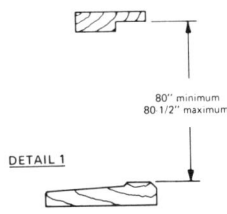

80" minimum
80 1/2" maximum

DETAIL 1

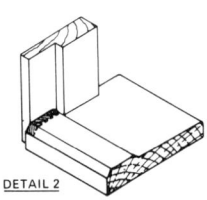

DETAIL 2

As Required

Actual Height

DETAIL 5

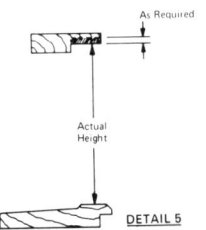

As Required

Actual Height

DETAIL 6

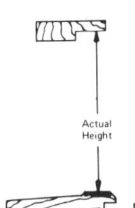

the dimension from the top f the threshold to the underide of head (see detail 1) is a ninimum 80", maximum 0½", install unit directly on op of oak sill/threshold.

The oak sill/threshold should be notched in each corner as shown in detail 2. The depth and width of the notch should be enough to allow the unit to seat properly on the oak sill/threshold. The notch can be made easily with a wood chisel and a hammer.

If the dimension from the top of the oak sill/threshold to the underside of the head is less than 80", the head can be notched as shown in detail 5. Subtract actual opening height from suggested minimum height. This will give the required notching dimension. For example, if the opening is 79⅝", it is ⅜" less than the minimum opening. Therefore the head must be notched out ⅜".

The head can be notched out as required with a wood chisel and a hammer, or if available, a power tool such as a router or sabre saw can be used. This rough cutout is concealed when installation is completed.

An alternate method for detail 5 is to remove the top of the oak sill/threshold to allow the Replacement Door Unit to slip into the existing opening (see detail 6.) The same procedure should be followed. Subtract the actual opening height from the suggested minimum height. This will give the required notching dimension. The notch can be made with a wood chisel and a hammer.

Anchor Down Screw   Aluminum Threshold   Anchor Down Screw   Aluminum Threshold

ak Sill   Caulking   Shim

ETAIL 3   DETAIL 4

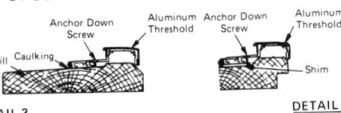

Caulk front lip of aluminum threshold as shown in details 3 & 4. If necessary place a thin wood shim under the front dge of the aluminum threshold before caulking. Anchor aluminum threshold to oak sill/threshold with screws supplied with unit.

Opening too high

When the height of the existing opening exceeds the suggested maximum height, fillers should be added to the head to allow the Replacement Door Unit to fit properly (see detail 7). Subtract suggested maximum height from the actual opening height. This will give the required thickness of the fillers. Use lattice strip or Ponderosa pine for fillers.

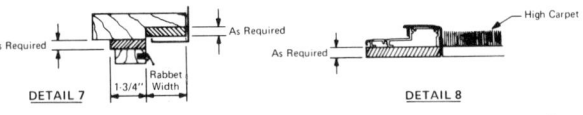

As Required

As Required

Rabbet Width
1-3/4"

DETAIL 7

High Carpet

As Required

DETAIL 8

After completing step number 1 of standard installation instructions install fillers as shown above. After fillers are installed, proceed with standard installation instructions.

If you have high carpeting, a riser can be placed under the aluminum threshold (see detail 8). This will reduce your existing opening height and will add clearance so that the door will clear the carpet when it is opened. This procedure can also be used if you do not wish to use fillers at the head as shown in detail 7.

Opening too wide

When the width of the existing opening exceeds the suggested maximum width, fillers should be added to the jambs to allow the door unit to fit properly (see details 9 & 10). Subtract suggested maximum width from the actual opening width: divide this figure by two, which will give the required thickness of the fillers. For example, if the opening is 33¼", it is ¾" wider than the maximum opening. Therefore the fillers will be ⅜" thick on both sides of the existing opening. Use lattice strip or Ponderosa pine for fillers.

After completing step number 1 of standard installation instructions, install fillers as shown in details 9 & 10. After fillers are installed, proceed with standard installation instructions.

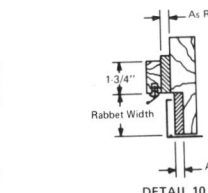

As Required

1-3/4"

Rabbet Width

As Required

DETAIL 9

DETAIL 10

square surface to fit the door to the frame. Planing the top, bottom and side edges may be required to fit the door to the frame once the old door has been removed.

Before hanging, chisel shallow recesses in one edge for the hinges and fit the lockset and handle at the height of the original latch plate. A properly fitted door should clear the sill, carpeting, and sides by about 1/32 in. The lockset edges of the door should also be planed at a slight bevel so the inner corner will clear the jamb when the door is opened. In planing, don't forget to allow for thickness of weatherstripping.

To fit the door to the existing hinge recesses in the frame, place thin cardboard pieces on the sill and stand the new door in position on these shims, which provide the bottom clearance. Then, make pencil marks to coincide with the hinge recesses in the frame. Stand the door on its side and chisel where four markings have fallen, to set the new hinges flush in the door.

Screw the hinges in place, stand the door in the open position and screw the door hinge to the frame. Open and close the door to check the fit. If necessary, plane any spots that bind or scrape against the frame.

After fitting the door, paint or stain it to suit the exterior and interior decor. All four edges should be finished, but pay particular attention to the top and bottom edges, which should be painted to minimize possible expansion in damp weather.

For installing the new latch plate, lock and handle, follow the manufacturer's instructions and use the templates supplied with the new lockset.

Installing a prehung entry door is even less complicated and usually consists of three simple steps:

(1) remove the old door, inside trim, threshold and hardware;
(2) set the replacement unit into the opening, shimming it where necessary to plumb the door jambs, and nail or screw where designated to secure the unit to framing members;
(3) apply weatherstripping, stop and trim, and fasten and caulk the threshold.

Hardware

During installation of a new entry door is an excellent time to update your home's security with a new lockset-deadbolt combination or separate units that provide complete protection.

Hundreds of lockset-knob-rose-escutcheon design possibilities permit a wide selection of "just the right hardware" to trim a new entry door. The choice, of course, should again reflect the architectural styling of the home.

Storm and Screen Doors

Like the entry door, today's combination storm and screen doors come in both wood and metal models for combined beauty and functionalism. Wood models are available at lumber dealers in stock sizes and a variety of styles that require virtually no maintenance. They can be permanently installed and preservative-treated against weather

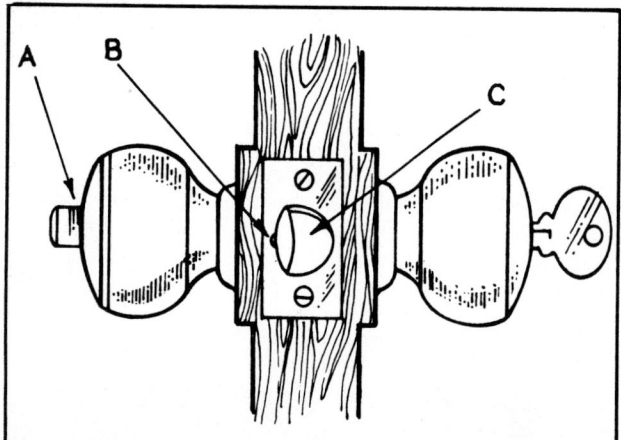

Key-in knob lock. This is the easiest lock to install. Locking button (A), is located inside house. Trigger bolt (B), is depressed when door closes, preventing latch (C), from being opened with a piece of celluloid.

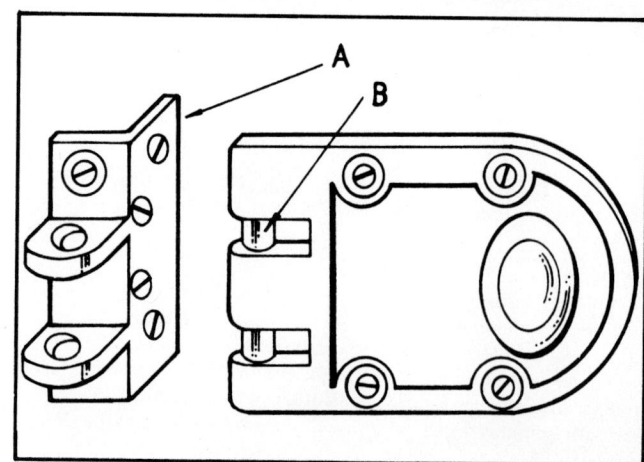

Vertical deadbolt lock. The lock is secured to the rim of the door with four long screws. Mating place (A), is secured with between four and seven screws. Vertical deadbolt (B), secures firmly to mating plate.

Installing a New Lock

a. Remove worn out, broken, or low-security lock.
b. Remove latch of old lock.
c. Use template packed with new lock to mark area to be enlarged.
d. If a jig is available (as shown), use hole saw to enlarge area to accept new lock mechanism.
e. If hole requires only minor enlargement use a wood rasp or similar tool.

f. Cut away excess wood in edge of door, if necessary, to accommodate new latch plate.
g. Install latch.
h. Insert lock mechanism from outside of door.
i. Attach mounting plate on outside of door and snap on trim and knob.

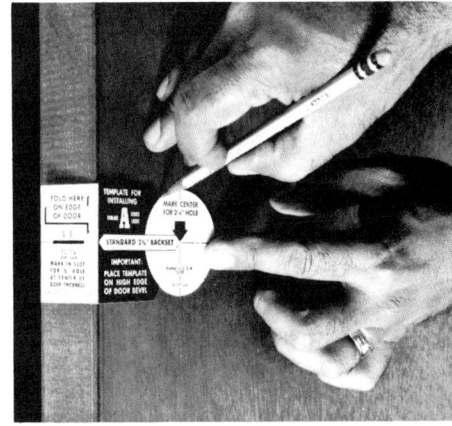

The long, narrow entryway of this home, designed by Architect Fred Langhorst, is protected from the elements by a solid roof open on the sides for sunlight and air. The effect of the entry is quite formal, and the solid overhang is massive enough to fit the scale of the larger redwood house. (Photo: California Redwood Assn.)

Exciting Entryways!

An open redwood trellis protects the large glass windows from sun glare at the entry of this home, yet still admits light and warmth in the winter. Designed by Architect David Leaf, the trellis entry ties the house into the landscaping. (Photo: California Redwood Assn.)

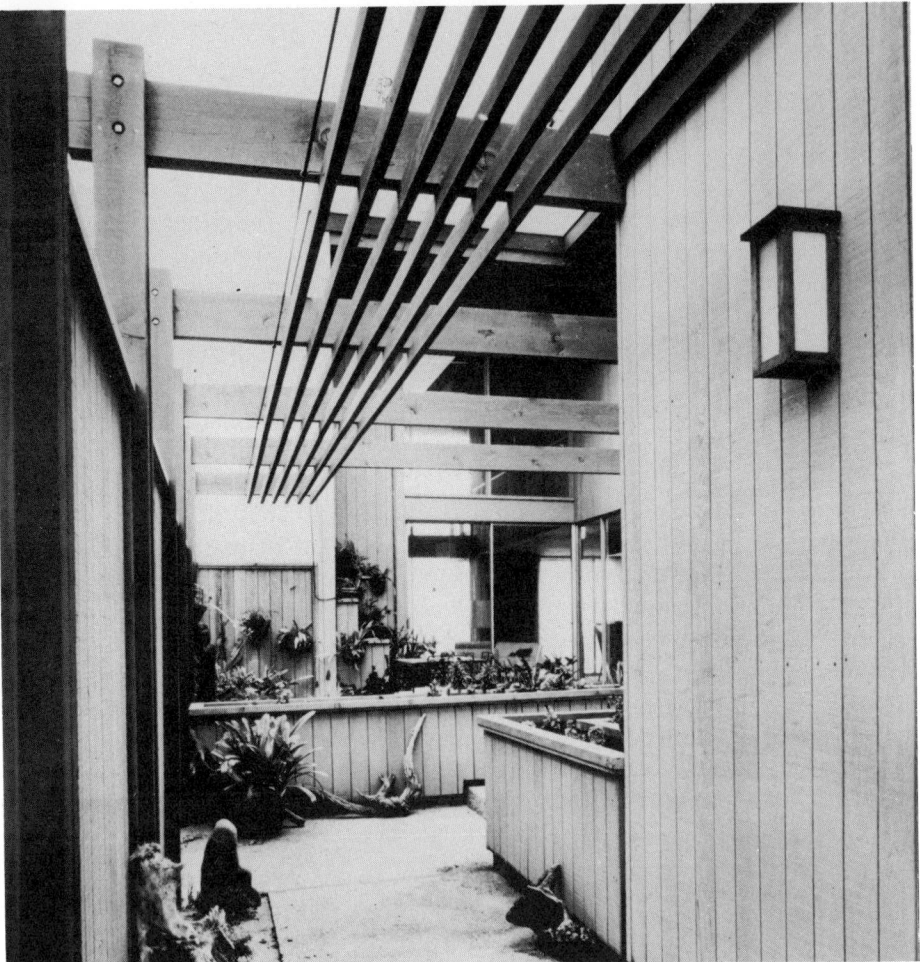

Driftwood, succulents, and redwood stained driftwood gray carry out the seascape motif at the entry of this beach house by designer David Rhame. The plants are contained in boxes which double as low walls. (Photo: California Redwood Assn.)

abuse. A quick change of glass panel to screen adjusts the door to the season.

All-extruded aluminum combination doors manufactured by several firms provide a self-storing feature which permits a quick switch from glass to screen, or vice versa. These doors are pre-hung and merely set in place and fastened to the door frame. Acrylic finishes in a choice of colors have been electrostatically bonded, eliminating periodic repainting.

Decorative Treatments

Treatment of the entryway (stoop, deck, porch) and entry walkway add distinction to the house, and can set it apart from identical or similar houses in a tract development. Successful utilization of this approach to remodeling can be far less expensive than trying to redo the house facade itself.

It's also well to keep in mind that appearance is just one consideration, and other effects of redesigning an entrance may offer even greater advantages—such as privacy, protection against sun, wind or passing showers, and the new relationship of a house to its surroundings.

Closing off the house from the street by means of a decorative fence, landscaping, or a trellised garden entrance can be a lasting asset, especially if the residence is on a route heavily traveled by noisy cars and boisterous children. The result is immediate privacy and peace, whatever the size of your front yard.

Depending upon orientation to the sun and the quirks of climate, a wide selection of plants can be grown on fences or in containers. Bougainvillaea —or in cold areas, hardy ivy—planted in hanging pots and cascading over a trellis is lovely and requires minimal attention. Lighting the entry (see lighting chapter) for safety and for emphasis offers creative possibilities. Many kinds of fixtures in wood, aluminum or glass are available with the source of light supplied by gas, electricity, kerosene or even candle.

Porches

Enclosed Porches

Many older homes have a wealth of added living area that is wasted most of the year—an outdated front porch. This space so common to the

1910-1940 era of homebuilding can be put to year-round use of simply enclosing the openings with nonload-bearing partitions or windows.*

The attached porch in most instances will have been constructed with a roof slope continuous with the roof of the house itself, or with a roof that ties into the wall of the house, pitched just enough to provide drainage. The floor construction will be a concrete slab on grade or a wood assembly above a crawl space, built in much the same way as interior wood floors with joists and decking.

Wood species used for your finished porch floor should have decay-and-wear resistance, be non-splintering and free from warping. Species commonly used are cypress, douglas fir, western larch, southern pine and redwood. Where moisture conditions are serious, only treated material should be used.

If a fully enclosed crawl space exists below the porch, it should be adequately vented or have an opening into the basement. Lack of same is one of the principal destructive elements that cause rot and force frequent repair projects. On an open porch, it's also a good practice to slope the floor slightly for drainage purposes, snow removal and the like. The slope, of course, should be downward from the house.

Supports for enclosed porches usually consist of fully framed stud walls, with studs doubled at openings and corners. If both interior and exterior finish coverings are used, the walls are constructed in similar manner to other walls of the house. They are attached with nails or a power stud driver, similar to placement of a wall on a new concrete slab. If insulated glass is used, you will have to call a contractor for installation.

Open Porches

Open porches frequently have decorative job-built or mill-made columns of a minimum 4 x 4 dimension. A formal design of a large house entrance, for example, often includes the use of round built-up columns topped by Doric or Ionic capitals. These

Basic framework for stud wall or partition

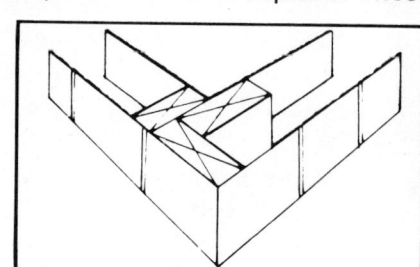

Inside and outside corner nailing surface, made up of three 2x4's and installed so it provides inside and outside nailing surfaces

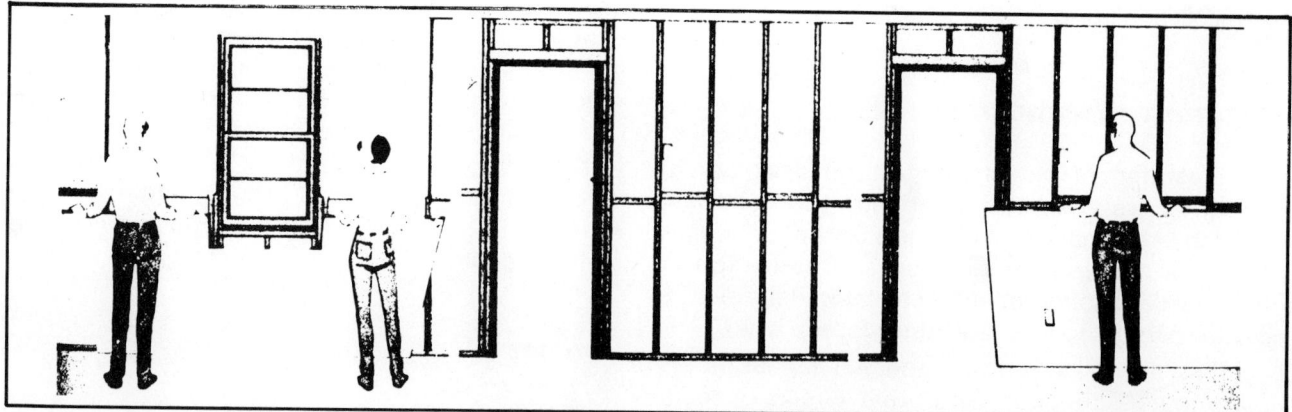

Once stud framework has been built (studs toe-nailed 16 in. on center) you can finish off with wallboard or plywood sheathing. Plywood can be nailed directly to frame, countersinking nails. Then stain or paint. Or install wallboard, horizontally, as shown. Mount upper sheet first, and work down. To cut wallboard, place on two sawhorses with 2x4's running the length of the sheet; mark cutting line; score panel deeply along mark. Lay a support under the cut; hold the panel rigid, and snap it off.

*Nonload-bearing walls or partitions do not support the weight of the roof.

BEAM CLIP
The Panel Clip Co.
POST BASE

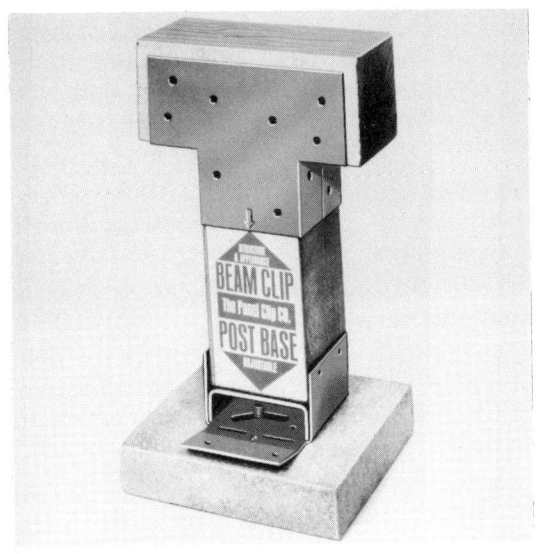

As an alternative to digging a hole, putting in a post and adding cement–or to utilize already-poured-and-hardened foundation slab–you can use an adjustable two-piece clip from Panel-Clip Co. It will position and anchor 4x4 posts to concrete even when bolts are out of line. It resists termites and moisture rot; the base cover has weep holes to allow moisture to escape. The base clip can be coordinated with the beam clip, as when adding porch or deck roofs. The beam clip is used to anchor the top of a post or a column to the header or beam. Two beams are recommended per post. Available at lumber yards; call or write to Panel-Clip (see Manufacturers' List) for nearest distributor.

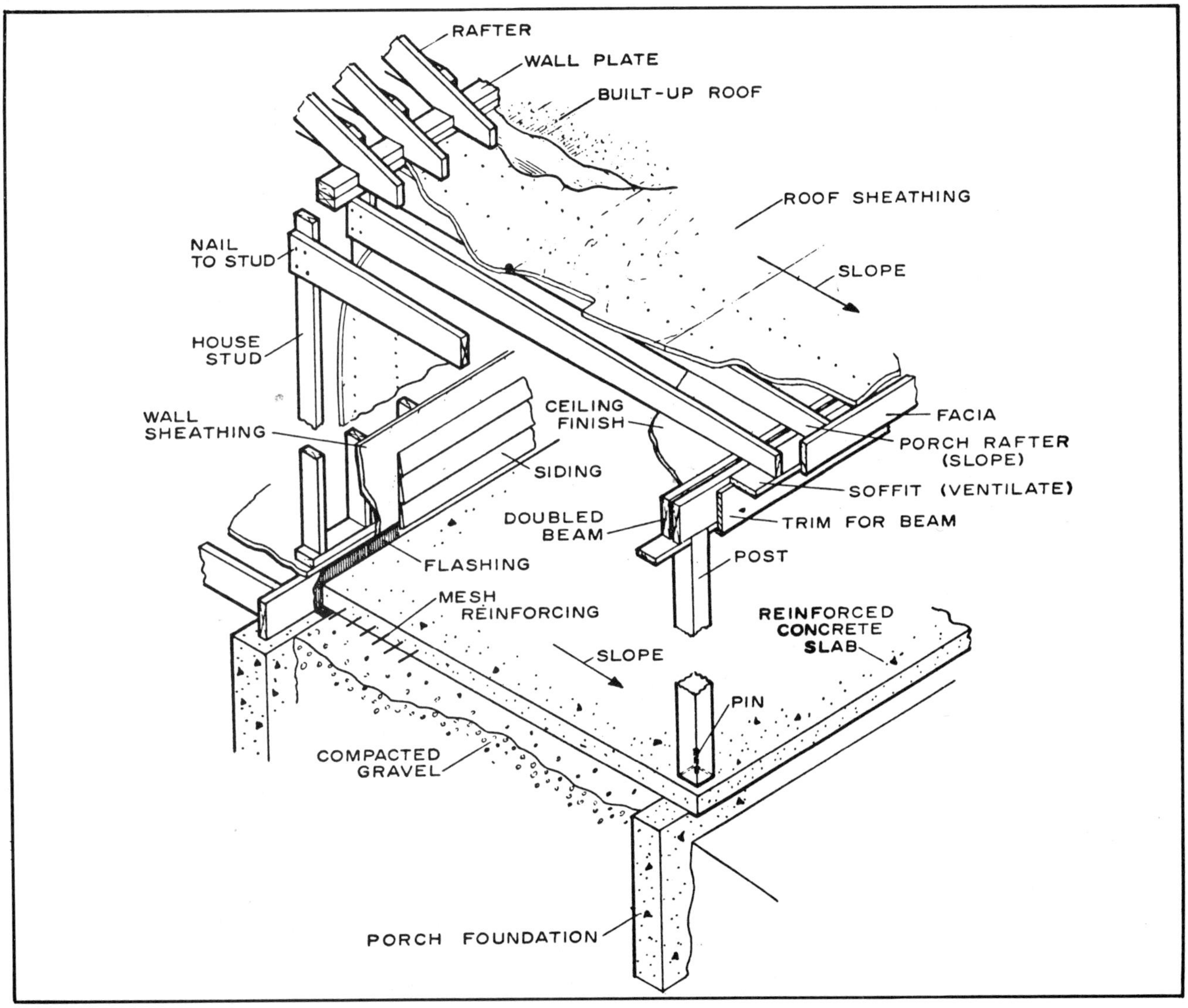
RAFTER
WALL PLATE
BUILT-UP ROOF
ROOF SHEATHING
NAIL TO STUD
SLOPE
HOUSE STUD
WALL SHEATHING
CEILING FINISH
FACIA
PORCH RAFTER (SLOPE)
SIDING
SOFFIT (VENTILATE)
DOUBLED BEAM
TRIM FOR BEAM
FLASHING
POST
MESH REINFORCING
REINFORCED CONCRETE SLAB
SLOPE
PIN
COMPACTED GRAVEL
PORCH FOUNDATION

Details of porch construction vary slightly when a concrete slab is used in place of a typical wood-framed floor system. Shown here are the suggested methods of attaching the porch to the wall studs located behind the home siding. (Sketch: U.S. Department of Agriculture Handbook No. 73.)

columns are factory-made and ready for installation at the building site.

The base of posts or columns in open porches should be designed so that no pockets are formed to retain moisture and encourage decay. In single posts, a steel pin may be used to locate the post and a large galvanized washer or similar spacer used to keep the bottom of the post above the concrete or wood floor. Commercially available metal post anchors and caps also may be used.

Railings

Porch balustrades (or railings) are fabricated in any number of designs usually with one or two railings with balusters between them. They are designed both for appearance and protection. A closed balustrade may be used with screens or combination windows above, a frequent midwestern approach to producing a year-round sitting area.

All balustrade members that are exposed to water and snow should be designed to shed water, with the bottom rail not in contact with the concrete unless the rail has been constructed of pressure-treated wood. It's also important to connect the railing to the post in such a way that prevents moisture from being trapped. One method uses galvanized angle iron attached to both rail and post, leaving a small space between the end of the rail and the post.

It's also recommended in building new balustrades or replacing existing ones that all exposed members, such as posts, balusters, and railings, be of all-heart, decay-resistant, or treated wood to minimize decay.

Outdoor Stairs and Steps

Porch stairs, like balustrades, exist in many different designs and have been constructed of various materials including brick, sandstone and wood. Whatever type, choose treads a minimum of 11 in. wide, and risers not higher than 7 in. or lower than 4 in. Proportioning of risers and treads in laying out porch steps should be as carefully considered as the design of interior stairways.

Normally, the porch riser is between 6 and 7 in. in height, with stringers used wherever there are two or more steps. With a single step, a simple inverted box can be used effectively.

Keep in mind when building safe exterior steps the need for a good support or foundation. Where wood steps are used, the bottom step should be

concrete or supported by treated wood members. Where the steps are located over backfill or disturbed ground, the foundation should be carried down to undisturbed ground.

Stringers should be anchored at the top to the porch framing and at the bottom anchored to the concrete pad or wood base. Stair treads can be set inside boxed stringers (stringers enclosing the ends of the treads), either on cleats or on notched stringers nailed to the inside of the boxed stringers. If the stairs are wider than 3 ft. 6 in., a third (center) stringer is required. (For diagrams and instructions see Chapter 10.)

Concrete steps should be at least as wide as the sidewalk and all risers should be exactly the same height. A landing is desirable to divide flights more than 5 ft. high. For safety and convenience, the tread should be at least 11 in.; all treads should be the same widths. The rise for each step should be not more than 7½ in. Allow a ⅛ in. pitch on each tread for drainage. The simple formwork shown here is 2-in.-thick material which is strong enough to keep from bending or bulging during the pour. An economical way to keep steps from sinking is to dig two 6-in. or 8-in. diameter postholes beneath the bottom tread. The holes extend below the frost line and are filled with concrete. The top step or platform is tied to the existing wall with two or more metal anchors. (See Chapter 10 for tips on using concrete). (Drawing: Portland Cement Assn.)

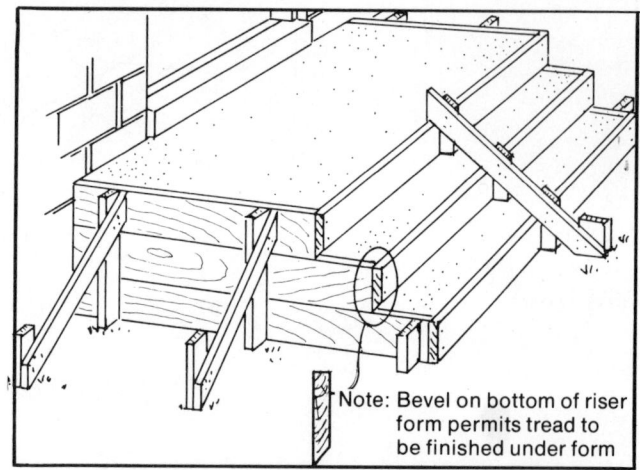

Note: Bevel on bottom of riser form permits tread to be finished under form

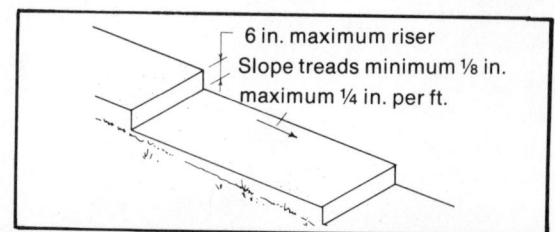

6 in. maximum riser
Slope treads minimum ⅛ in.
maximum ¼ in. per ft.

Building a stepped ramp is often the best way to handle foot traffic on a long slope. Ramps should have a tread length to provide two easy paces between risers, which should be a maximum 6 inches in height. Treads should be sloped a minimum of ⅛ in. per foot and a maximum of ¼ in. per foot. (Sketch: Portland Cement Assn.)

2. Exterior Trim

The outside of a home can readily be compared to a woman's dress or man's suit—it either fits well and enhances the wearer's appearance, or it's ill-suited for one or many reasons and does little beyond providing the required outer covering. Thus, it's important that every item of the house exterior be considered on its own merits and for its compatibility to all other elements.

Later chapters of this book will deal specifically with roofing and siding and the many options offered today's homeowner. This chapter is more concerned with what could be called the "trimmings"—the windows, shutters, dormers, overhangs, chimney, and garage doors.

Restyling or updating can bring about dramatic changes: all the proof one needs of this is a quick tour of an inner-city redevelopment program where old and ugly houses have been made new and attractive. In some instances, a world of change has been made by chopping off an old porch, while another house has been improved with an addition.

Windows

Most people look *through* windows, not *at* them as they should. Beyond the primary functions of providing light, air and protection, windows play a major role in the appearance of a home. Window designs should suit the architecture of the house, and each window should be chosen carefully for insulatitive quality and good design.

Most new and replacement windows being used today are of wood or aluminum construction. There are pros and cons for both types, including the basic facts that: wood acts as an insulator while metal conducts heat; wood windows require painting but metal windows do not; wood does not corrode or pit and metal does, etc. The architectural style of your home, and your design preferences, and cash availability will help you to sort this out and make a decision.

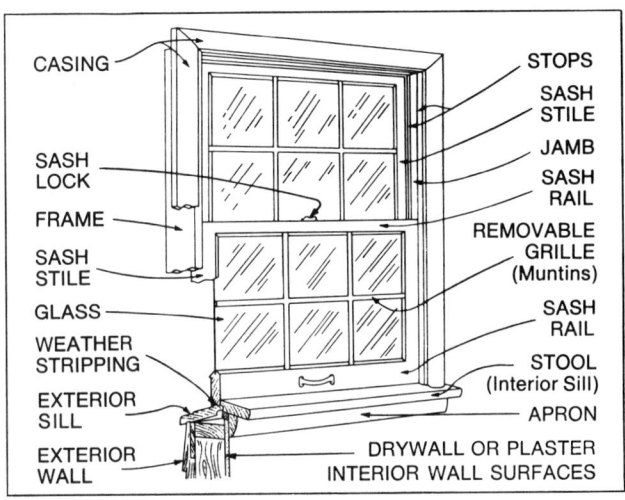

Technical names given to various parts of a window are detailed in this sketch. Most windows can be purchased as assembled units minus the trim (casing, apron and stool), which are cut to fit on the job.

In choosing windows it's well to keep in mind that the least expensive is not always the best solution. Select units that are best for your climate and give consideration to using double-glazing or insulating glass that eliminates the need for storm windows in colder climates.

There are six basic types of window styles used in bay, bow, box and picture windows:

- Double-hung units have two sash, one above the other, that move up and down. These windows have long been used for traditional homes.
- Casement windows are sash hinged at the side to swing out. They are opened and closed by rotary operators, providing maximum ventilation when opened to a 90° angle. Casements are ideal for awkward locations, such as above sinks and countertops.
- Gliding windows, or sliders, have sash that slide in tracks. This design is popular with contemporary architecture, yet is also compatible with Colonial and Traditional homes.

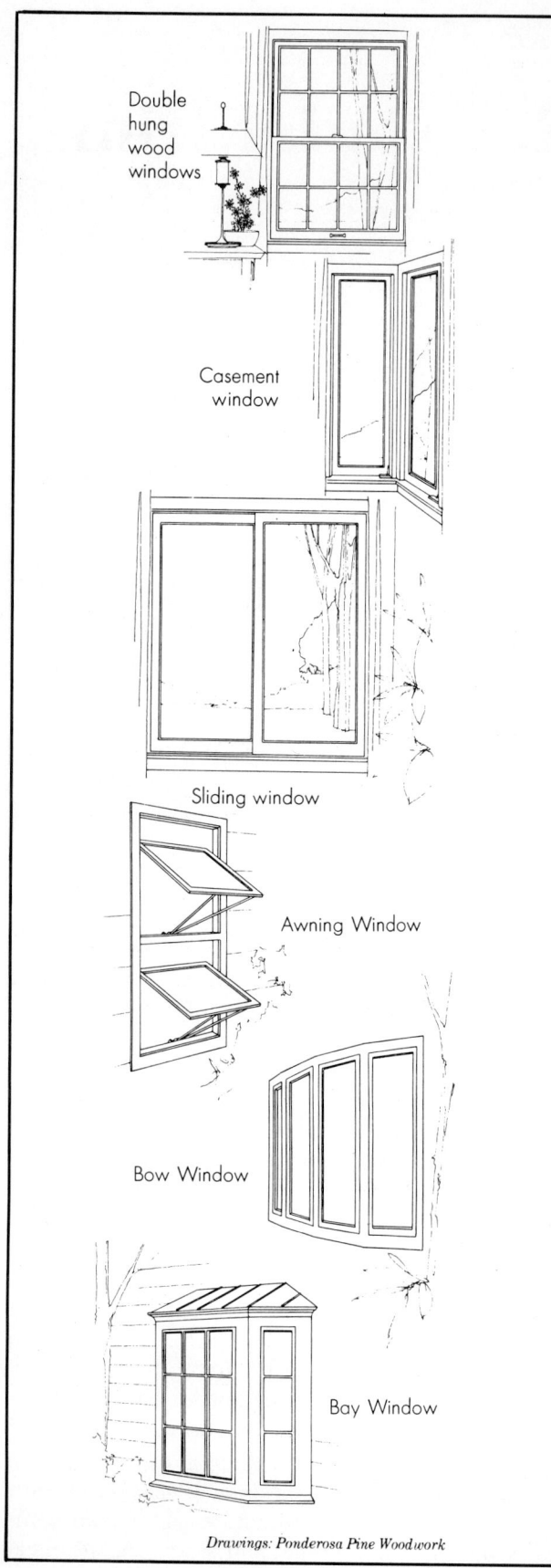

Double
hung
wood
windows

Casement
window

Sliding window

Awning Window

Bow Window

Bay Window

Drawings: Ponderosa Pine Woodwork

- Awning windows have sash hinged at the top to open out, providing a shield from the rain even when open. This window is sometimes used stacked, one above the other, or can be located below a fixed window to provide natural ventilation.
- Hopper windows are similar to the awning style, except sash are hinged at the bottom so the window will open inward. This style is frequently used in basements but should be avoided in other walls where it would interfere with furniture placement.
- Fixed windows have glazed glass that does not move, such as the typical picture window that provides light and a view where ventilation is supplied by other means.

Most existing homes have two or more of these window types in use. Newer models available from retail lumber dealers are design-engineered to open easily and close tightly, and are equipped with precision-made hardware and built-in weather-stripping. And some wood windows are preservative-treated or plastic-encased for minimum maintenance.

Cutting of wall and installation of most new windows should be left to an experienced contractor. The damage possible to your home if you cut inaccurately into a load-bearing stud wall can be considerable.

Window installations can be used to provide extra space and more light in a living room or dining room. Replacing a double-hung or fixed window with a stock bay window will give a room a more spacious feeling. With windows angled to catch the light from three directions, a bay brightens the room all day long and widens the view to 180°.

The center section of a bay window is usually a fixed window, one that doesn't open. Ventilation is provided by the two side windows, which can be casements or double-hung. Further customizing is provided by a choice of removable grilles in rectangular or diamond shapes for a traditional small-paned look.

Bow windows are similar to the bay, but curved instead of angled out from the wall. Casements or fixed units may be used, combined with a few awning sections for ventilation.

New townhouse construction with mansard roof styling is doing much to popularize box style windows, flat units set out from the wall in a box-like frame. The shadow-box frames or surrounds provide dramatic architectural treatment. The window

Preparation of the Rough Opening

Installation techniques, materials and building codes vary according to area. Contact your local material supplier for specific recommendations.

The same rough opening preparation procedures are used for Wood and Perma-Shield Windows.

Brick veneer with a frame back-up wall is similar in construction to the frame wall in the following illustrations.

When enlarging the opening is necessary, make certain proper size header is used. (Contact your supplier for proper header size.) For installation of a smaller window—frame the opening as in new installation.

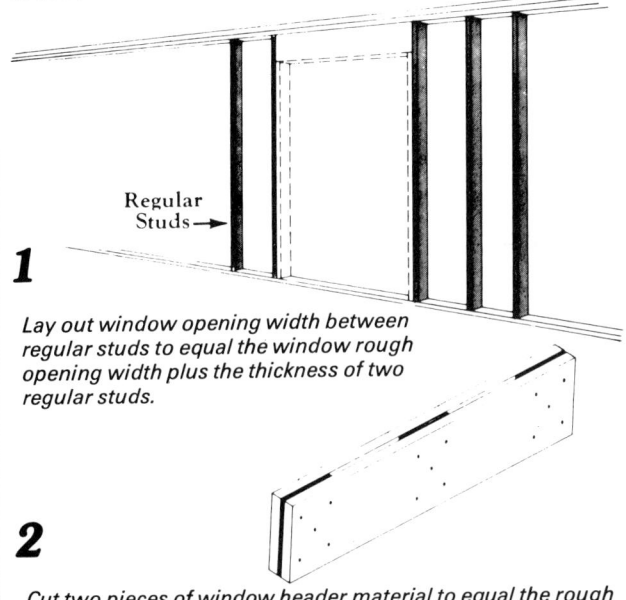

1

Lay out window opening width between regular studs to equal the window rough opening width plus the thickness of two regular studs.

2

Cut two pieces of window header material to equal the rough opening of window plus the thickness of two jack studs. Nail two header members together using adequate spacer so header thickness equals width of jack stud.

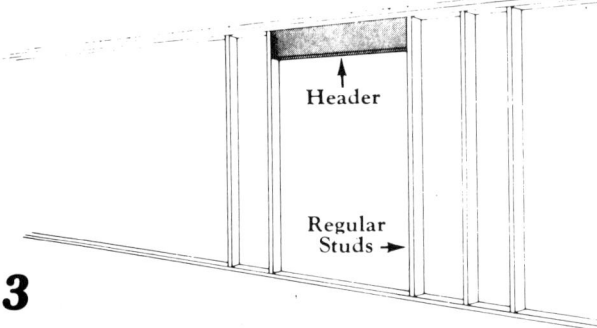

3

Position header at desired height between regular studs. Nail through the regular studs into header with nails to hold in place until completing next step.

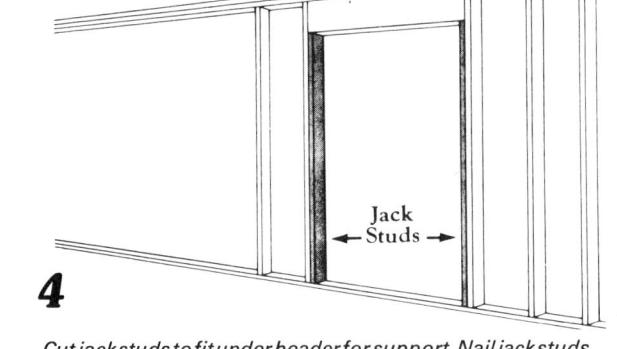

4

Cut jack studs to fit under header for support. Nail jack studs to regular studs.

5

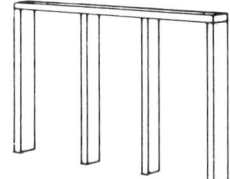

Measure rough opening height from bottom of header to top of rough sill. Cut 2"x4" cripples and rough sill to proper length. Rough sill length is equal to rough opening width of window. Assemble by nailing rough sill into ends of cripples.

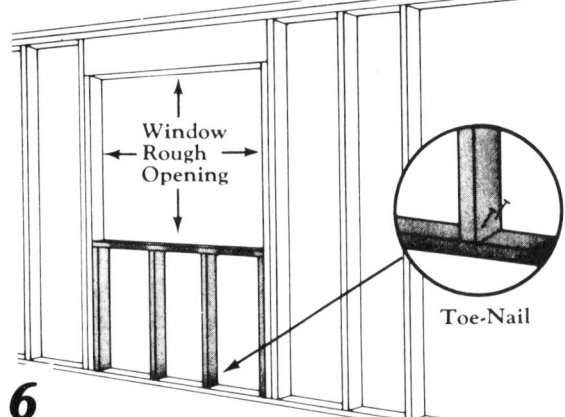

6

Fit rough sill and cripples between jack studs. Toe-nail cripples to bottom plate and rough sill to jack studs at sides.

7

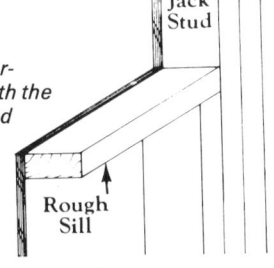

Apply exterior sheathing (fiberboard, plywood, etc.) flush with the rough sill, header and jack stud framing members.

Old and damaged windows can be replaced with a new unit, even if the wall opening is not the same size for both units. Installation techniques, materials and building codes vary according to the area, but the framing system illustrated here is generally accepted across the country (Drawings: Andersen Corporation).

Prefinished wood windows are factory-assembled in complete easy-installing units, with all hardware mounted and ready for immediate operation. Shown here are the two principal types of wood windows, double-hung in the top photo and, below, casement units formed into a bow combination installation.

Bay windows lend an added dimension to home exteriors as well as affording extra interior space. Shown here is Andersen's casement angled bay unit, which has a low-maintenance rigid vinyl sheath over preservative-treated wood frame and sash.

or windows can be casements, fixed, double-hung, or a combination. A pair of casements provides the look of French doors.

Most stock windows can be washed from the inside. Casements open wide enough to reach both sides of the panes, and some double-hung and gliding window sash can be lifted out or tilted. This makes washing them safe and easier.

With growing concern being expressed about fuel saving, many cities are adopting resolutions that new construction and remodeling must incorporate insulating glass when new windows are installed. Long in use, this type of glass is the modern method of providing double window pane protection against the weather.

Insulating glass is actually two panes of glass sealed together at the edges to form an insulating layer of air between. The glass can be plain or color-tinted to reduce glare, and comes in many standard sizes. A key feature of this type of glass is its ability to keep window temperatures stable, thus preventing condensation from forming on the glass.

Shutters

Few windows or doors today are equipped with shutters for their original purpose—closing and opening for light control and weather protection—but millions of shutters are being used for decorative purposes.

You may now choose from wood or plastic shutters in louver or raised panel designs to complement almost any window or door. Depending

Removable grilles make window washing easier, as shown in this sketch of a casement window. Usually made of rigid vinyl, the grilles snap out from the inside of the window and are easily replaced. (Sketch: Ponderosa Pine)

upon manufacturer, these units come in widths of 12, 14, 15, 18, 19 and 20 in. and in heights 23 through 80 in. A general rule is that 14 in. shutters are used with windows up to 2 ft. 8 in. wide; greater widths are used for windows wider than 2 ft. 8 in.

Shutters may be purchased unfinished as standard wood millwork or may be obtained prefinished from several manufacturers. Andersen Corporation, for example, offers 14 and 18 in. widths in either black or white Perma-Shield, a rigid vinyl sheath with pine grain appearance that gives a real wood look but won't chip, flake, peel, blister or need painting. Benson Mfg. Corporation makes exterior plastic shutters in 12, 15 and 19 in. widths in a choice of black, white, Virginia green, Dominion brown and sunset red (rust).

1

3

2

4

Wood window installation is relatively simple using today's precision-made units. Shown here are the main steps for an Andersen casement type window: (1) the window is set into the frame opening from the outside with exterior casing overlapping the exterior sheathing, using a 3½-inch casing nail partly driven temporarily at one upper corner, with the nail going through the head casing and into the header. In (2), the window is adjusted for level and a second nail driven in the other top corner. A check for plumbness is made followed by (3) further casing nails spaced about 10 in. apart. All nails are driven at a slight angle inward toward the

framing members. Head flashing is applied before siding to extend over head casing and up along face of sheathing. After siding has been applied, complete perimeter of the window is caulked as shown in (4).

Decorative wood shutters enhance most window settings, such as this pair of Andersen Perma-Shield narrowline double-hung windows, which are glazed with double-pane insulating glass. This eliminates the need for storm sash. Removable vinyl grilles provide the traditional look.

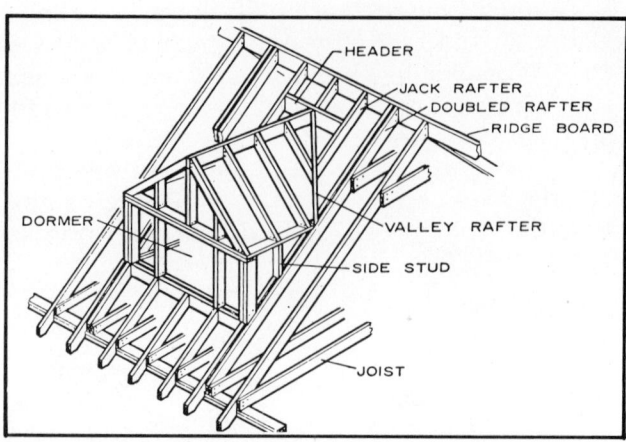

The typical house dormer added to an existing home requires partial removal of the finish roofing and reframing of the roof structure itself. In most instances, a series of rafters must be removed and the new dormer framed as shown here. (Sketch: U.S. Department of Agriculture Handbook No. 73.)

Shutter installation has been greatly refined in recent years, in most instances eliminating the need for templates which previously were used to align the units accurately with adjoining windows and doors. Now you need only nail simple clips to any wall surface and snap the shutters on the clips. The total job can be accomplished in five to ten minutes.

An even newer style shutter now finding favor on the West Coast is called the Roll-A-Matic, which is custom fitted to the exterior of the window with controls located inside the home. In these applications, the shutters are used to filter air flow, protect the room from sun, insure privacy and seal out traffic noise. Made by Continental Customs, they can be opened fully, closed partially or completely, as you desire.

Another variation of the popular European-type rolling shutter made by Pease Co. can be used with new construction or remodeling. The units are installed on the outside of the window, yet operated manually from inside the home to control light, protect privacy, and provide weather protection. The manufacturer reports that these rolling shutters, even used on a window with a storm window, will act as a heat saver, gaining 2650 btu's per window when the outdoor temperature is at 15°.

Dormers

Dormers, or upright windows in a sloping roof, most often exist or are added to add daylight to spaces inside the roof, whether used for storage, added bedrooms or other modern space needs. These units must have their own separate roofs and thus are treated in the same way as the overall house roofing to provide uniform appearance. Generally speaking, to handle a dormer in other fashion is courting design disaster.

A dormer roof may be flat or curved (as is popular in mansard roofs); it may have one slope in the same direction as the main roof but at a lower pitch; or, it may be a span roof with a ridge, the front being either hipped or gabled, as typically found in Cape Cod architecture.

Depending upon the house styling, the dormer "cheeks" or sidewalls may be treated in several ways. If the home is roofed with slate, the cheeks are usually of the same material. If the roofing is asphalt shingles, the sidewalls are finished with this exterior siding material. If the main roof is wood shake or shingle, use of this same material will provide a pleasing appearance to the sidewalls.

Adequate flashing, of course, is absolutely necessary to prevent leaks in the roof. Still another successful method of providing the cheek triangle is to use glass, which increases the natural light reaching the interior.

Overhangs

Lack of a roof overhang is the cause of many a home's unattractive appearance. While this absence didn't detract from New England saltboxes, the ommission is clearly detrimental to many lower-priced homes built in recent years. In both instances, rafters were cut off at the outer edge of the exterior wall and a frieze or facia board applied to the rafter ends.

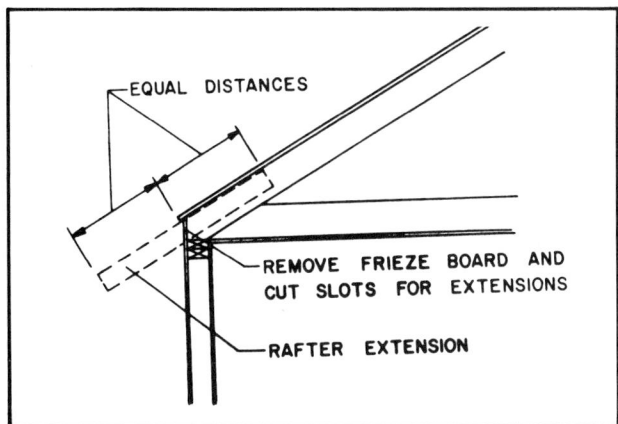

Extending the overhang to provide better weather protection to the wall of a house requires removal of the frieze board and cutting of slots for rafter extensions. The added overhang should extend an equal distance (broken line) into the existing roof structure, with half the length of the new rafter becoming the overhang. (Drawing: U.S. Department of Agriculture Handbook No. 481.)

The New England architecture compensated for the lack of a cornice by steeply pitching the roofs from the ridge to the ground on the "weather side" of the house and maintaining this same pitch for the other (front) side of the two-story homes.

More modern homes built without the cornice often suffer severe water problems in colder climates, where snow and rain will freeze in the gutters and back up into the wall of the dwelling. The lack of the overhang also permits gutter overflow water to run down the face of the house and stain the siding or leave spots around the windows, doors and trim.

Roof overhangs should be at least one foot and preferably two feet all around the house both for weather protection and appearance. Even greater widths are most popular for contemporary houses where exposed laminated or solid beams are used with wood roof decking to provide a contemporary or rustic look.

A good time to correct the lack of roof overhang is when re-roofing (a better time, of course, would be during the original construction). Fascia or frieze boards can be removed, exposing the ends of rafters, and rafter extension pieces of 2 x 4 or 2 x 6 can easily be nailed to the sides of the existing rafters, extending into the wall a distance equal to the new overhang. The rafter extension is then covered with tongue-and-groove boards or plywood and the entire upper surface roofed in the same manner as the rest of the house.

Soffits can be treated in several ways, from leaving the rafters exposed to completely enclosing

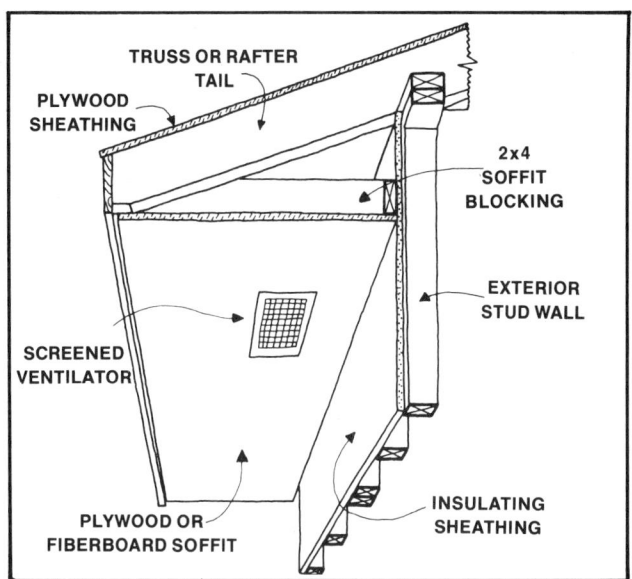

Boxed eave overhang and soffit is probably the most common method for finishing off roof overhangs except in many Western states where rafter tails are left exposed. In some areas it's common practice to use special fascia boards pregrooved on one side to receive the edge of the soffit material. At house ends, boxed overhang is usually finished with a cornice return. After application of siding material, the soffit-wall corner is trimmed with a cove mold. Readily available, but not recommended for the first-time owner-builder, are metal soffit-and-vent systems. Joints in the soffit material should occur where lookout blocking will provide a nailing base for both sheet ends. Normal practice is to leave soffit nail heads exposed but with entire soffit receiving a paint finish.

Vinyl plastic soffit system consists of V-grooved panels in either perforated (for ventilation) or nonperforated types. These panels, produced by Bird & Son, are adaptable for sloping soffits as well as horizontal installations.

Some manufacturers of soffit and siding materials of rigid vinyl offer a full assortment of accessories such as base flashings, starter strips, inside-outside corner units, window-door caps and so on. With a small and simple one-story home, the cost of these materials may be minimal and justified by their easier application. For larger and more complex homes having more corners, different eave heights and greater areas involved, the extra costs of these materials may be considerably more than conventional wood-based sheet materials with wood trim.

Installing Overhang & Soffit

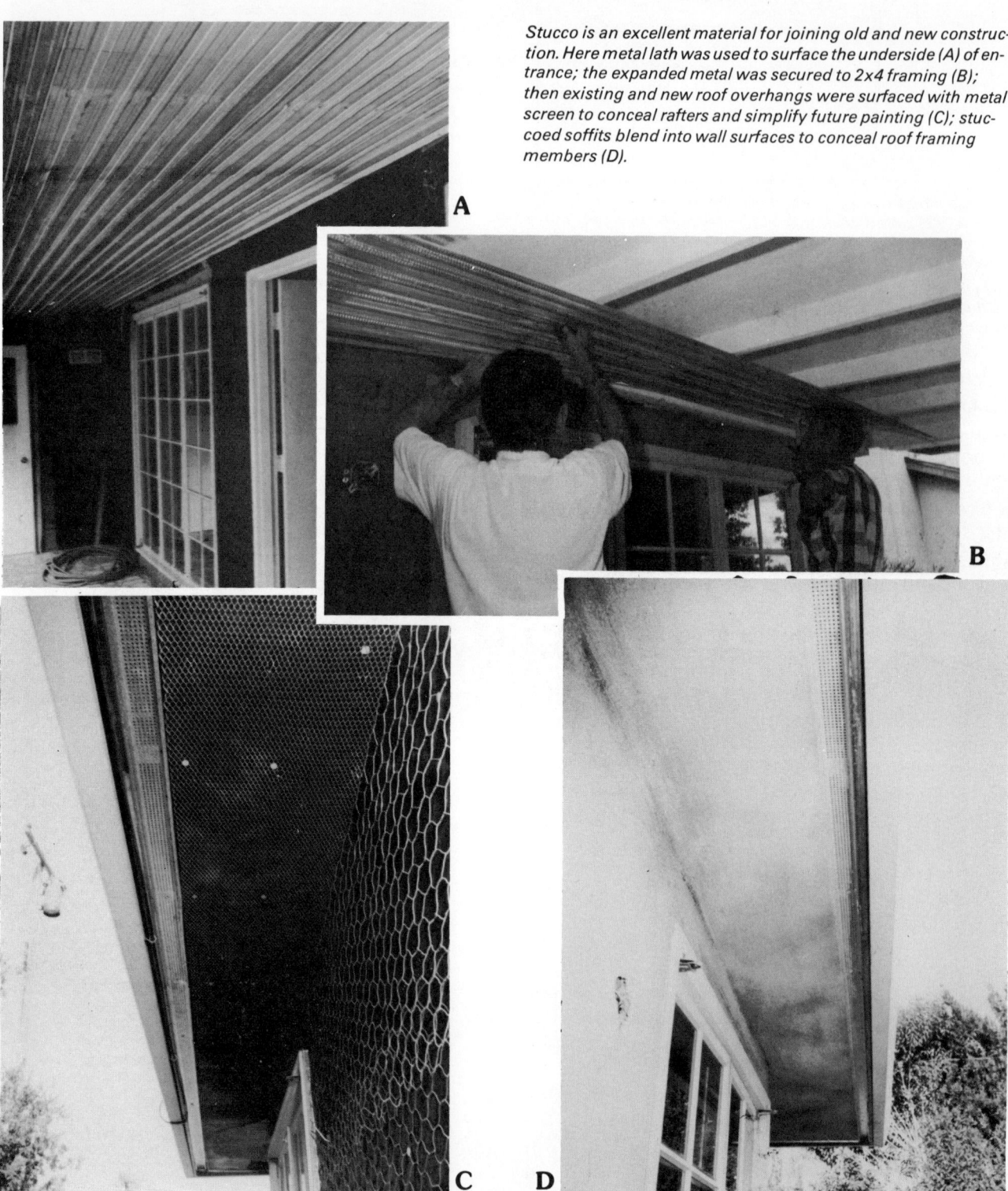

Stucco is an excellent material for joining old and new construction. Here metal lath was used to surface the underside (A) of entrance; the expanded metal was secured to 2x4 framing (B); then existing and new roof overhangs were surfaced with metal screen to conceal rafters and simplify future painting (C); stuccoed soffits blend into wall surfaces to conceal roof framing members (D).

them for a smooth appearance and easier painting maintenance. In either instance, provision should be made to provide ventilation to the roof with screen ventilators.

Attic Ventilation

A warm attic that is inadequately ventilated and insulated may cause formation of ice dams at the cornice. During cold weather after a heavy snowfall, heat causes the snow next to the roof to melt. Water running down the roof freezes on the colder surface of the cornice, often forming an ice dam at the gutter that may cause water to back up at the eaves and into the wall and ceiling. Ventilation provides part of the answer to these problems.

In hot weather, ventilation of the attic and roof areas offers an effective means of removing hot air and thereby lowering the temperature in the rest of the house.

Hip-roof houses are best ventilated by inlet ventilators in the soffit area and by outlet ventilators along the ridge. The difference in temperatures between the attic and the outside will then create an air movement independent of the wind, and also a stronger movement when there is a wind.

Decorative Chimney Treatments

Of all exterior home trim, the chimney tops the list of items least likely and most difficult to change. For the most part, initial appearance is the view that will be seen for the life of the house, with the exception of possibly painting the bricks a different color or framing the chimney in wood as is now common when prefabricated metal chimneys are used in place of masonry materials.

The important consideration here is that the chimney be maintained in the best working condition and that, if masonry, the brickwork is not allowed to deteriorate to the point of dangerous loose bricks or stonework.

Both custom- and factory-built chimneys come in a variety of sizes and materials. You can select from models designed for contemporary or traditional style architecture, but once the decision is made and the unit in place, changing it becomes difficult as well as costly.

Perhaps the best opportunity to better the appearance of a chimney is available if a masonry or decorative metal surround was not used as part of

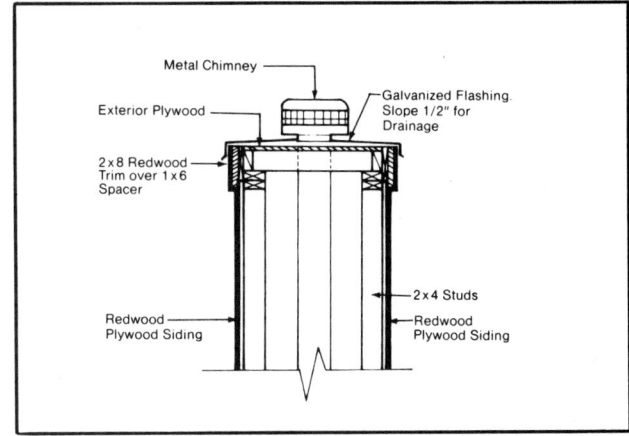

Wood as well as masonry materials may be used to enhance a home chimney. This sketch by Simpson Timber Co. details how a prefabricated metal chimney may be surrounded with redwood plywood siding secured to a wood frame. If desired other siding treatments, such as panels of simulated decorative brick, can be applied to frame.

the original construction. In these instances, lightweight prefabricated housings giving a brick appearance can be added. Or plywood frame boxes can be fabricated to extend the siding used.

Typical roof housing assemblies that simulate the conventional chimney are made of corrosion-resistant construction. The embossed aluminum side panels are finished in red brick pattern. Size is determined by the vent diameter, and height varies with the type of roof.

Garage Doors

Whether the garage is attached to the home or sits away from the home, the garage and its door or doors present a massive part of one view of the home. Style is important, for the garage door is the largest single element of the house and should enchance it, not detract from it.

Selection of a new garage door for replacement purposes should be considered carefully. Keep in mind that the typical garage door has more moving parts than an automatic washing machine and when not properly installed you have continual problems.

It's essential to consider your home's particular architectural styling: Colonial, Rambling Ranch, Cape Cod, English Tudor, French Normandy or any other of the basic home styles popular today. A ranch home might stress maximum horizontal lines in the door selection to emphasize the wide, low, long appearance; the Spanish style might benefit from a door with cathedral light windows.

For details, consult How to Cut Your Energy Bills, a Successful book by Derven and Nichols.

Three basic types of garage doors are offered for today's home: wood, metal (steel or aluminum), and fiberglass. All come in single-door and double-door sizes for modern overhead operation, with or without an automatic door opener.

Single-size garage doors can be 8, 9 or 10 ft. wide, and, depending upon brand selected, are 6 ft. 8 in., 7 ft., 7 ft. 6 in., and 8 ft. high. Double-width doors come in 15, 16, 17 and 18 ft. widths, and the same heights as single doors. Other custom-size doors may be ordered at higher cost.

Within the basic types of doors available, there are a number of specific design selections including:

- Flush panels of tempered hardboard which provide an unbroken surface that does not trap dirt or dust. This door style blends with most architectural stylings and can be painted any color. The flush door also offers the homeowner the opportunity to create a special design through the use of decorative wood trim offered in numerous kits by the door manufacturers. Light inserts also are possible in one section or several sections of the door.

- Raised and carved panel garage doors also provide an almost endless selection of self-created designs. The decorative wood panels may be ordered in square or horizontal styles, with or without routed designs, which may be specified. Thickness of the raised and carved panels usually is $^{11}/_{16}$ or ¾ in.

- Fiberglass doors are offered in various translucent, colored panels. The panels transmit up to 60 per cent of the outside sunlight into the garage, making the area brighter for home projects. Fiberglass doors are said to rarely need painting and weigh approximately one-third as much as a wood door, making the units easy to operate. Designs are limited, usually to a series of deep ribs.

- Metal garage doors also rely heavily on deep ribbed designs that provide a horizontal appearance. This type door comes with or without a lightweight plastic insulating core, can be ordered with window lights, and is factory-painted to minimize future maintenance.

Most overhead sectional doors are assembled at the site with four or five horizontal sections, de-

Fiberglass and metal overhead garage doors feature a rib design that blends well with lap siding, as shown here. The doors are easily maintained by an occasional hose rinsing.

Maximum daylight transmission is another feature of the fiberglass overhead garage door, making the garage a playroom, if desired. At night, when lit from the inside, the door also provides lighting in front of the garage.

pending upon design. Window lights can be specified in the third, fourth or fifth panel from the base, with the latest trend toward using the top panel for both better design and security reasons. When the top panel is used, lights are generally fan-shaped with smaller panes installed, with or without lead tape for further decoration.

One-piece wood or metal overhead and sliding garage doors also are available and have been used extensively in the West. The overhead style extends outside the door frame when lifted and generally is harder to operate for a woman or child. By-passing

wood doors frequently are used for Western residential garages, but such units provide only half access to the garage at any given time.

While not a design factor of the home exterior, automatic garage door operators are worthy of consideration when updating. These units permit you to open and close the door from inside your car, in all kinds of weather. The electronically controlled units have been greatly improved in recent years, nearly eliminating the early problems of others opening your door (with their controls) or of the doors going up and down with the passage of an airplane.

Before

After

3. Siding

Siding can add new dimensions to the looks and efficiency of an old home. This is widely accepted, but most homeowners are amazed to discover they have over 500 different styles and selections to choose from.

Careful attention should be given in selecting the proper siding material for both new homes and major remodeling projects. Aside from providing weather protection, the siding material selected must do justice to the architectural styling of the home, and be as maintenance-free as possible.

Today you may choose from a number of "basic" types and styles of siding such as: wood and wood-base materials, metal, plastic, masonry and mineral composition. Each has its own characteristics and may be found in most locales. Siding can be obtained in many different patterns and can be finished naturally, stained, or painted.

Fundamentals

Before further detailing the specific types you may wish to consider for your home, it's well to have a basic understanding of a few fundamentals. First, most sidings may be applied directly over existing siding if you choose to not remove the original material. However, badly damaged or insect-infested material is best removed before re-siding. Likewise, homes with extensive moisture problems evident on the exterior siding surface may well require the

The 1940 tract house has been modified in many ways across the country, but probably no more dramatically than this Los Angeles dwelling restyled by Widom/Wein and Associates, architects. The stucco-frame structure today has an entirely new appearance with soaring roof lines and exterior walls sheathed with 1x6 resawn square joint tongue and groove clear grade redwood lumber. Original front-of-the-house dormers gave way to a flat roof area with recessed windows; the rear of the home was completely transformed with a large fixed window and sliding glass doors opening onto a brick patio. (Photos: California Redwood Assn.)

removal of some interior wall surfacing, and installation of insulation with a vapor barrier that faces the warm side of the wall.

The main difficulty you can anticipate when applying new siding over existing siding is adjustment of the window and door trim to compensate for the added wall thickness. The window sills on most houses extend far enough beyond the siding, so that new siding should not affect them. However, the casing may be nearly flush with the siding and require some type of extension. One method of accomplishing this extension is by adding a "same size" trim member over the existing casing. The drip cap at doors and windows can be either replaced or removed, and blocking installed behind to hold it out from the wall a distance equal to the new siding thickness.

Contractors

Re-siding a home is a major undertaking that is often left to professionals. It should be added, however, that the re-siding business has been a major source of homeowner discontent, with "fly-by-night" contractors signing up jobs where materials and labor may never be supplied or the quality is questionable. Be certain of the firm you select and check them out thoroughly with the Better Business Bureau; get references from previous customers. Any time spent in this direction will be well worthwhile.

Contractor-applied re-siding projects can range in cost from $2000 to $6000 or more, depending on the size of the home and the material selected.

How Much to Order

To estimate how much siding is needed to cover a house, you must first calculate the total surface area. For each exterior wall, multiply the length by the height. To calculate the area of a gable, multiply the length by the height and then divide the re-

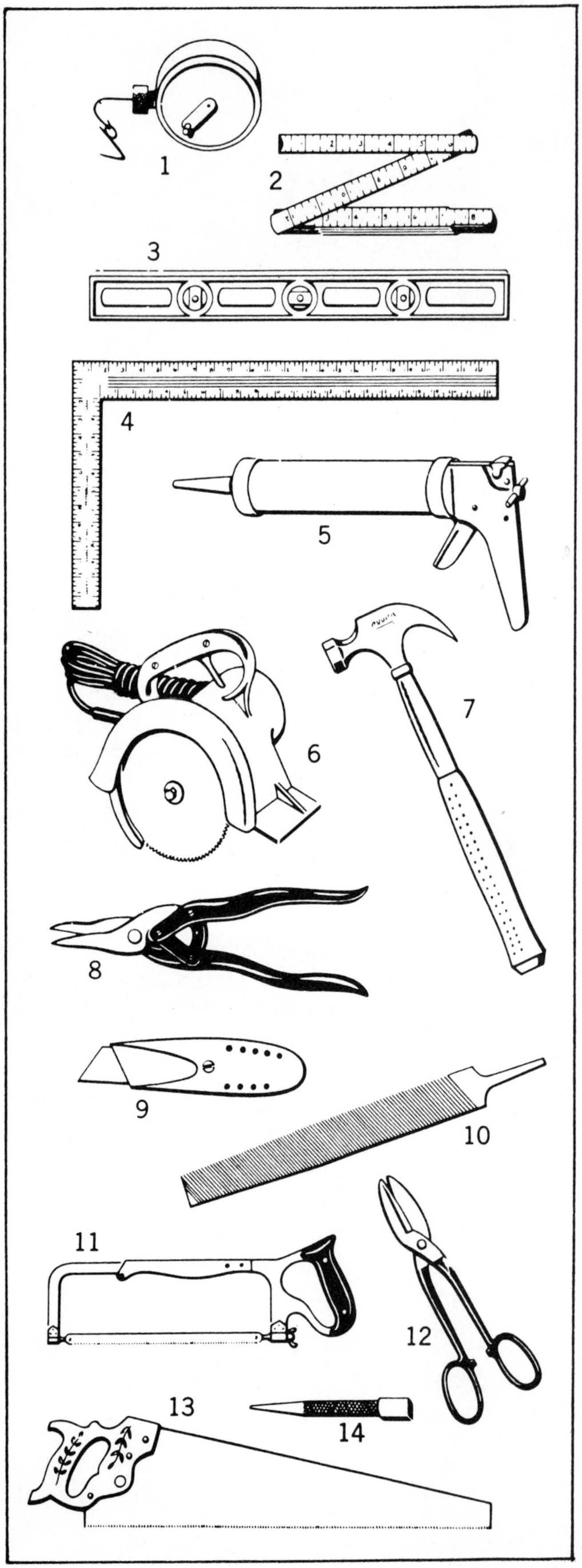

1

2

3

4

5

6

7

8

9

10

11

12

13

14

Hand tools for siding application, when using aluminum shown at left, are suggested in the Installation Manual for applications of Alcoa Building Products. Practices and tools used by siding specialists may vary from one area to another. The tools shown are identified as follows: (1) chalk line reel, (2) folding rule, (3) 2- or 4-foot level, (4) carpenter's steel square, (5) caulking gun, (6) electric saw with aluminum cutting blade, (7) claw hammer, (8) double-action aviation snips, (9) utility knife, (10) metal file, (11) fine-tooth hacksaw, (12) tinsnips, (13) conventional cross-cut handsaw, (14) nail set.

Obtain the Proper Tools and Equipment

Cut and crimp tools for use with vinyl siding include the precision aviation-type curved-blade snips whose double-acting blades easily follow cutting marks in vinyl (photo above) and a pliers-like hand tool (photo below) called a "Snap-lock Punch." It makes a depression crimp in vinyl cut edges that allows the edge to be inserted into trip strips and locked into position.

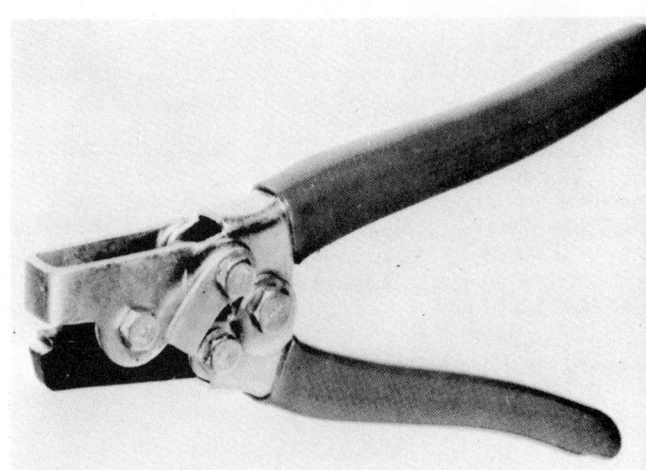

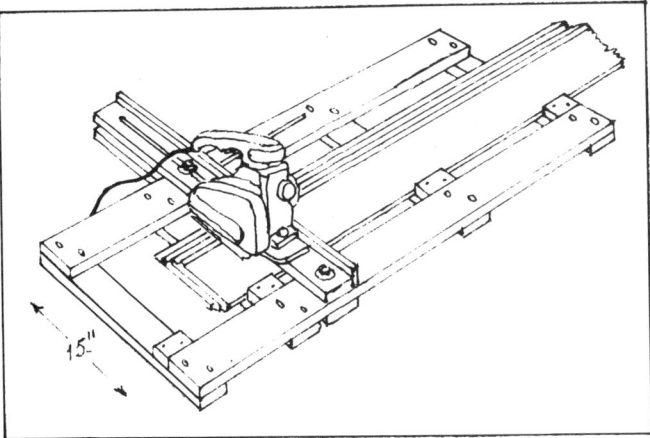

Power cutting of aluminum or vinyl siding may easily be done with a standard table-type radial saw (photo at right) with saw-horses of proper height to rest long siding panels on. With an electric handsaw, cutting is best done using an easy-to-make cutting jig (drawing sketch above); the saw guide member pivots to provide angle cuts. The device, which is shown in the installation manual of Lifeguard Aluminum Siding, permits cutting of several pieces of siding at one time.

Metal brake with a portable mount base that can rest on saw-horses is shown placing a right-angle bend in a piece of aluminum sheet. The brake, made by Tapco Products, and called a "Port-O-Brake," is a necessary device for siding applicators who custom fit prefinished aluminum into cover pieces for window casings, frieze boards and other wood shapes. In braking long strips such as this, care must be used to bend upwards evenly. The edge of material in the brake is clamped down tightly before the bend is made.

Typical equipment setup for a siding applicator is shown here. Using customer's two-car garage, the table-type radial saw is at the right with saw-horses holding siding panel packages. In the center, the portable brakes are laid on saw-horses; the newer brake shown in front is for bending, the older one in back is used simply for straight-edge marking. At left you see part of an aluminum coil-stock roll, and in the front a small air compressor for powering the pneumatic stapler used for soffit installation.

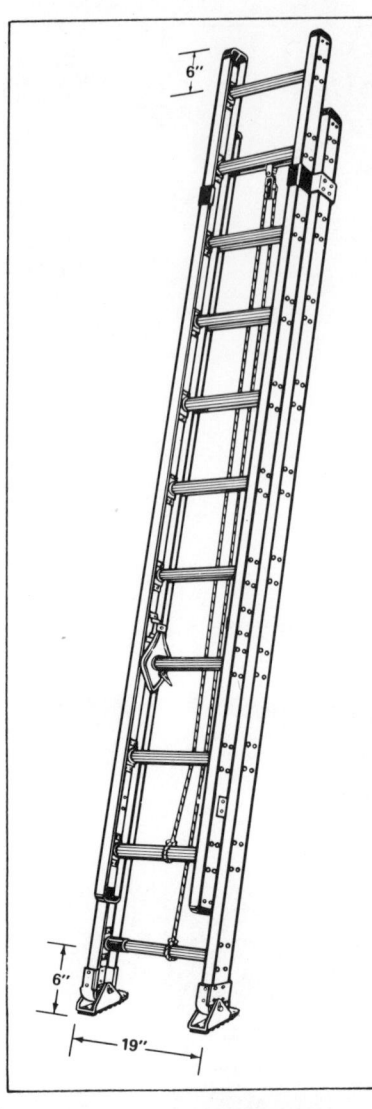

Ladders come in many varieties. At far left, the smaller ladder with its angled flat steps is a good type for siding work. For higher levels, the extension type is necessary. Shown in the drawing is a new nonconductive reinforced-fiberglass extension ladder that combines light weight with safety near electrical lines. This ladder is sold by R.D. Werner Company (see appendix).

Other features to look for in extension ladders of fiberglass or aluminum are: nonslip safety shoes, plastic caps on top ends to avoid marring or scratching, extension life rope and pulley, strong rail-rung joints, plastic wear sleeves on rungs.

When ladders are placed against sidewalls, they should be neither too steep nor too shallow an angle. Recommendation: the distance of the foot of the ladder from the bottom of a vertical wall should be about one-fourth the overall length of the ladder (not the maximum length of an extension ladder, but the length being used).

Be Alert for Safe Practices When Using Scaffolds & Ladders

Saw-horse and plank scaffolds are quite suitable when working on the siding or soffits of a one-story home. A scaffold using three or four 2x10's or 2x12's will allow several men to work in the same area with relative safety.

Use care in attempting to suspend scaffold platforms from ladders. Before doing so, investigate availability in contractor supply firms of special suspension brackets that provide proper attachment to ladders.

When using ladders either for working purposes or simply to reach scaffolds, always face the ladder while going up or down. Lean toward the ladder when working, and try to keep one hand in a holding position or free to make a quick grab.

Uneven ground can be licked when using ladders by the "Ladder Leveler" extension legs shown above in use on brick steps. Made by Alproco Inc. (see appendix). The extension legs have non-skid feet and are adjustable to 9 in. in ¼-in. increments.

U-Shaped aluminum arm at the top of the extension ladder in above photo is called the "Saf-T-Arm" because it holds the ladder away from the vertical surface allowing ample working room. No bending backward necessary. This inexpensive device bolts on any ladder made by the Fracon Company, Inc.

Aluminum scaffold devices of use in residing work include the multi-position folding ladder offered by Goldblatt Tool Company (photo above); it can be used in inverted-U form as a low scaffold or in inverted-V form like a stepladder.

At right, the aluminum scaffold planks made by R.D. Werner Company are able to do double-duty as ladders. The metal devices on which they rest are foot-operated jacks that the workman on the scaffold can raise or lower without stepping off the scaffold. They ride up and down a pair of 2x6 posts held in vertical position by roof plates, and are made by the Hoitsma Adjustable Scaffold Bracket Co.

sult in half. Add these square-footage figures together, plus the areas of any other elements that will be sided such as dormers, bays and porches.

With the total surface area of the house calculated you can adjust this figure to allow for window and door areas that will not be sided. This is done by adding all of the door and window-surface areas and dividing the figure in half (the other half allows for some waste, to be expected in cutting, etc.). Subtract the window-door figure from the total area of the house to arrive at the total square footage of siding required to cover the house.

Fastenings

Installation of metal, plastic and mortar siding is accomplished with various types of fastening devices engineered to the respective materials. Wood siding may be applied with corrosion-resistant nails, usually galvanized steel or aluminum. The length and type of nail varies with the thickness of the siding and type of sheathing.

Materials Available

Here, in alphabetical order, is a rundown on the various types of siding now on the market.

Aluminum

Aluminum siding is one of the most-used residing materials on the market, and is produced by such major firms as Alcoa, Reynolds and U.S. Steel-Alside. The material usually carries a 20-year guarantee against manufacturing defects (not normal weathering or fading); one brand, Alcan Building Products, comes with a special free Hail Protection Limited Warranty that covers 100 per cent of the cost of labor and materials in excess of a $100 deductible for the first two years of service, and coverage prorated at 5 per cent per year for the next 18 years.

Aluminum siding is manufactured in numerous colors, styles and textures including a "shingle-wood" coated with the special Pollution-Resistant Vinyl (PRV) Dualcoat finish that bonds the color tight.

This lightweight material is applied directly over tight sheathing or old siding or masonry surfaces that can be leveled with furring strips. Horizontal-style aluminum siding comes in double 4 in., double 5 in. and 8 in. sizes with prepunched nail-

Alcan Building Products' Shingle-Wood aluminum siding looks and feels like wood shingles and is sold with a 30-year warranty in a wide range of colors.

ing slots. Interlocking action of the panels conceals nail heads and insures a firm seal. Each succeeding panel locks securely into the one before, forming a protective shield.

Aluminum siding also is available in vertical panels providing a 12- or 16-in. plain, grooved, or ribbed surface and again interlocks to conceal nailing. A 12-in. wide panel is offered for use as soffit, fascia and siding. Both lap and vertical styles are made with color-matching accessories.

Asbestos

Asbestos siding has long been one of the least expensive materials for exterior surfacing, yet it is one of the most easily damaged. It will shatter from a heavy blow, but can be easily replaced when applied in 12 x 24-in. shingle form. This type of siding also is available in panels 4 ft. wide and 4-to-12 ft. long in woodgrained and grooved types.

Asbestos shingles come with prepunched nail holes and may be maintained with an occasional washing with a garden hose.

Cedar Shingles

Cedar shingles and shakes offer a natural insulative value as well as excellent resistance to heat transfer, both factors in this age of energy saving. Although each is an attractive product of the western red cedar tree, there are some important differences between the terms "cedar shingle" and "cedar handsplit shake," which are frequently confused in referring to roof and wall applications.

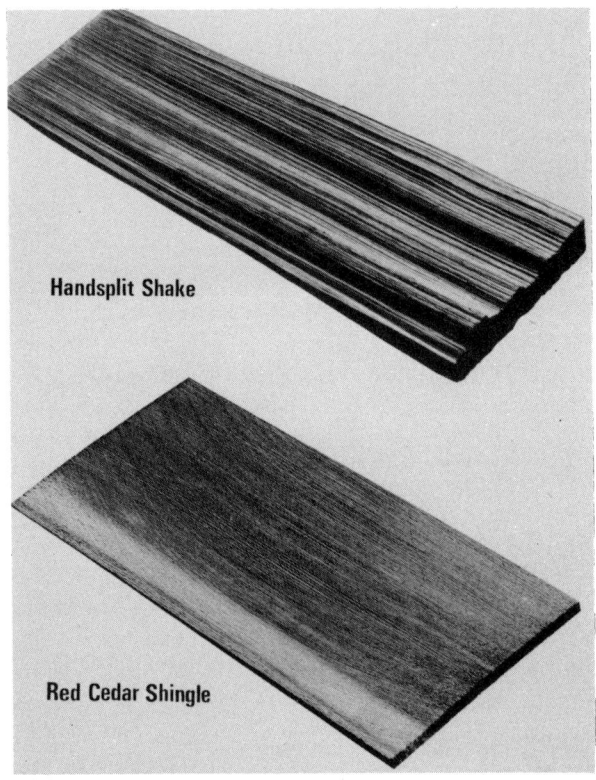

Handsplit Shake

Red Cedar Shingle

Handsplit shakes differ from shingles as shown here in the surface texture. Still another variety is the machine-grooved shake (not shown) which may be used for sidewall applications to give a rough appearance. (Photo: Red Cedar Shingle & Handsplit Shake Bureau)

One basic difference is that the red cedar shingle is machine-sawed to achieve a flat surface; the handsplit shake is—literally—split from the log, retaining its natural texture. The shingle therefore is smooth, and the shake rugged, in appearance. The industry also has a machine-grooved sidewall shake which in reality is a processed shingle.

Either regular or re-manufactured shingles can be used for sidewalls. The latter include: rebutted-rejointed shingles, whose edges have been re-trimmed to make them strictly parallel and at exact right angles to the butts; and, machine-grooved shakes, which additionally have one face grooved or furrowed. Spacing between shingles is optional in wall application.

There are two basic methods of shingle wall application: single-coursed and double-coursed. In single-coursed construction, weather exposures are employed which are slightly less than one-half the nominal shingle length, as follows: 16-in. length exposure—7½-in.; 18-in. length exposure—8½-in.; 24-in. length exposure—11½-in.

In double-coursing, two layers of shingles—one directly over the other—are applied. The top course, machine grooved shakes or shingles, normally are of No. 1 grade with lower grades used for the inner and completely concealed layer. With the doubled courses, extended weather exposures are permissible: 16-in. length—12-in. exposure; 18-in. length—14-in. exposure; 24-in length—16-in. exposure.

Several nailing methods may be used to apply shingles to side walls: On solid sheathing, the shingles are applied directly over a good grade building paper; on open sheathing (2 x 4 vertical studs), paper is applied over the studs and 1 x 4 nailing strips spaced so the course lines fall 2 inches below strip centers; on old wood walls, shingles or shakes can be applied directly as on new sheathing; in overwalling over stucco, nailing strips should first be nailed over the wall to provide a good base for nailing double courses.

Grooved sidewall shakes aside from being available in natural color are offered in either prime-coated or finish-coated in a wide range of colors. Where the building code permits, 8-ft. shingle and shake panels (plain or in color) may be nailed directly to studs on 16- or 24-in. centers.

Cedar shingles and shakes are sold in 25-sq. ft. bundles.

Hardboard

Hardboard siding combines many of the features found in prefinished hardboard paneling used indoors, such as resistance to dents and scratches, together with the special toughness required in an exterior material. Hardboard is a long-lasting material that is seldom damaged.

Exterior hardboard comes in many finishes and styles to simulate rustic planks, clapboard, board-and-batten, contemporary V-groove paneling and stucco surfaces. Some hardboards are preprimed; others are prefinished. Hardboard has no knots or grain to rise or check, and it doesn't splinter, split or crack. It is easy to work with using standard carpenter tools.

Hardboard may be applied over sheathed or unsheathed walls, and generally holds paint longer than lumber sidings. Manufacturers recommend for re-siding applications that the old siding first be removed. If this is neither possible nor practical, a flat level plane should be provided by applying furring strips or plywood sheets.

Mansard roofs such as the one above are named after a French architect who made the style quite popular in the early 17th century. A popular revival of the style in the U.S. began in about 1970 and has grown extensively for remodeled buildings. The above home, a formerly boxy-looking two-story, was remodeled with steep rafter framing on the second floor, plus a new garage. The upper roofing is conventional asphalt shingles. The steep portions are finished with thatch-type hardboard panels painted to match the roofing shingle color.

When is a Roof a Wall?

A mansard roof with recessed windows has asphalt shingles on both the shallow and steep roof areas. Bottom photo shows the complications that can arise with mansard styling when fireplace chimneys are encountered. Flashings must be custom-fitted, and it's no job for an amateur.

The big question here may be where the change occurs from a roof to a wall or vice versa. With materials such as cedar shingles, it makes a difference in the amount of shingle exposure. One answer has been given by the International Conference of Building Officials. In the ICBO's Uniform Building Code, a ruling indicates that a roof becomes a wall when the angle of slope reaches 60 degrees or greater. This is roughly equal to a 20-in.-12 pitch (a rise of 20 ft. in a horizontal run of 12 ft.).

Typical of thousands of modest ranch houses, this home enjoyed a wooded setting but lacked effective landscaping as well as sufficient living area for the owner's family. Following a major remodeling program, the house took on a new appearance complete with new landscaping, relocation of the front door, new windows and a complete re-siding with Masonite Colorlok. The garage was converted to living area.

Before

After

Before

After

This 52-year-old dwelling originally housed one family with living room, dining area, kitchen and sun porch on the first floor; three bedrooms and a bath were on the floor above. In the reworked floor plan the stairwell was walled off from the first floor and an outdoor stairway and entrance created for the second floor which now serves as a separate apartment. A screened porch was added at the rear of the home, topped with an open deck for the second-floor inhabitants. The front stoop was replaced by steps and a brick planter, and prefinished Masonite Colorlok lap siding was used to transform the exterior of the house.

39

Re-siding with Hardboard

Re-siding a home with hardboard siding is much like working with natural wood. First, inspect the home to determine any unusual problems and estimate the amount of hardboard siding needed. With all materials on hand, you are ready to begin.

(1) Nail any loose existing siding firmly into place and replace any broken boards. Remove old trim, molding, and caulking for proper fit of accessories around doors and windows.

(2) Remove downspouts. If new fascia will be installed, remove gutters as well. Measure distance from lower edge of the existing siding to top wall of each corner. Using the longest measurement obtained, measure downward at each corner and mark the low point at bottom of wall. This will aid in aligning the bottom starter strip parallel with top of wall and will avoid irregular or wedge-shaped piece of siding at top next to soffit. Make second mark 2

in. above mark already made at each corner. This locates top of starter strip. Stretch chalk line from corner to corner and snap reference line to mark starter strip location. Starter strip must meet all corners.

(3) Because few older homes have straight walls, it may be necessary to install furring strips behind starter strip to insure that new walls will be straight. Install starter strip, nailing 16 in. on center. Starter strip should end about 2 in. from corners to allow for corner accessories if used.

(4) Install continuous inside and/or outside corners.

(5) Apply caulking around existing window or door trim, seat J-trim in caulking, and nail J-trim in place on 12-in. centers. Install J-trim wherever necessary to cover and protect ends of siding laps. Or, if window/door trim protrudes beyond siding, butt siding

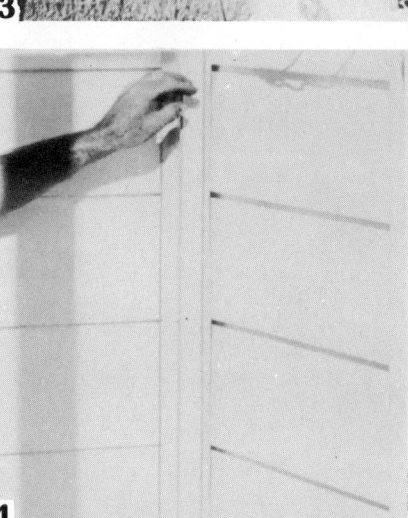

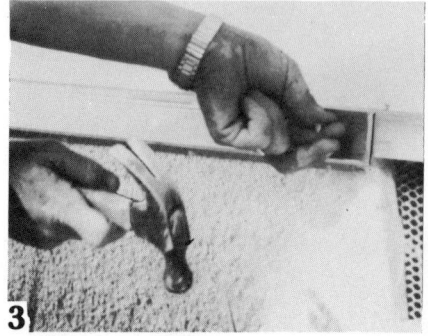

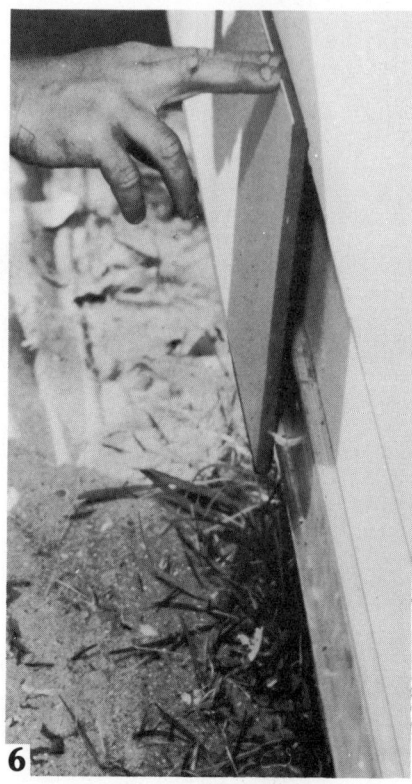

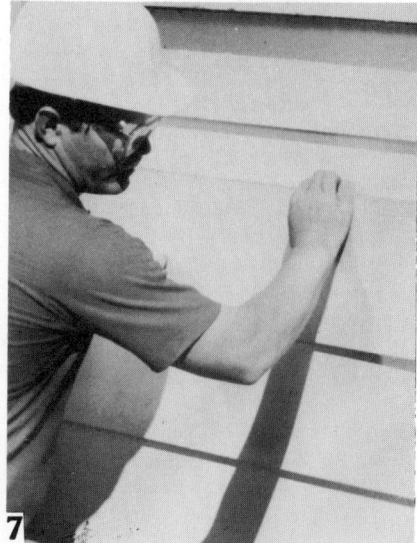

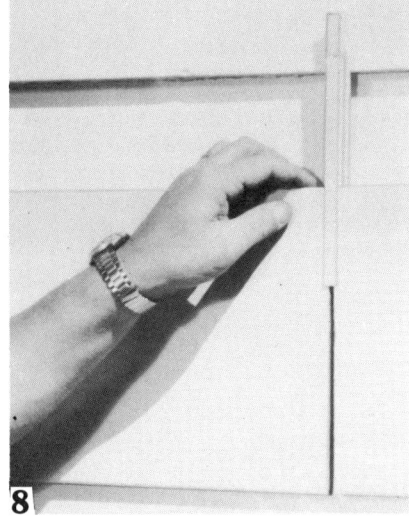

8

9

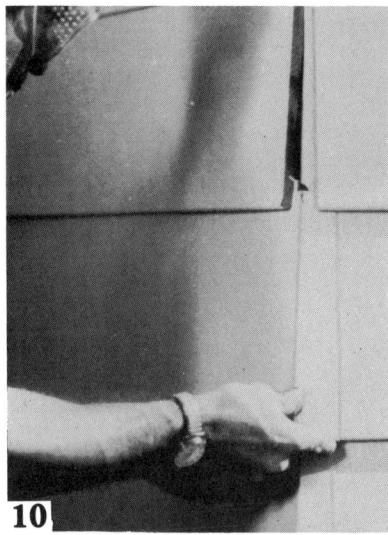

10

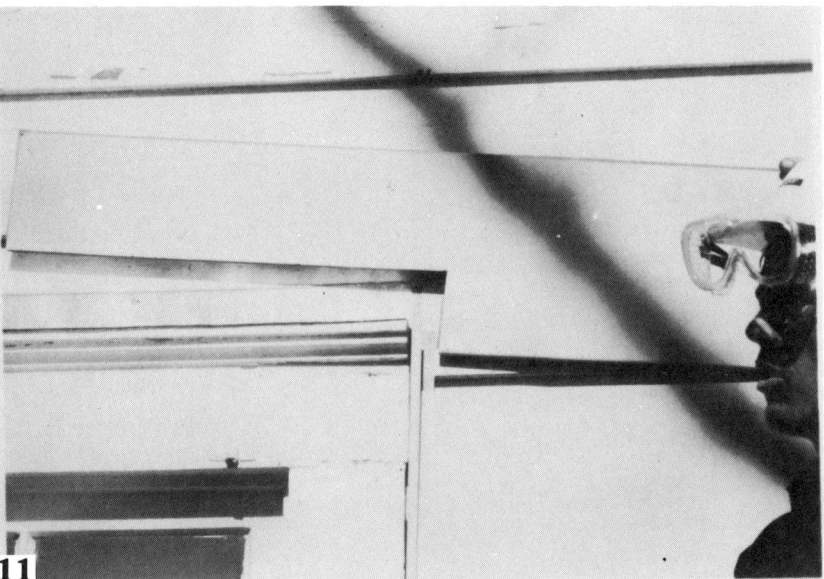

11

12

against trim and caulk the joint. This eliminates need for J-trim.

(6) Install first lap of siding, engaging interlocking spline with starter strip. Nail ½ in. below top edge of siding, using galvanized nail that will penetrate at least 1¼ in. into existing wood siding. Pull downward slightly when nailing to insure spline engagement. Do not countersink nails.

(7) When measuring and fitting pieces which fit end-to-end, allow ⅛-in. gap between pieces for insertion of butt joint molding. Also allow ⅛-in. gap around all trim to be caulked later.

(8) Insert joint molding into ⅛-in. gap from top. After insertion, nail ends of both siding pieces in place ½ in. from top edge. For best appearance, stagger joints at least three ft. apart horizontally or three laps vertically. It might be noted that when going over old horizontal siding, it may be necessary to install horizontal furring strips to provide a straight nailing base and a straight uniform appearance. This also brings nailing base out far enough to insure proper locking of spline with next lap.

(9) Be sure to engage mounting spline on the beveled top edge of the siding, pressing down firmly on each piece of siding to

insure proper seating. (Note horizontal furring strip in illustration.)

(10) Outside corners can be installed as work progresses or after entire wall is sided. Slide corners up into place, slipping top under course above and seal tabs under lower edge. Drive nails through exposed hole at top of corner.

(11) Siding may have to be cut or notched to fit around windows and doors. When cutting more than 1 in. or 2 in. into siding, make a joint as shown. When fitting under windows, cut as needed and caulk later.

(12) On gable ends, install J-trim along existing or trim boards. Make template to match angle of roof and cut shorter pieces to install along the angle. Then measure length needed between two end pieces, allowing for two butt joint moldings, and cut piece to fit. Stagger joint moldings for best appearance.

When the re-siding job is finished, caulk wherever the cut edge of the siding may be exposed, such as over or under windows. It is not necessary to caulk at joint moldings or individual outside corners. (Photos: Masonite Corporation)

The combination of different siding materials can add substantially to the architectural styling and appearance of a home. Pictured here in the "before" version, this house was expanded with a one-story add-on styled in Tudor wood and stucco, only the "stucco" used for the addition is actually hardboard paneling that blends with the original stucco and brick. (Photos: Masonite Corporation)

After

Before

Hardboard lap siding is 7/16-in. (nominal) thick and comes in 16-ft. lengths. Widths range from 6 to 12 in. Panels for vertical application are 4 ft. wide and 8, 9 or 10 ft. long. Thickness is 7/16-in. (nominal). These panels come in a variety of grooved patterns and frequently are used with battens.

Plywood

Plywood siding offers a great range of sidewall surfacing treatments for both new construction and remodeling. Wood species such as redwood, fir, cypress and cedar are used in the manufacture of various overlaid, grooved and textured plywoods, some of which are factory-primed and others of which are factory-finished.

There are over a dozen general types of plywood sidings, including self-aligning lap and the many vertical panel types. Groovings range all the way from wide 1½-in. furrowed grooves that are 12 or 16 in. on center (reverse board and batten) to the popular Texture 1-11 type and other grooves 2, 4, 6,

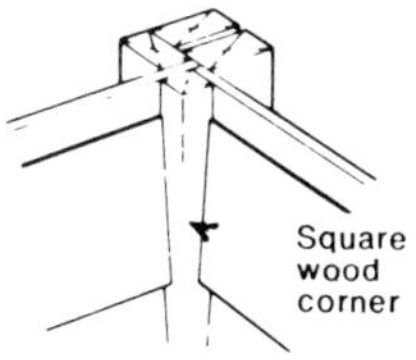

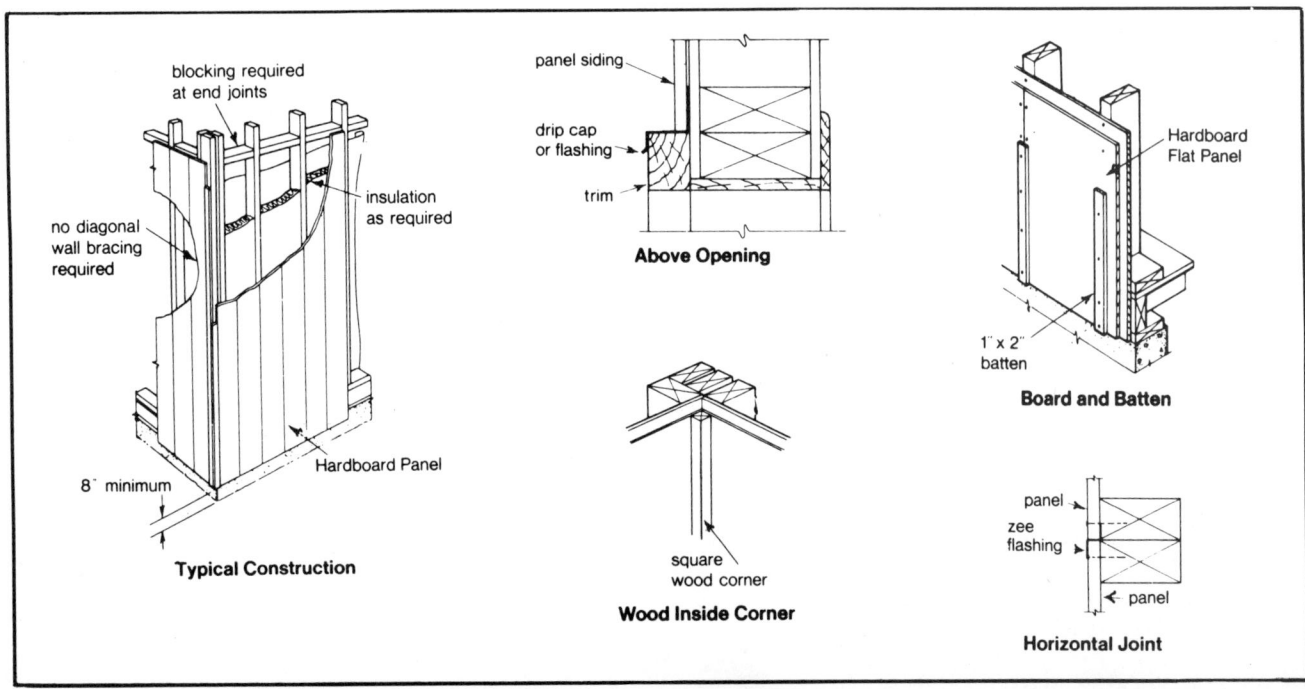

Square wood corner

Wood Inside Corner

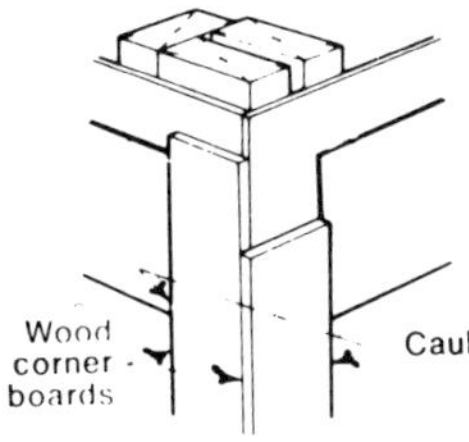

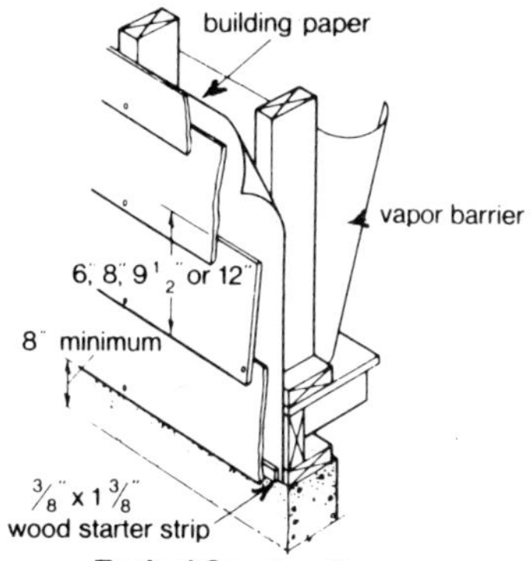

building paper

vapor barrier

6, 8, 9½ or 12"

8" minimum

3/8" x 1 3/8" wood starter strip

Typical Construction

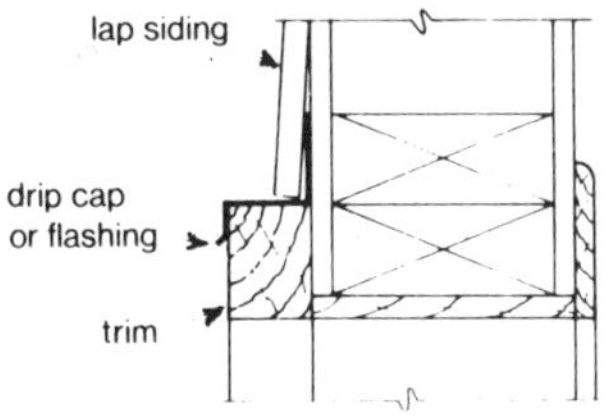

lap siding

drip cap or flashing

trim

Above Opening

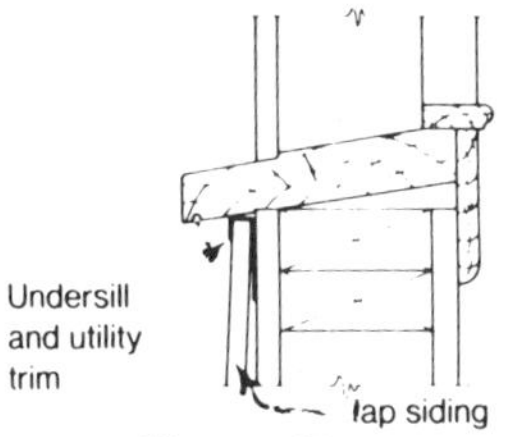

Undersill and utility trim

lap siding

Window Sill

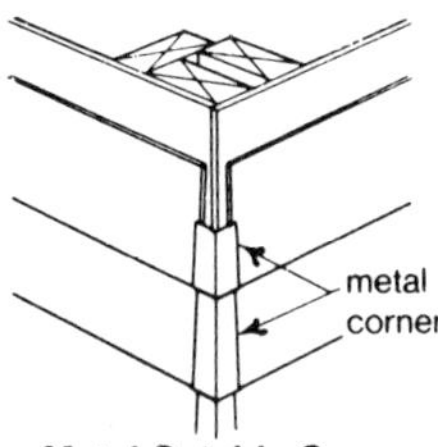

Wood corner boards

Caulk

Wood Outside Corner

metal corners

Metal Outside Corner

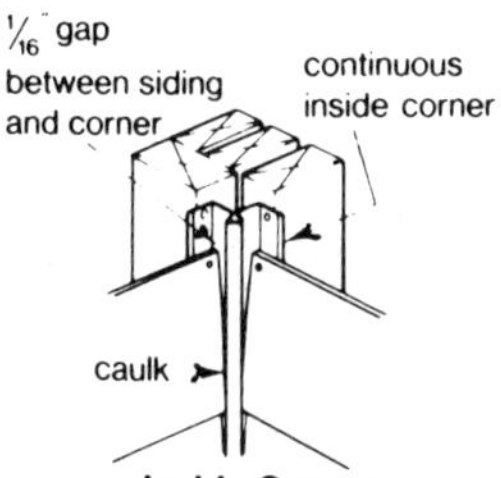

1/16" gap between siding and corner

continuous inside corner

caulk

Inside Corner

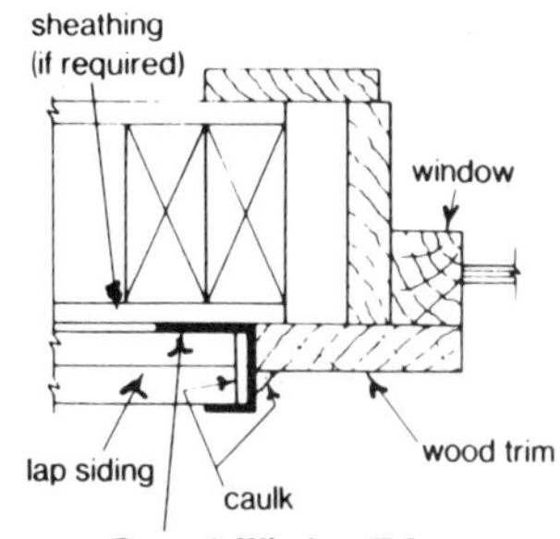

sheathing (if required)

window

lap siding

caulk

wood trim

Door & Window Trim

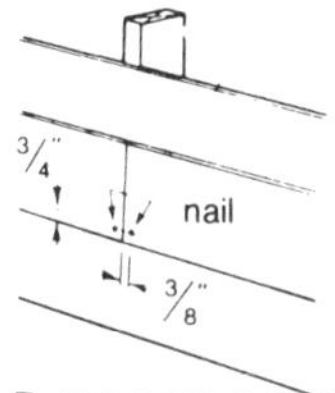

3/4"

nail

3/8"

Butt Joint Detail

Hardboard Lap and Panel Details

Corners and joints of hardboard siding installations are handled in certain common ways indicated in the drawing sketches above for lap or bevel siding and below for sheet or panel siding.

These installation details appear in the hardboard siding catalog of Champion Bldg. Products for the firm's "Sundance" and "Cadence" siding lines, and the procedures will generally be

applicable for hardboard sidings made by other companies as well. However, some firms producing plastic-film surfaced sidings may recommend installation in a slightly different manner. Note: sketches shown are intended for new construction applications, but joint and corner treatments when re-siding will be essentially the same.

blocking required at end joints

insulation as required

no diagonal wall bracing required

8" minimum

Hardboard Panel

Typical Construction

panel siding

drip cap or flashing

trim

Above Opening

square wood corner

Wood Inside Corner

Hardboard Flat Panel

1" x 2" batten

Board and Batten

panel

zee flashing

panel

Horizontal Joint

8 or 16 in. on center. There also is narrow saw kerfing. Most types of panels have shiplapped or tongue-and-groove edge choices. All standard plywood siding thicknesses are represented.

Plywood surfaces ranged all the way from sanded to rough sawn, striated or brushed, and in various grades including such faces as knotty cedar. There are medium density overlaid surfaces, paint-primed and even acrylic-overlaid in permanent colors.

Lap siding comes in various plywood lengths up to 16 ft. with one-piece overlaid faces. Vertical plywood sidings are generally available in 4-ft. widths, and up to 10-ft. lengths; some come up to 12 ft., and a few to 16 ft.

Aside from the standard sidings made by most firms (reverse board and batten, rough sawn, brushed, kerfed, etc.), a number of leading manufacturers offer proprietary plywood sidings for more than 13 additional exterior treatments.

Redwood

Redwood siding is an all-weather siding widely used throughout the United States because of its excellent combination of physical and aesthetic qualities. The material is available in a wide range of attractive grades, patterns and sizes. A choice of rough sawn or smooth textures enchances the pleasing contrasts of deep red heartwood and creamy sapwood. Its character runs so deep that even construction grades are frequently choosen for highly visible applications.

The California Redwood Association and most manufacturers recommend clear all heart and clear grades for siding applications, and stress that both should be "Certified Kiln Dried" or bear the initials "CKD". Also recommended is preapplication treatment with a water repellent, which will improve the finish performance no matter what type of finish is used.

Among the styles of redwood siding currently

Patterns in Plywood Siding

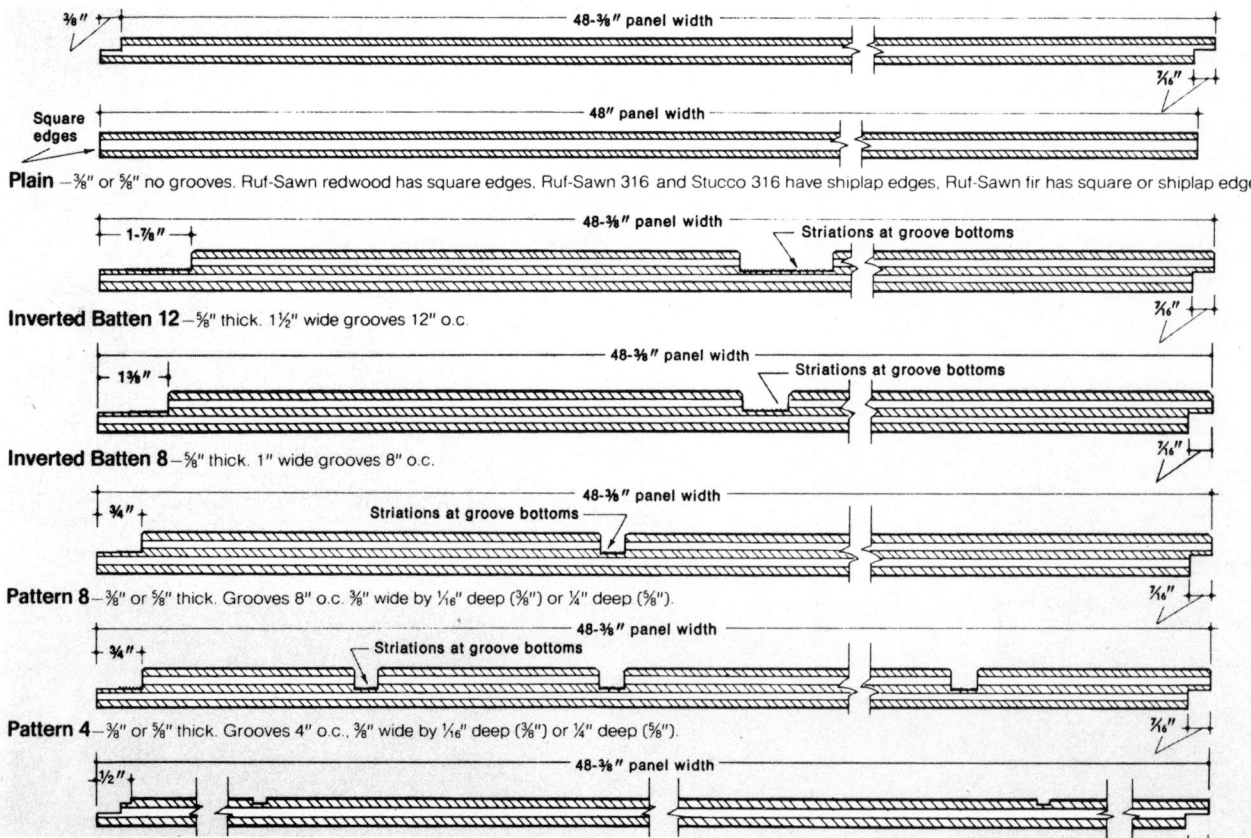

Plywood siding panels are produced in various thicknesses as well as face surfaces. (Drawing: Simpson Timber Co.)

offered are: plain bevel, rabbeted bevel, shiplap, V rustic, tongue and groove, channel rustic and board and batten. This highly insulative material can be ordered with factory-applied water repellent, primed with paint, or finished with stain. No other commercial softwood produced in America takes and holds stain or paint better than redwood; yet, without a finish, redwood performs equally well and with the seasons its deep reddish-brown coloring turns gradually to a silvery driftwood gray.

Redwood Magic

What was a 1930-ish small, ordinary, seven-room bungalow is now a contemporary home. Located near Muir Beach, San Francisco, the house was redone with redwood plywood siding, trimmed with redwood battens and finished with water repellent for a natural appearance. The "after" view illustrates how an old chimney can be encased for a "today" look and new windows installed for better visibility. Architect William Weber Kirsch also redid the interior. (Photos: California Redwood Assn.)

Before

After

Redwood Application and Finishing

Exterior Nailing

Proper nailing is a factor to a successful re-siding. Shown here are approved methods for applying various types of redwood siding. Note the suggested spacing required in several cases. (Drawings: Simpson Timber Co.)

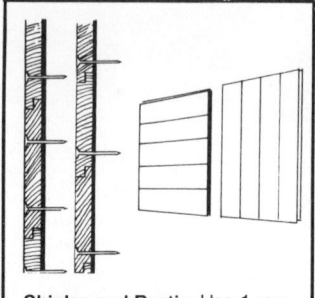

Shiplap and Rustic: Use 1 row of nails for siding 6" or less in width and 2 rows for wider.

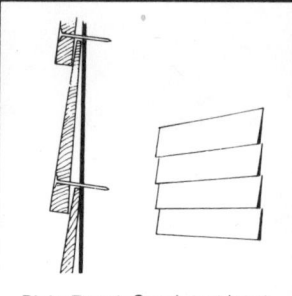

Plain Bevel: Overlap at least 1"—nail must clear tip.

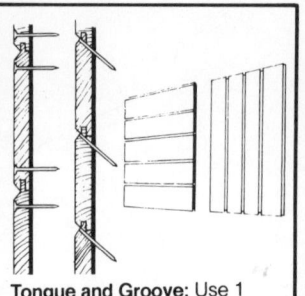

Tongue and Groove: Use 1 row of nails for siding 6" or less in width and 2 rows for wider.

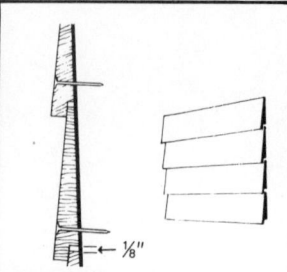

Rabbeted Bevel: Nail 1" from lower edge and leave ⅛" expansion clearance between courses.

- Use only corrosion-resistant hot-dipped (or hot-tumbled) galvanized or stainless steel nails. A small-headed nail such as Maze Stormguard Splitless ring shank nail is especially recommended. Electro-galvanized nails should be avoided.
- For vertical siding use 8d ring shank siding nails into ½-in. minimum thickness plywood or 1-in. nominal thickness lumber sheathing; one or two rows as noted below at 24 in. o.c. maximum.
- If ring shank nails are not used when nailing vertical siding to sheathing, use horizontal blocking at 24 in. o.c. to provide solid nailing.
- For applying horizontal siding use nails long enough to penetrate 1½ in. into studs or wood sheathing and studs combined.
- On mansard or similar type roofs, do not exceed 20° from vertical.
- For additional information refer to CRA Data Sheet 4A1-1 on nails and nailing.

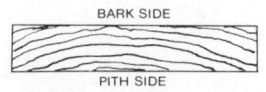

- Prevent shell-out; to prevent flat grain boards from shell-out, be sure to nail with bark side out.

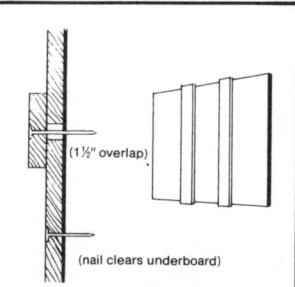

Board and Batten: 8d siding nail for underboard. 10d siding nail for batten.

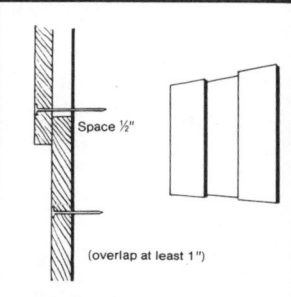

Board on Board: 8d siding nail for underboard. 10d siding nail for batten.

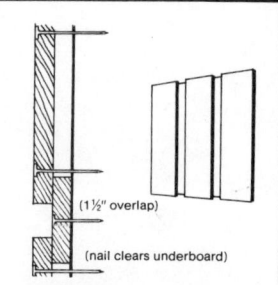

Reverse Batten: 8d siding nail for underboard. 10d siding nail for batten.

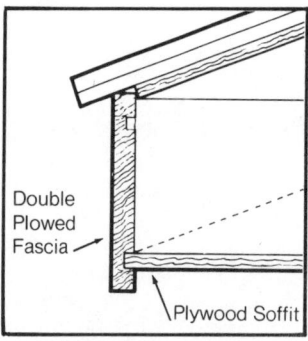

Double Plowed Fascia

Plywood Soffit

Fascia Installation

Nailing: In applying fascia use 8d nails that penetrate 1" into structural member. Use 2 nails per rafter for 1x6 (3 per rafter for 1x8).

Interior Paneling Installation

Easy to apply, Redwood Paneling can be attached to furring strips or directly over dry wall areas using a construction grade adhesive. For vertical application use nails, staples or panel adhesives. For overhead use, Redwood Paneling should either be nailed or stapled with a power stapler.

Redwood Paneling: Horizontal or vertical. 6" widths or narrower. 1-4d finish nail, blind-nailed.

Note: Redwood Paneling (⅜") should not be used in exterior applications.

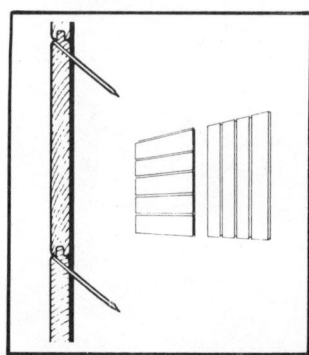

PATTERNED SIDINGS

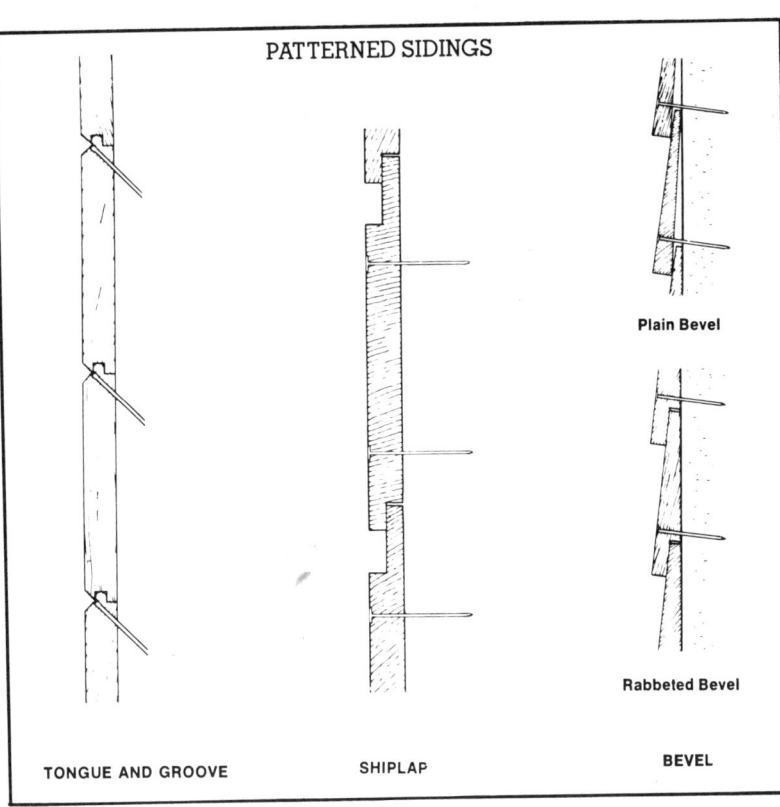

Plain Bevel

Rabbeted Bevel

TONGUE AND GROOVE   SHIPLAP   BEVEL

Solid Wood Siding

Solid wood sidings in various wood species are still sold by many lumber suppliers, but principally the bevel type is available. In redwood, however, a wide range of patterns is available (see sketches at left) and, for a still further choice of exterior appearance, square-edged siding boards in redwood can be used as indicated below. These sketches are taken from the application literature of the California Redwood Association (see appendix).

BOARD SIDINGS

Nominal and standard dressed sizes for boards, strips, and dimension lumber are shown in the table below.

THICKNESS		WIDTH		
ROUGH (Nominal)	DRESSED S1S or S2S Green or Dry	ROUGH (Nominal)	DRESSED S1E or S2E Green	DRESSED S1E or S2E Dry Finish
3/4	11/16	3	2 9/16	2 1/2
1	3/4 *	4	3 9/16	3 1/2
1 1/4	1 1/16	6	5 5/8	5 1/2
1 1/2	1 5/16	8	7 1/2	7 1/4
2	1 5/8	10	9 1/2	9 1/4
		12	11 1/2	11 1/4

*The standard for green 1" is 25/32 but is frequently manufactured to 3/4" net.

Vertical grain has greater stability than flat grain, and weathers exceptionally well. It is usually preferred for exterior finish carpentry. Flat grain redwood is highly figured as compared to the more subdued, uniform pattern of vertical grain redwood.

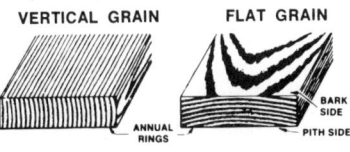

VERTICAL GRAIN   **FLAT GRAIN**

ANNUAL RINGS   BARK SIDE   PITH SIDE

STANDARD BOARD AND BATTEN: *Drive one 8d nail midway between edges of the underboard, at each bearing. Then apply batten strips and nail with one 10d nail at each bearing so that shank passes through space between underboards.*

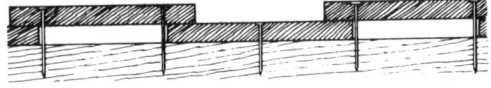

BOARD ON BOARD: *Space underboards to allow 1 1/2-inch overlap by outer boards at both edges. Use one 8d nail per bearing for underboards. Outer boards must be nailed twice per bearing to insure proper fastening; use 10d nails, driven so that the shanks clear the underboard by approximately 1/4 inch.*

REVERSE BATTEN: *Nailing is similar to board on board. Drive one 8d nail per bearing through center of under strip, and two 10d nails per bearing through outer boards.*

Steel

Steel siding on the market today is expected to provide up to 30 years of service under normal conditions, with manufacturers suggesting that all scratches and indentations be touched up immediately to prevent rust conditions. This material is one of the most costly of sidings, but boasts nearly maintenance-free features. Because it can be easily damaged during applications, it is often installed by a professional contractor.

Steel siding is a highly sophisticated product offered in many different colors achieved with silicone resins and color pigments. These coatings provide chalk resistance, gloss and color retention, and re-

sistance to erosion and abrasion. Standard styles include clapboard and vertical panels plus a full range of accessory items including gutters, downspouts, soffit and fascia systems.

Solid Vinyl

Solid vinyl sidewall covering combines acoustical and thermal insulation properties with the aesthetic appeal of natural wood. This siding has the look of painted wood, yet requires little or no maintenance or painting since the color runs throughout the material. It is impervious to pollutants in the air, and unaffected by fungi and termites.

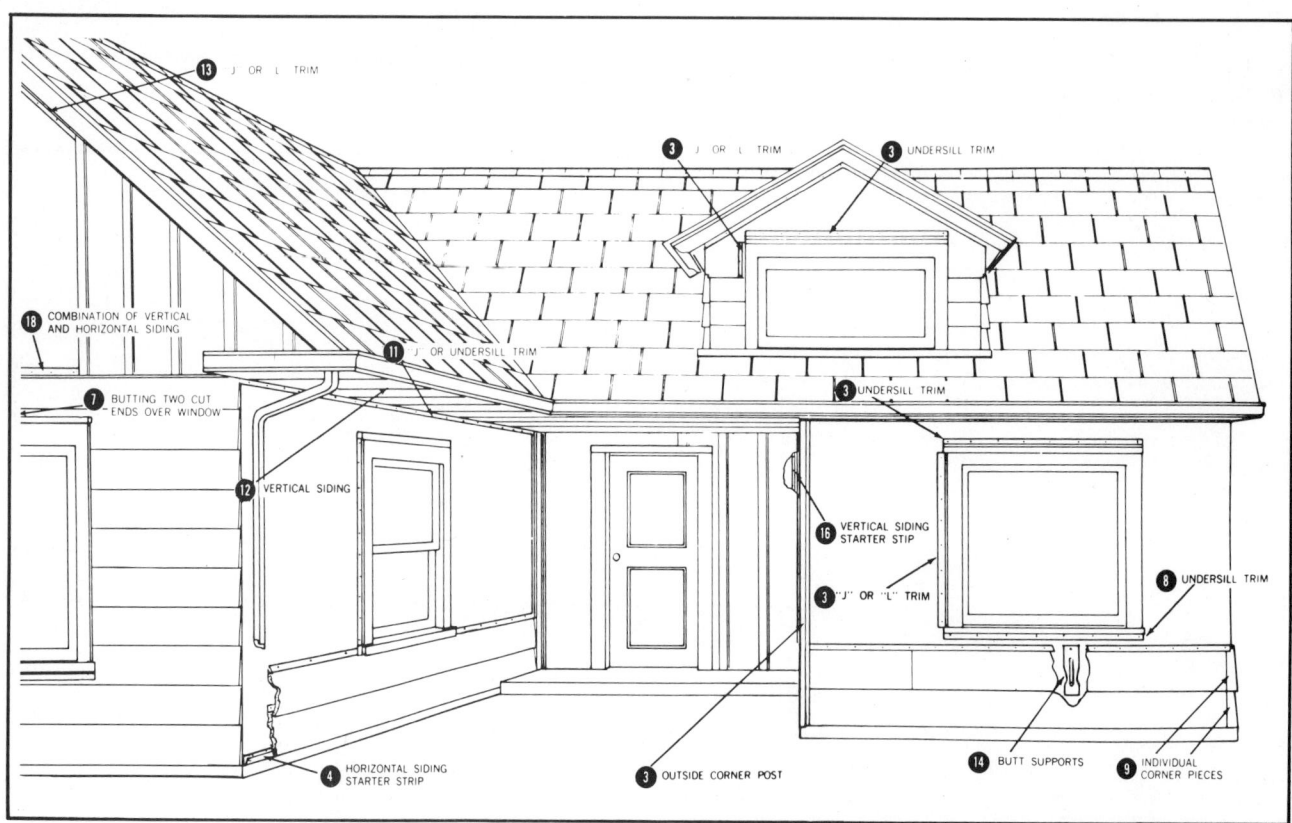

Wood-grain textures and prefinished colors make steel siding an attractive remodeling material. Both clapboard and vertical panel styles are offered, plus a full line of accessories: "J" and "L" trim and undersill trim installed around existing windows and doors (3 & 8), at eaves (11), and at gables (13); starter strip (4) placed at lowest paneling points, with siding panels installed from

bottom up; bottom flange of each panel locks into the top flange of panel beneath it and top flanges are secured with galvanized steel nails; panels butt together where necessary (7) using special supports (14); soffit (12) can be covered with vertical siding applied similar to horizontal siding (Art: American Iron and Steel Inst.).

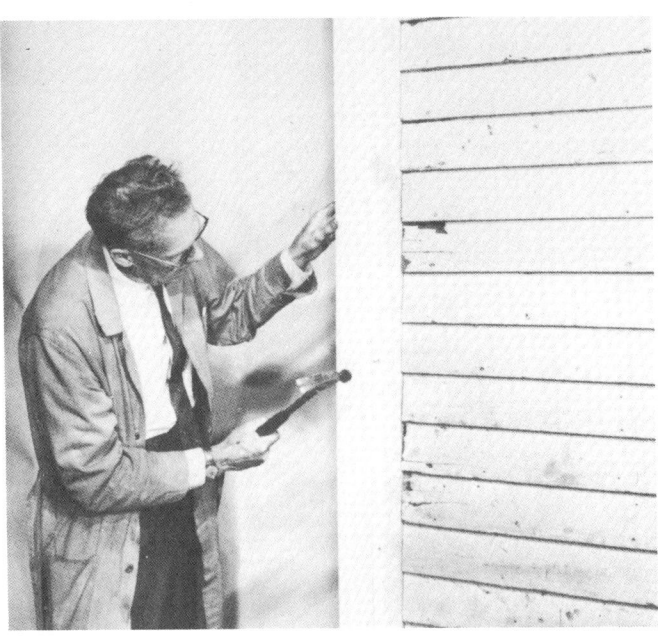

Installation of Solid Vinyl Siding

Outside corner post is positioned on building corner with ¼-in. gap at top for expansion; nails spaced 8 to 12 in. Metal corner units are normally not used with vinyl siding.

Starter strips, as in drawing at right, are kept back 3 in. from building corners so that corner posts can extend downward to point just below bottoms of the strips.

The extruded vinyl starter strips are nailed in slot centers, not quite driving nails up tight. The strips butt to each other, again leaving a ¼-in. expansion gap.

Use of a chalkline and level is recommended around both sides of each building corner, in order to assure that starter course is accurately level and conceals bottom of old siding.

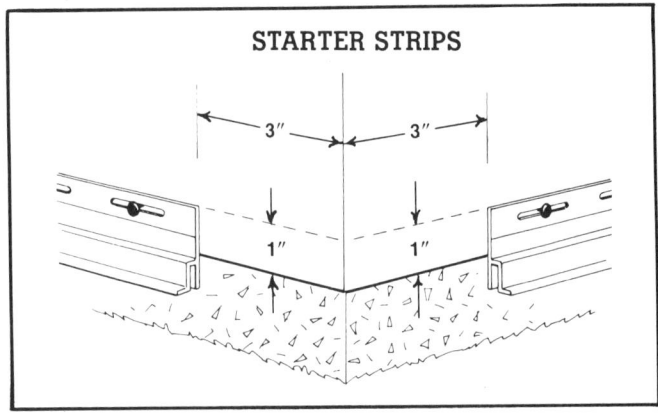

STARTER STRIPS

Inside corners apply in similar way to outside corners with gaps on each side to starter strips. Note that siding panels must be cut to sufficient length to fit within the corner post channels but not fit tightly; there should be a ¼-in. gap between the panel end and the channel back. Corner posts are of extruded vinyl in matching colors.

Photos in this series on this and following pages are from the application manual issued by the Society of the Plastics Industry, while the drawings have been adapted from those appearing in the vinyl siding installation instructions issued by the Certain Teed Corporation.

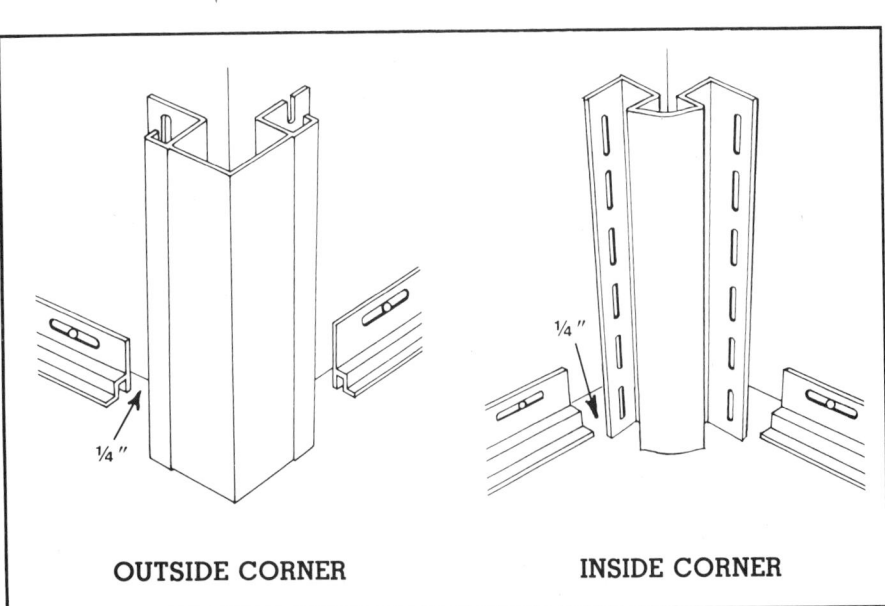

OUTSIDE CORNER   **INSIDE CORNER**

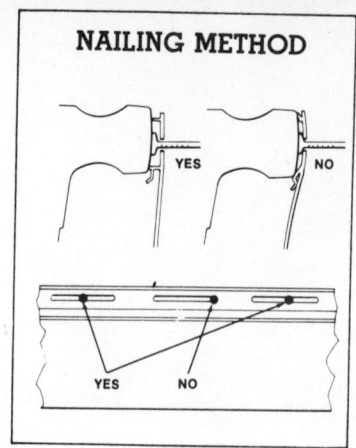

NAILING METHOD

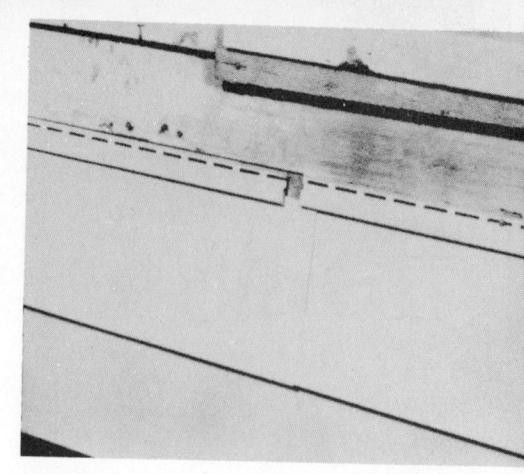

Proper nailing of vinyl siding shown at the right. Corrosion-resistant nails are used and positioned in the centers of the nailing slots at about 16-in. spacings. Be careful not to drive nails fully home; they should be left just slightly loose so the siding hangs on the nails. This permits siding panel movement in expansion and contraction due to temperature changes.

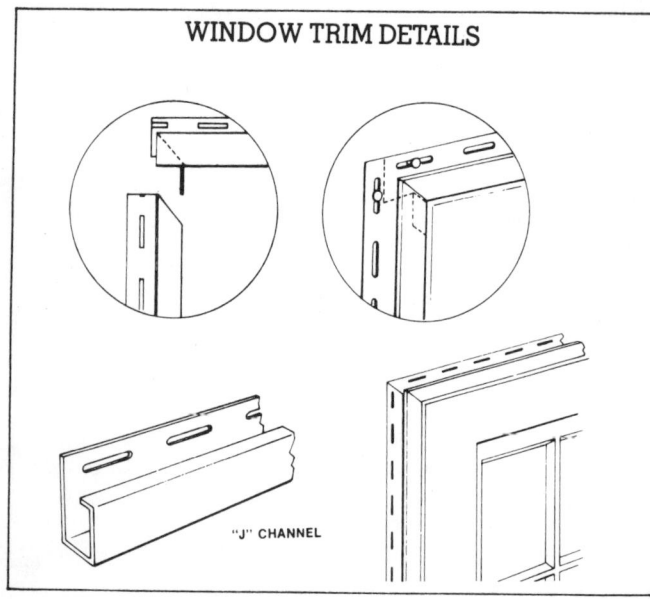

WINDOW TRIM DETAILS

"J" CHANNEL

Fitting Vinyl Around Windows and Doors

Window trim moldings of J-channel shape are of extruded vinyl in colors matching siding. They are placed at sides and top (jambs and head) of each window. Mitered corners with top fold-down tabs are used as indicated in sketches at left.

Below-window fitting is handled by use of a vinyl undersill trim strip whose shape is shown in the sketch at left. Blocking will ordinarily be needed under the trim strip, unless the siding panels happen to fall, so no panel cutting is needed below the window.

Photo at right shows the use of tinsnips for making vertical cuts to fit sides of window. Photos at right below indicate use of utility knife to make horizontal cut using steel square as guide, and the U-shaped under-window cut completed, with waste piece to be discarded.

Crimping tool is used horizontally along raw cut edge to place projecting nubs which will lock into the undersill trim when the panel is slipped upward into position.

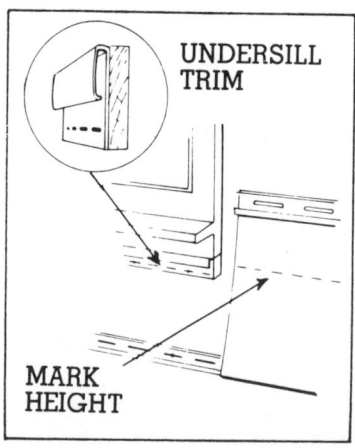

UNDERSILL TRIM

MARK HEIGHT

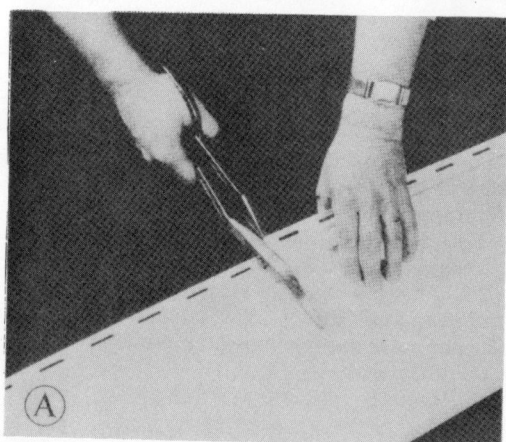

Ⓐ

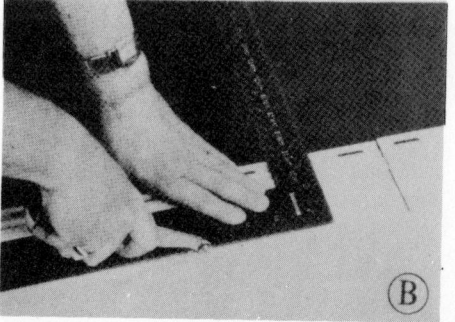

Ⓑ

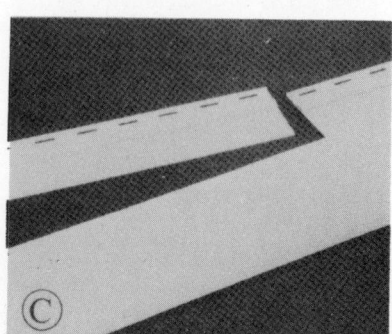

Ⓒ

Siding panels progress upwards with pieces cut to proper length for fit between windows or between window and building corner. Endlaps of panels, if needed, should be staggered one course to another, and overlying lap end should face away from entrance doors.

Over windows, siding panel receives a U-cutout similar to that for under windows but made from the bottom of the panel.

Be sure to measure width carefully between J-channel backs leaving ¼-in. gap at each side.

If old siding doesn't fit window frames well at head and jambs, caulk the cracks before installing the J-channel trim members.

Siding bottom edge slips upward to lock into top edge of the siding course below. If a panel is damaged or marred after being installed, it can be removed and replaced. A special siding zipper tool is used along the bottom edge of the panel above the damaged one. When this edge is unlocked, the damaged panel can be slid downward and removed.

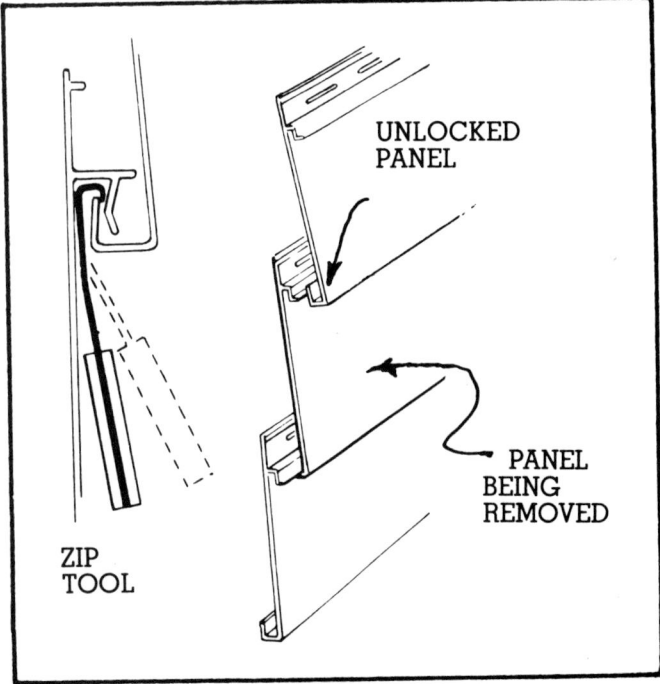

UNLOCKED PANEL

PANEL BEING REMOVED

ZIP TOOL

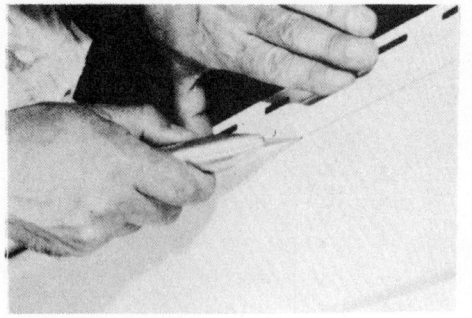

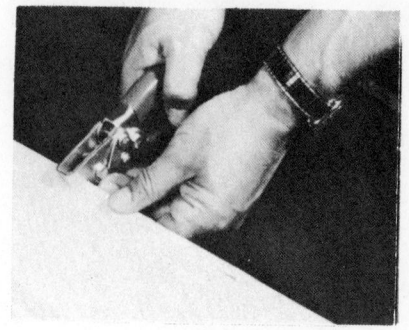

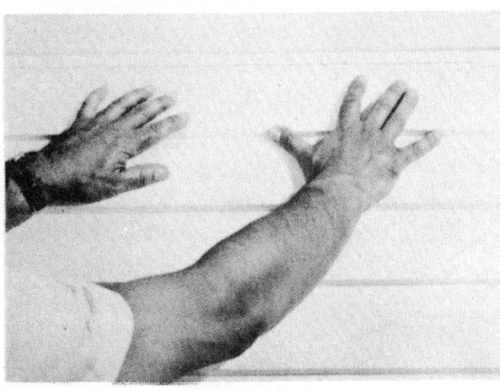

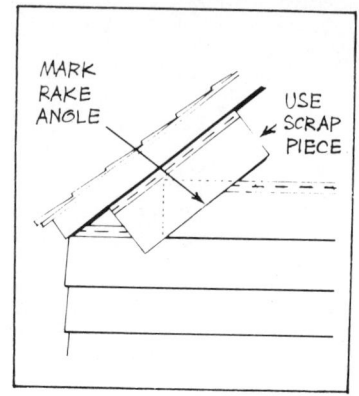

MARK RAKE ANGLE

USE SCRAP PIECE

Finishing Up at the Eaves

Approaching soffit or eave height, the final siding panel will, in all probability, have to be cut or trimmed lengthwise to f a narrower-than-the-panel space. Before measuring for this last step's width, understill trim should be continuously applied with its top edge touching the soffit or eave trim board.

Siding panel is then cut length-wise to a width that will allow it to fit into the under-sill trim. The panel is then punched every 16 to 24 in. so that the raised ear or nub is on the outside face of the panel. Panel is then pushed upward so its bottom edge engages the panel interlock of the course below and the cut upper edge slides into and locks with the undersill trim.

Where panels go up a gable end, J-channel trim is installed along the rake fascia board. Siding panel ends are then angle-cut, as shown in sketch, to fit into the J-channel.

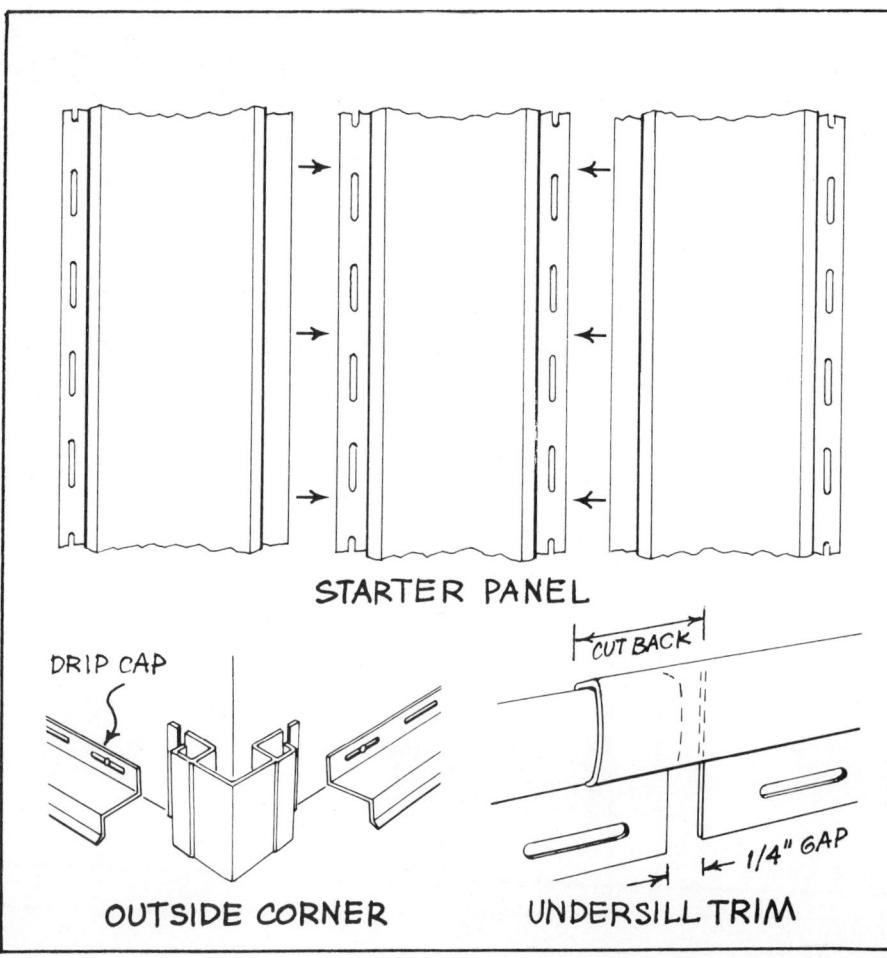

STARTER PANEL

DRIP CAP

CUT BACK

1/4" GAP

OUTSIDE CORNER

UNDERSILL TRIM

Applying Panels Vertically

Another type of vinyl siding is that show in the drawings at left. Wall installation o vertical siding begins with a double-side starter panel at the center point between outside wall corners. Then additional standard panels are slipped into the inter lock edges on each side of the starter panel.

At the base of the vertical panels, a drip-cap trim member is installed instead of a starter strip. Outside and inside corner in-stallation is the same as for horizontal siding panels. The undersill trim pieces are installed to hold the tops of vertical panels in place.

Solid vinyl siding comes in an embossed wood grain texture or smooth finish, in a choice of colors including gold, yellow, white, green, gray and others. Both clapboard and vertical-panel styles are offered, along with a full line of accessories including gutter systems and soffit systems.

Long life is a key feature of this material, for it is expected to last the normal life of the house. Manufacturers offer limited guarantees which cover manufacturing defects for as long as 40 years.

Application of solid vinyl siding can be over existing siding that is solidly secured to framing and without bows. The new siding is installed with ordinary carpenter tools.

Wood

Wood siding has a character and personality all its own, clear or knotty, rough-sawn or smooth. This material comes in the broadest range of patterns, installation styles and textures. Its beauty can be enriched and protected by oils, deepened by stains, or painted for special effects.

Manufacturers recommend that all wood siding and exterior trim be thoroughly dry when installed, and free of dampness or moisture condensation when painted. Most firms offer siding that has been water-repellent treated, or paint-primed on the back or both surfaces. Such applications are beneficial in

The beauty of brick sidewalls has long been accepted in American architecture, and the material's durability is beyond question. Built in the 1770's, this structure was the home of William Geddes, His Majesty's Collector of Customs, for the port of Chestertown (Md.). The house recently was re-roofed and is listed on the National Register of Historic Places. (Photo: Certain Teed Corp.)

Old Brick
Still a Good Value

Professional wearing apparel for sandblasting provides complete protection from the air-conveyed sand. This helmet has an air intake hose connected to the back and an integral protective neck bib.

protecting the siding from any later effects of adverse moisture conditions.

Preprimed siding, also available, has a complete prime coat on the siding face, as well as protective prime or treatment on the reverse side. This provides superior base for additional coats of quality paint.

Installation Notes

Where wood sheathing is used, siding may be nailed at 24-in. intervals with corrosion-resistant nails, usually galvanized steel or aluminum. Where other types of sheathing are used, nails should be driven through the sheathing into the studs at each bearing. Lengths of nail will vary with the thickness of the siding and type of sheathing.

Bevel siding and square-edge boards, applied horizontally, should be lapped, with nails driven just above the lap, to permit possible movement due to change in moisture conditions. The preferable spacing of siding is such that the bottom of a piece coincides with the top of the trim over door and window openings. This arrangement requires careful planning by the carpenter or homeowner before starting to apply the siding. A liberal coating of water repellent, on the end surfaces, is a good practice.

Corner treatment of siding depends upon the overall house design and may involve corner boards, mitered corners, or alternately lapped corners.

Siding is frequently applied vertically in order to produce a desired architectural effect. Where tongued-and-grooved boards are used, the siding should be blind nailed to wood sheathing at 24-in. intervals.

Square-edge boards used with battens, are spaced about ½ in. apart and nailed only at the center. The batten is attached by one nail driven through the center so it passes between the boards. The arrangement permits movement with change in moisture conditions. Where sheathing other than wood is used, blocking should be provided between studs to permit nailing of the vertical siding. During installation always take protective measures; wear eye and head coverings, and be sure ladders are safely and correctly placed.

Sandblasting

The stately brick home can be given a more pleasing appearance by the ambitious homeowner with an occasional sandblasting. This work can be performed by a professional service located through the telephone Yellow Pages, or the homeowner can rent the necessary equipment and tackle the job himself.

The average one-story, three-bedroom brick home can be sandblasted in a single day; two-story homes requiring the use of scaffolding and ad-

Climbing ladders and scaffolding may be required for buildings of two or more stories. Note how window glass has been completely covered. Tarps have not as yet been placed over the doorway.

Sandblasting of stucco can provide a new look to an older home, similar to the effect on brick and stone.

Plants adjacent to sandblasting operations should be covered with polyethylene film. Note the distance of the workman from the surface being sandblasted.

Light and dark areas of this home wall graphically demonstrate the results achieved through sandblasting. One workman is shown here using the gun while another continues with protection of glass and other items that could be damaged by the sand.

All photos: W.L. Bipes, Co., Inc.

ditional preparation will lengthen the required work hours.

Brick and stucco homes updated with sandblasting first are "protected" by placement of tarps over all wood surfaces that could be pitted by the sand "blasted" through the gun applicator. Duct tape is most often used to hold the tarps in place over windows, doors, wood columns, adjoining wood siding and the like. Glass surfaces, like wood, are easily damaged by sandblasting and must be protected from the flow of the sand. Light fixtures, mail boxes and other decorative items should be removed, if possible, or at least covered with tarp.

Normally a 150 CGM portable compressor is used for home sandblasting operations. Hoses connected to a sand pot and the compressor propel the cleaning sand to the hand-operated gun equipped with a $3/16$ to $5/16$-in. nozzle. The smaller nozzle is recommended for homeowner use, with the blasting operation starting at the top of the wall and moving downward, just as with exterior house painting.

Aside from the application equipment, it is recommended that the person doing the work be fully protected with goggles and face guard to keep sand out of eyes, nose and mouth. Professional suits for this purpose are much akin to those worn by astronauts, complete with air intake hoses.

Brick veneer lay-up, like the concrete block foundation work, starts at building corners with carefully leveled and plumbed units that provide a base for stretching mason's line to give a straight edge for intermediate coursing to follow. In large photo at left below, veneer work has begun and brick ties have been nailed to the studs ahead. Loose bricks are conveniently piled nearby and mortar mixed and ready for use from any of several mortar boards placed on folding-leg supports to be at convenient work height. Then two brick layers work well together on a resi-dential wall with a third person providing a continuous supply of mortar and bricks. In the lower photos, beginning at the left, a continuous offset of veneer brick provides the outer face of a fireplace chimney integral with the wall veneer. Center photo shows staggered brick ends where day's work finishes off and next day begins. Last photo indicates completed wall; tubular scaffolding in place was used for higher courses; rental mortar mixer is in foreground.

4. Roofing

On any residence, regardless of style or location, a lot of roof surface will be clearly visible and have a great effect on the overall home appearance. A strong roof design ties the house together, is essential to the entire architectural compostion, and should at all times provide necessary protection from the elements.

The roof of a home must blend with the surroundings. At the same time, this area is exposed to the sun, wind, rain and other elements more than any other area of the house, and should be well maintained to protect the financial investment in the home.

Why Re-roof?

There are two reasons to re-roof a house: (1) your present roof leaks and is aged beyond simple repair; (2) you've determined that a new roof will improve the appearance of your home. Both reasons are valid, and in the case of No. 1, repair or replacement is mandatory if you place any value on the home and its contents. If the roof leaks, it should be taken care of immediately.

Reason No. 2 is discretionary, but is gaining ground as people become more aware of how an attractive, good-quality roof can improve the appearance and increase the value of a home.

Inspecting the Roof

Periodic inspections will help you to determine the need for roof maintenance or replacement. The best place to start is inside the home under the roof. Under the roof you may be able to detect leaks early. Also look for telltale signs of leaks or dampness on ceilings and walls. Look for little streaks of water, tiny bits of light, or discolored wood on the rafters.

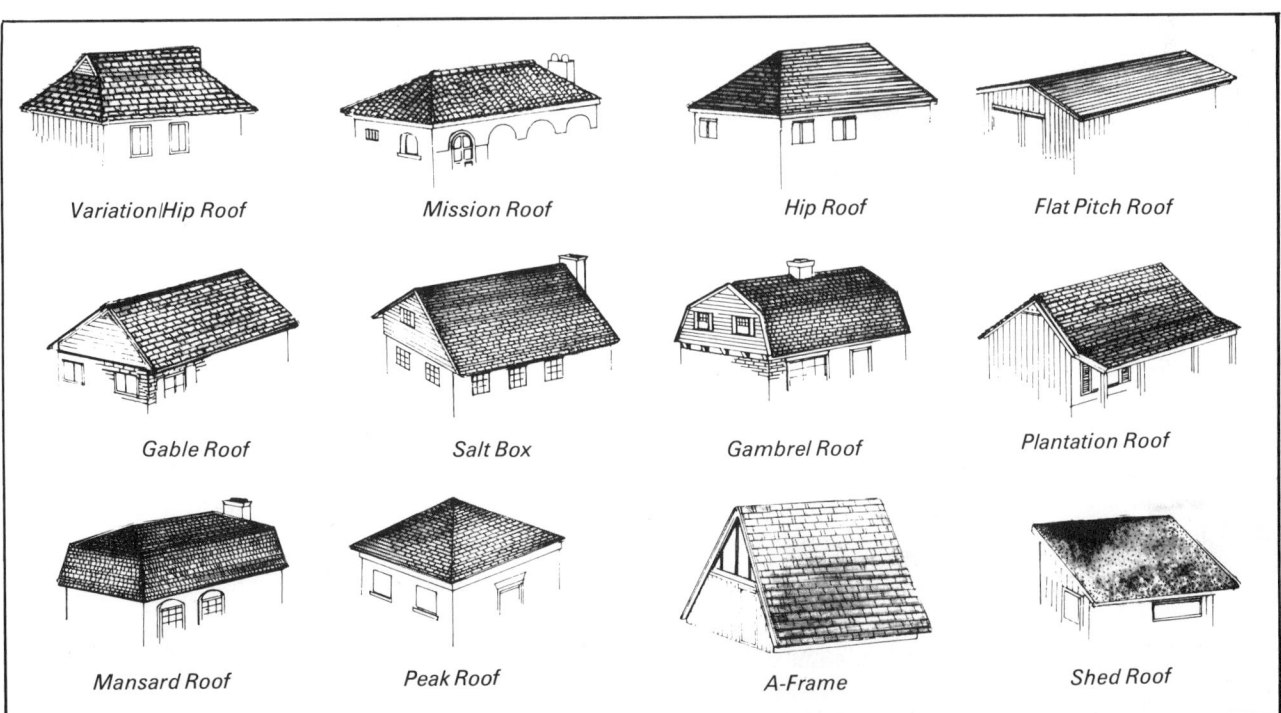

Variation/Hip Roof   Mission Roof   Hip Roof   Flat Pitch Roof

Gable Roof   Salt Box   Gambrel Roof   Plantation Roof

Mansard Roof   Peak Roof   A-Frame   Shed Roof

It's a good idea to check during a rain to find the exact spot where water enters. Shove a piece of stiff wire through the opening so you can find it on the roof when the weather clears.

Check the roof from above. Look for cracked, missing, rotted or torn shingles. Check valleys, joints around vents and under the chimney. Check for loose or cracked boards under gables and gutters that may be rusted or clogged.

A roof tends to wear uniformly and even the best roofing materials will eventually succumb to weathering. Most of today's roofing materials are designed to provide satisfactory service for a period of 15 to 25 years with little maintenance. A roof of standard asphalt shingles, 15 years old for example, is a prime candidate for re-roofing.

Preventive maintenance can ward off major roof jobs. Local building materials dealers offer a wide range of materials for both wet and dry patching leaks.

Should old roofing be removed? It depends. If the old roofing shingles lie flat without curl, thereby presenting a fairly even base for the new shingles, then removal is not indicated and the new roofing can be applied over the old.

Should You Do the Job Yourself?

Depending upon your handyman abilities and interests, you may wish to take on roof repair or replacement yourself; or, you may seek the aid of a professional roofing firm. The trained roofer can provide useful information on such things as material and labor costs and how to use color and texture to advantage. He can also help you to determine whether the new roof can be installed over the old one. In many cases it can, thus eliminating the cost of tearing off the old roof.

Another major decision factor is the steepness of your roof. Steep roof slopes, for example, with a pitch of 12 in. rise per ft. of run or horizontal distance, often involve special instructions. Also, the factory-applied adhesive spots work best for lower roof slopes where the weight of the shingle plus the sun's rays soften the adhesive and complete the bond. Steeper slopes particularly around dormer valleys and ridges, are more hazardous and should usually be undertaken by a professional with safety equipment.

Special care should be taken in selecting a roofer. This area of home repair, unfortunately, has been a prime rip-off target for door-to-door hucksters involved in disreputable home improvement schemes.

Before choosing a roofer, find out how long he has been in business. Is he known for getting the work done on schedule and for living up to his promises? Is he willing to provide references? Does he back up his work with services?

Generally, it's a good idea to get estimates for comparison. But be sure the contractors are bidding on the same materials and the same quality of workmanship. If financing is required, a good place to seek it is the bank where you have a savings or checking account.

Before signing a contract, be sure it spells out the work to be done, materials to be used, completion date and final price. If you are in doubt about a roofer, contact the local roofers' association or the Better Business Bureau.

Choosing a Roof

Styles

American homes are constructed with a choice or combination of nine basic roof styles: gable, but-

Footing holds for roof work can be provided simply by temporarily tacking 2x4's in place. Photo at right shows new plywood sheathing being applied over old roofing. At right, the footing 2x4's are tacked through wood shingle courses, nail holes filled with caulking after removal. Some roofers use sheet metal straps slipped between shingles to hold the footing 2x4's.

terfly, shed, mansard, hip, gambrel, flat, dome and vault. Of these, six are most popular and can be described as follows:

Gable. This inverted V-shape is the most prevalent style. This style is widely used for one-story Cape Cod cottages, two-story New England Colonial homes, Tudor, Greek Revival and Spanish Monterey residences. The roof of the New England "salt box" combines both gable and shed styles. A-frame houses are essentially gable-roofed, with the eaves continued down to form the side walls.

Butterfly. Wide-angled V's, butterfly roofs are found most often on homes of contemporary design, including many beach houses and other vacation homes.

Shed. Shed roofs consist of one straight, sloped plane. Again, this style is popular in more contemporary architectural designs.

Mansard. Steeply sloped, mansard styles add an element of classic French architecture especially popular in townhouse and commerical construc-

tion, where the design dresses up an otherwise uninteresting "flat-top".

Hip. These roofs have four sides sloping down from the ridge, and are typical of French Provincial architecture; they are often used for garage construction as well as for the home itself.

Gambrel. A gambrel design looks somewhat like a gable roof folded down once on each side. Of Dutch origin, this style dots the Pennsylvania Dutch countryside, where the roofs angle over the big, hex-marked barns. Today, the design also adds variety to look-alike development houses.

Energy Savings

Roof design has a considerable effect on energy conservation. For example, in warm climates, steeply pitched roofs absorb less heat, making the house easier to cool in the summer. Light-colored roofing materials reflect rather than absorb sunlight, considerably reducing the load on cooling

Asphalt shingle terminology includes the roofing terms indicated. Whether a homeowner contracts the work or does it himself, he should acquaint himself with the basic fundamentals of the work so that he can talk intelligently with contractors or suppliers. The drawings here come from the "Asphalt Shingle Installation Manual" put out by the Asphalt Roofing Manufacturers Assn.

TOP LAP
HEAD LAP
EXPOSURE

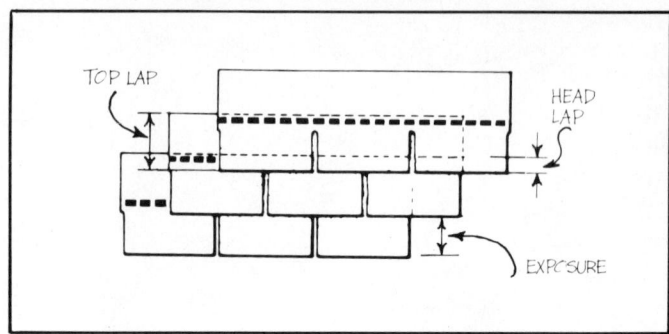

Roof slopes portrayed in this sketch indicate the suitability of asphalt shingles for various slope conditions. Rise, run and pitch are common terms used when discussing roof slopes. And it is common practice to describe a slope or pitch in rise-to-run figures, such as "3-in-12".

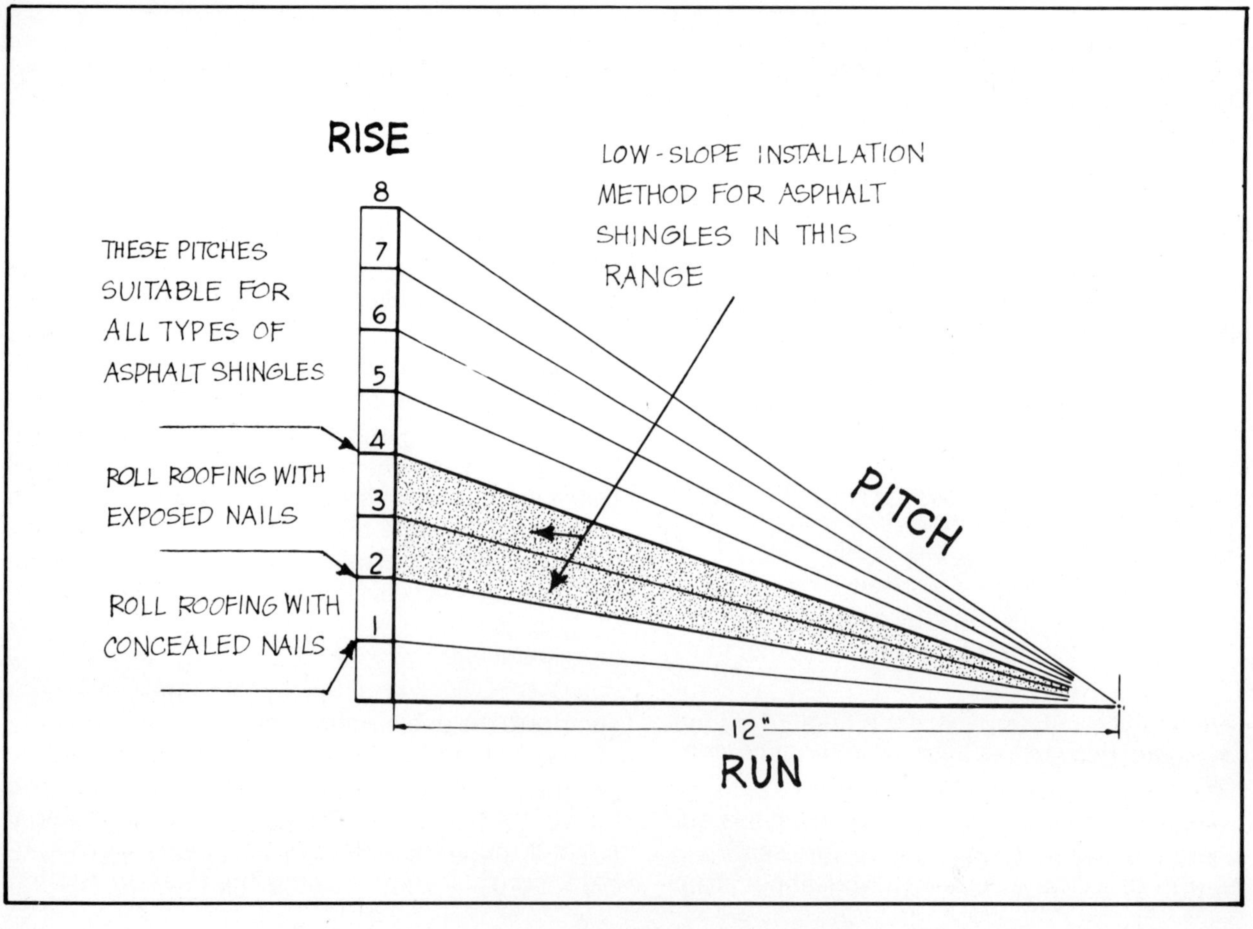

RISE
8
7
6
5
4
3
2
1
THESE PITCHES SUITABLE FOR ALL TYPES OF ASPHALT SHINGLES
ROLL ROOFING WITH EXPOSED NAILS
ROLL ROOFING WITH CONCEALED NAILS
LOW-SLOPE INSTALLATION METHOD FOR ASPHALT SHINGLES IN THIS RANGE
PITCH
12"
RUN

equipment. It's estimated that on a hot day, a roof of white asphalt shingles is about 20 degrees cooler than a dark roof.

Materials In Use

Roofing materials on the market today include common roll roofing, asphalt shingles, slate, terne metal, ceramic tiles, wood shingles and shakes, aluminum shingles, asbestos-cement shingles and built-up roofing assemblies. Selection of a given type involves both the roof structure and its design. For example, a flat roof should not be covered with anything other than built-up roofing, while commonly pitched roofs generally can be surfaced with any of the other types of finish roofing.

Asphalt shingles today are used on more than 80 per cent of U.S. homes, generally for roofs with slopes of 4 in. or more per horizontal foot. These shingles come in a variety of styles, the most popular of which is the square butt strip shingle, elongated in shape and available with three tabs, two tabs or one tab (without cutouts).

Selecting a Roof Color

Many architects and designers suggest that the exterior color treatment of the home should always begin with the roof. They point out that the roof is usually the largest unbroken visual expanse; its color will be obvious. Also, roofs last a long time, so the color must be acceptable for a long time.

In building a new home or reroofing, select a roof color you won't tire of, and one that will blend easily with changing siding and trim shades. Don't choose gaudy or "fad" colors for the roof.

Color can affect the architectural appearance of a house. By using a dark-colored roof, you can make a tall house look shorter; a light-colored roof makes a squat house look taller. "Hot" colors, such as red or gloss yellow, make sidewalls seem to advance and thus are not recommended for outsides of houses.

The site on which a house is located should be considered; color can be used to coordinate the house and grounds. Earthtone browns, forest greens and slate grays are natural colors designed to blend the roof with the site.

Designers further recommend you not use more than three colors for roof, siding and trim. Gutters and downspouts should be kept in the same color as their background and not treated as accent

Thermoplastic adhesive spots factory-applied to shingles are set by the heat of the sun once the shingles have been installed. This gives each shingle an independent gripping power that resists high winds (Photo: Bird & Son).

items. Accent colors are recommended for doors, shutters and trim.

Asphalt Shingles

Asphalt shingles get their color from the ceramic-coated mineral granules that are embedded in the shingles. These coarse granules also contribute to the shingles' ability to resist fire. And in the case of white roofing, many manufacturers offer homeowners the option of shingles with fungus-resistant granules. In hot and humid areas of the South, where white roofing is popular for its heat-reflecting qualities, fungus-resistant shingles are often recommended to retard ugly discoloration and staining of the roof cause by fungi and algae.

For protection against high winds, self-sealing asphalt shingles have a factory-applied adhesive which, when activated by the sun's heat, bonds each shingle to the one below.

Asphalt shingles that bear the UL label for Class C fire resistance have been tested to assure that they will not readily ignite or contribute to the spread of flame. Shingles rated Class B or A afford even better fire protection.

Roofing Color Guide

HOUSE STYLE: MODERN, RANCH, MODERNIZED COLONIAL, ETC.

HOUSE COLOR	DOOR	SHUTTERS	ROOF COLOR
DEEP RED	WHITE, BLACK	BLACK, BEIGE	DARK GREY, BROWN, WHITE, DARK GREY/GREEN, BLACK
DEEP YELLOW	DEEP GOLD, BLACK, WHITE	BLACK	WHITE, GREY/GREEN, BROWN DARK GREY, DARK BUFF, BLACK
BEIGE	RED, YELLOW, BLUE, BLACK, CHOCOLATE, WHITE	BLACK, CHARCOAL, DARK GREEN, WHITE	BROWN, DARK BUFF, GREY/GREEN, DARK BLUE, DARK GREY, WHITE, BLACK
WHITE	RED, YELLOW, BLUE, BLACK, WHITE, BEIGE	BLACK, CHARCOAL, DARK GREEN, BEIGE	DK. GREY, DK. BLUE, GREY/GREEN, DK. GREEN, BUFF, BROWN, CORAL, TURQUOISE, BLACK
DARK GREY	BLACK, RED, BLUE, YELLOW, WHITE, BEIGE	BLACK, CHARCOAL, BEIGE	WHITE, DK. GREY, DK. GREEN, GREY/GREEN, BUFF, CHARCOAL DK. BLUE, DARK BUFF, BLACK
CORAL	BLACK, WHITE, BEIGE, DARK RED	BLACK, CHARCOAL, BEIGE	BUFF, BROWN, DARK GREY, TAN, WHITE, BLACK
DARK GREEN	LIGHT GREEN, BLACK, GREY, WHITE	LIGHT GREEN, WHITE, CHARCOAL	DARK GREY, WHITE, GREY GREEN, BLACK

HOUSE STYLE: PENNSYLVANIA DUTCH, DUTCH, MODIFICATION OF STYLE

HOUSE COLOR	DOOR	SHUTTERS	ROOF COLOR
RED	WHITE, BLACK, DARK BLUE	BLACK, DARK GREY	DARK GREY, WHITE, BLACK
WHITE	RED, YELLOW, BLUE, BLACK, WHITE, BEIGE	BLACK, DARK GREEN, CHARCOAL	DARK GREEN, BROWN, DARK GREY, DARK BLUE, GREY/GREEN, BLACK
YELLOW	DEEP GOLD, BLACK, WHITE	BLACK	BROWN, DARK GREY/GREEN, DARK BUFF, BLACK
BEIGE	RED, YELLOW, BLUE, BLACK, CHOCOLATE, WHITE	BLACK, CHARCOAL, DARK GREEN, WHITE	WHITE, DARK GREY/GREEN, BROWN, BUFF, TAN, DARK CORAL, BLACK
GREY	BLACK, RED, BLUE, YELLOW, WHITE, BEIGE	BLACK, CHARCOAL	DARK GREY/GREEN, DARK GREY, DARK BLUE, BROWN, BLACK

HOUSE STYLE: CAPE COD, SALT BOX

HOUSE COLOR	DOOR	SHUTTERS	ROOF COLOR
RED	WHITE, BLACK	WHITE, BLACK	DARK GREY, WHITE, BROWN, BLACK
WHITE	BLACK, RED, YELLOW, BLUE, BEIGE	BLACK	DARK GREEN, BROWN, DARK GREY, GREY/GREEN, BLACK

Source: 3M Company

HOUSE STYLE: CAPE COD, SALT BOX (CONTINUED)

HOUSE COLOR	DOOR	SHUTTERS	ROOF COLOR
DARK GREY	RED, YELLOW, BLUE, BEIGE, WHITE, BLACK	BLACK, WHITE	WHITE, TAN, BUFF, RED, BROWN, BLACK
YELLOW	GOLD, BLACK, WHITE	BLACK	DARK GREEN, WHITE, BROWN, BLACK
LIGHT GREY	RED, YELLOW, BEIGE, BLUE, BLACK, WHITE	BLACK	DARK GREEN, GREY/GREEN, DARK BLUE, BLACK

HOUSE STYLE: GEORGIAN, WILLIAMSBURG, GREEK REVIVAL

HOUSE COLOR	DOOR	SHUTTERS	ROOF COLOR
WHITE	BLACK, WHITE, NATURAL WOOD, DARK GREEN	BLACK	DARK GREEN, DARK GREY, DARK BLUE, BLACK
DARK GREY	BLACK, WHITE, DARK GREEN	BLACK	WHITE, DARK GREY, DARK GREY/GREEN, BLACK
YELLOW	BLACK, WHITE, CHARCOAL	BLACK	DARK GREY, BROWN, BLACK
DEEP BLUE	LIGHT BLUE, GREY, BLACK, WHITE	BLACK, WHITE	DARK BLUE, DARK GREY, GREY/GREEN, BLACK
BUFF BEIGE	BLACK, WHITE, DARK GREY	BLACK, CHARCOAL	DARK GREY, DARK BUFF, TAN, BROWN, DARK GREEN, BLACK

HOUSE STYLE: VICTORIAN, GOTHIC, RENAISSANCE, TUDOR

HOUSE COLOR	DOOR	SHUTTERS	ROOF COLOR
WHITE	RED, BLUE, YELLOW, BLACK, GREEN, BEIGE, WHITE, GREY	BLACK, CHARCOAL	DARK GREY, GREY/GREEN, DARK GREEN, BROWN, BUFF, BLACK
DARK RED	BLACK, WHITE, BEIGE	CHARCOAL, BLACK	WHITE, DARK GREY, BROWN, BUFF, BLACK
GREY	RED, BEIGE, YELLOW, BLACK, WHITE, GREEN, BLUE	WHITE, BLACK	DARK GREY, DARK BLUE, DARK GREEN, BUFF, GREY/GREEN, BROWN, BLACK
DEEP YELLOW	BLUE, GREEN, TURQUOISE, BLACK, BEIGE, WHITE	WHITE, BLACK	DARK GREY, DARK GREY/GREEN, BROWN, DARK BUFF, BLACK
MASONRY (STONE)	BEIGE, WHITE, BLACK, GREY, YELLOW	WHITE, BLACK, BEIGE	WHITE, SILVER GREY, DARK GREY, GREY/GREEN, BROWN, BLACK

Quantity Required

Shingles are purchased and installed by "squares" or 100 square feet of roof area. To properly estimate the quantity of material you will need you first must know the slope or pitch of the roof which is found by: (1) measuring the distance between the ceiling joists and the ridge; (2) dividing this number by the run of one half the distance between the front and back walls of the house.

For example: (see attached sketch) the house measures 36 ft. between the front and back walls.

The ridge is 12 ft. above the joists. Slope equals 12 ft. divided by 18 ft.—or 2 ft. of rise for every three linear ft. In inches, that's 24 in./36 in., which reduces to 8 in./12 in.

Determine the area of the house by multiplying the length by the width. Multiply that total by the "factor" shown in the sketch at the right for the slope of your roof. Divide the resulting answer by 100 which gives you the number of squares. Another square should be added to the total for each 130 running feet of hip and ridge.

1. First re-roofing strip along eave will be a 5x36-in. strip, so this width is measured and cut so that the 5-in. strip has the black adhesive seal-down striping near the bottom.

2. Balance of the cut strip then is further trimmed down 2 in. to provide another 5-in.-wide strip without seal-down adhesive, which can be applied later at the ridges.

Starting Over Old Asphalt Shingles

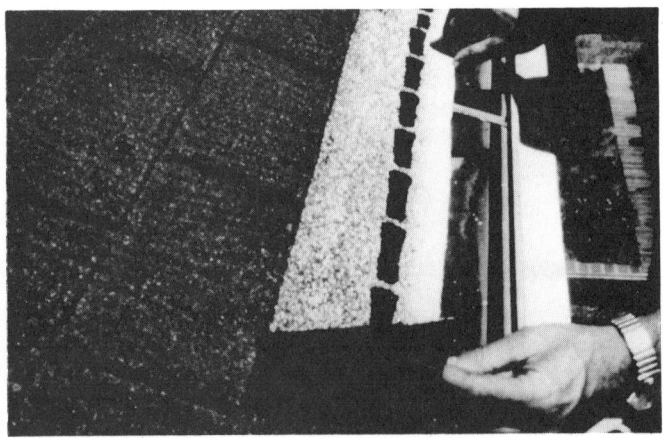

3. Beginning or starter course of the 5-in. wide strips is then positioned against butt of the second course of old asphalt shingles, with the seal-down striping near the eave edge.

4. Nailing of the starter strip takes four nails per strip, placing the nails at a point just below the seal-down adhesive striping.

5. Second course of shingle strips is then placed, the strips having been trimmed down to 10-in. widths. This course is positioned butting to the third course of old shingles.

6. Third and following courses are then placed conventionally, each butting to an old shingle course. This series is from a complete installation set covering Johns-Manville fiberglass shingles.

Roofing Preparation

Before re-roofing, the base upon which new shingles are to be placed needs attention. Nail down or remove protruding roofing nails. Renail split shingles. Replace broken or missing ones. Whether the old roofing is asphalt or wood shingles, get a smooth firm foundation for the new roofing material.

Roofing felt application is needed, on pitches below 4|12, when old roofing is removed. Again, remove old nails or drive them down before applying the felt strips. Use care in alignment of strips so that the white shingling guidelines are kept parallel with the eaves and ridge lines.

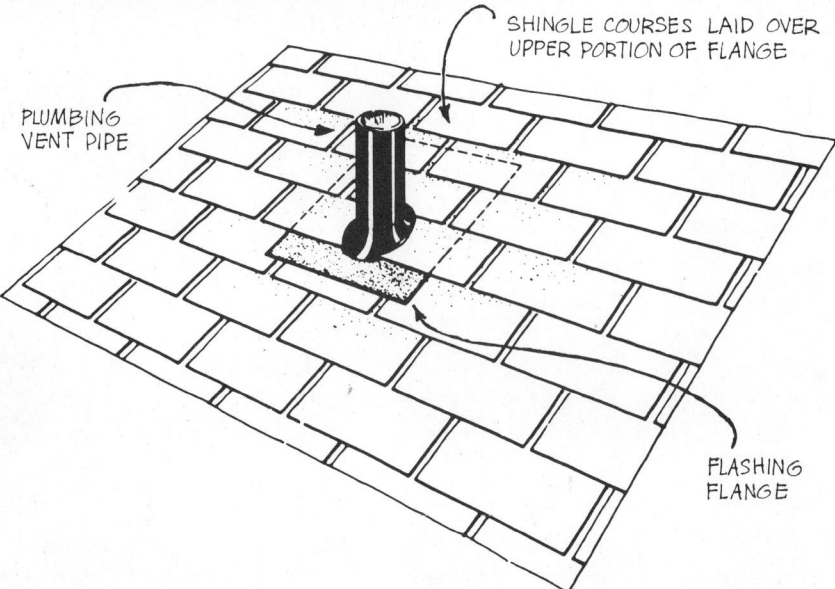

SHINGLE COURSES LAID OVER UPPER PORTION OF FLANGE

PLUMBING VENT PIPE

FLASHING FLANGE

Check flashings at all plumbing stack and vent projections through the roof. Flashing flanges should be interleaved as indicated with the new shingling. If old roofing remains in place, so does the flashing, and the new shingles are cut to fit the projection and cemented down around it.

The elegance of older homes is being perceived throughout the United States as wise buyers and investors quickly calculate the sound values of such homes in today's marketplace. This turn-of-the-century home, with its wrap-around porch, was re-sided recently with Johns-Manville solid vinyl siding.

The perfect home exterior is a combination of many elements: the natural beauty of the site, the architectural design, and a coordination of basic materials. This home in Edina, Minnesota features Andersen windows throughout, and is highly attractive from any angle.

Doors, windows and shutters, when in proper scale with the total facade, provide exceptional architectural beauty. (Photo: Johns-Manville.)

Well conceived overhangs can provide weather protection for guests who come calling at the front door. This protected area provides a small-size porch as well. (Photo: Johns-Manville.)

The graceful styling of New Orleans French Quarter residences is being duplicated in many cities through use of wrought iron columns and railings. Popular French doors at the second level lead from bedrooms to balcony, which shelters the double-door entry below. (Photo: Johns-Manville.)

Decking of 2x4 Douglas fir creates level area on a sloping site. (Photo by Fred Rola for Western Wood Products Assn.)

This deck was constructed from pressure-treated Outdoor Wood. (Photo: Koppers Co., Inc.)

Just steps away from a sandy beach is this redwood-plywood-sided vacation home by architect Richard Stowers. Redwood was selected for the exterior because of its superb resistance to the adverse effects of salt spray, fog, and wind. (Photos: California Redwood Assn.)

Use of regional woods and natural features is popular with many homeowners. This setting at the base of a mountain range employs redwood and various sizes of rock and gravel to enhance the southwestern flavor of the home. (Photo: Simpson Timber Co.)

This 100-year-old house looks like new with application of Masonite prefinished green Colorlok siding. This material avoids frequent re-painting for up to 15 years. Older homes such as this often occupy exceptional sites no longer available in many cities, especially near the water.

Masonite hardboard siding gave new life to this well-built home, which for several years had clearly shown its age.

Half-timber style architecture of this home exterior was accomplished with prefinished hardboard panels that give the appearance of skip-trowel stucco. Joints of the panels were concealed with the battens and boards. (Photo: Masonite Corp.)

Redwood has become a most popular exterior wood trim for homes of all architectural stylings. This residence, designed by Huxley, Clemons & Colbourn, AIA, includes both upper and lower decks overlooking a well-appointed patio and swimming pool. Note the treatment of the chimney, which carries forth the redwood siding pattern. (Photo: Simpson Timber Co.)

Outdoor extensions of the modern home are as numerous as the families who enjoy summertime living. This post-and-beam assembly was constructed with a redwood slat roof that permits free flow of light and air while affording sun control. (Photo: Simpson Timber Co.)

Weather-resistant urethane gives the appearance of rough-sawn, hand-hewn wood in the design of this Lightcraft of California outdoor lantern. A similar design is offered for post use.

Outdoor wood pressure-treated with preservative chemicals was used in the construction of this good-neighbor fence which looks the same from either side. The wood has long-lasting protection against decay and termites for outdoor, in-ground installation. (Photo: Koppers Co., Inc.)

Replace shingles on an old wood-shingled roof if there are broken or missing shingles. Simply insert the replacement up under the course above, and nail down.

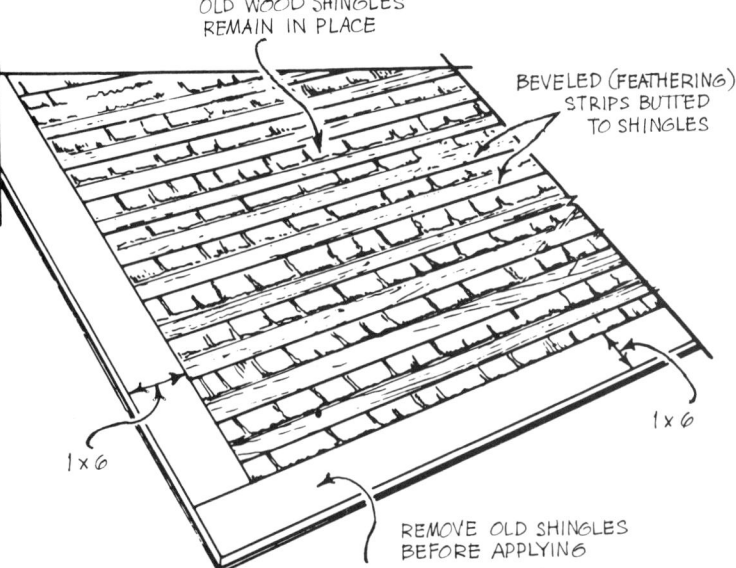

OLD WOOD SHINGLES
REMAIN IN PLACE

BEVELED (FEATHERING)
STRIPS BUTTED
TO SHINGLES

1 x 6

1 x 6

REMOVE OLD SHINGLES
BEFORE APPLYING

Add wood strips to firm up the base to which the re-roofing materials will be attached. The drawing indicates new six-inch wide strips along eaves and rakes, since these areas are most likely to show decay. Apply strips so top surface is flush with old roofing. At far right, feathered strips butt to old wood shingles. Beveled wood siding boards make good feathering strips.

Metal edging applied along eaves and rakes will provide a proper drip edge and prevent moisture backup under the roofing material. Instruction details on these pages and the drawings have been excerpted from the application manual issued by the Asphalt Roofing Manufacturers Association.

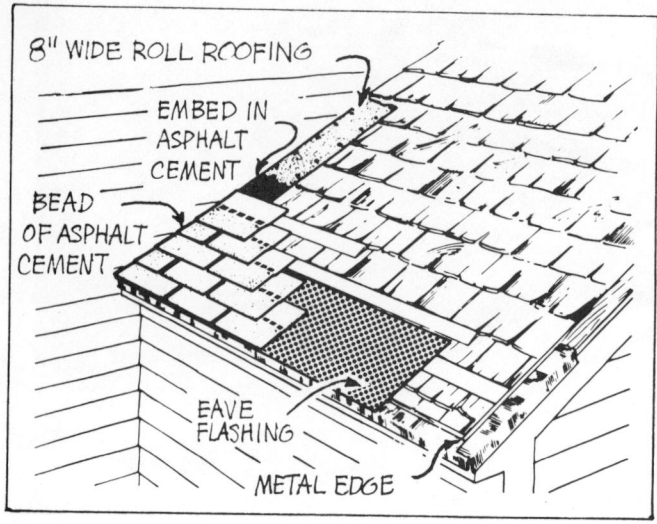

Eave flashing and sidewall flashing with roll roofing cemented down is desirable when new asphalt shingles are being applied over old roofing.

Edge shingles that meet a sidewall or the rake of the roof can be pre-cut quickly by using a template shingle that's a half tab in width.

Shingling Begins at the Eaves

Random spacing of strip shingles is achieved by removing different amounts from the rake tab of succeeding courses. Sketch shows amounts of cuts, minimum being 3 in. With a five-course repeat pattern, the eye tends not to follow the vertical alignment of cutouts and the spacing appears random. Cut-off pieces may be used at opposite end rakes or at sidewalls.

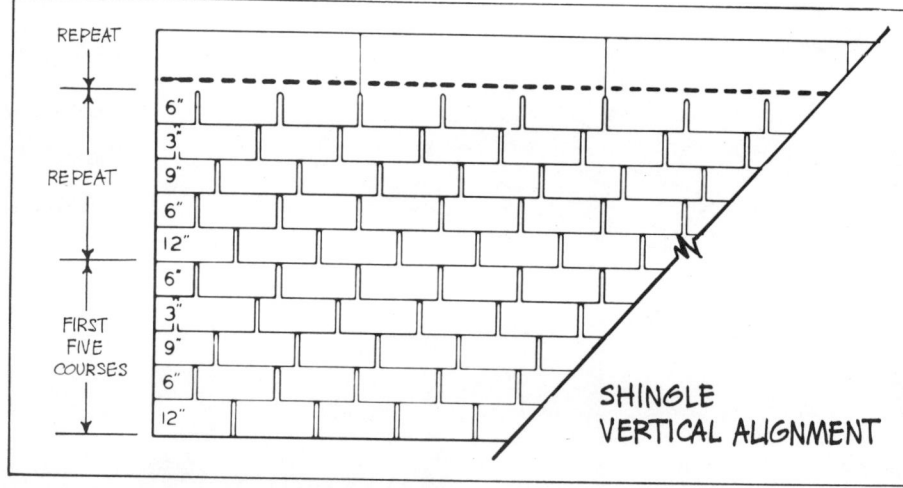

SHINGLE VERTICAL ALIGNMENT

Diagonal application makes for easier shingle handling according to expert roofers; this method is preferred, rather than applying full shingle courses across the roof horizontally.

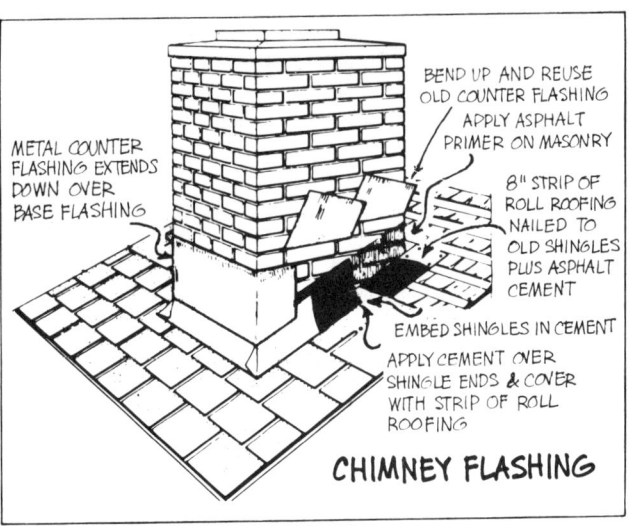

METAL COUNTER FLASHING EXTENDS DOWN OVER BASE FLASHING

BEND UP AND REUSE OLD COUNTER FLASHING

APPLY ASPHALT PRIMER ON MASONRY

8" STRIP OF ROLL ROOFING NAILED TO OLD SHINGLES PLUS ASPHALT CEMENT

EMBED SHINGLES IN CEMENT

APPLY CEMENT OVER SHINGLE ENDS & COVER WITH STRIP OF ROLL ROOFING

CHIMNEY FLASHING

Use Care with Roof Flashings

Chimney flashing when re-roofing can often make use of old counter-flashing when the old material is still serviceable.

Cementing down of new shingles all around the chimney should be done whether old counter-flashing is used or not. If not, then additional cement caulking should be applied along the joint between shingles and the chimney faces.

Sidewall juncture, the point where a roof surface meets the siding of an upper story, also requires the use of a roofing-felt underlayment strip of flashing plus the cementing down of the adjacent shingles, as indicated in this photo.

Two ways of flashing through-roof projections such as plumbing stacks or ventilators. At far left, the technique when re-roofing over an old roof, new shingles are cut to fit around the stack or vent and cemented down. In near left photo, where old roofing has been removed, the regular flashing flange interleaf with shingles is used as though it were a new construction job.

Making an Open Valley

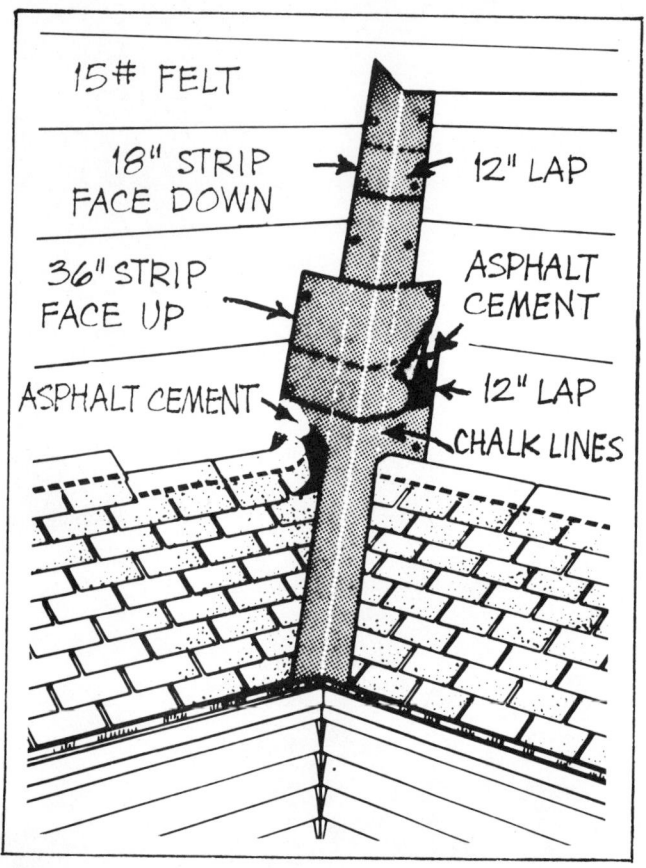

15# FELT

18" STRIP FACE DOWN → ← 12" LAP

36" STRIP FACE UP → ASPHALT CEMENT

ASPHALT CEMENT → ← 12" LAP CHALK LINES

Open valley method uses two layers of mineral-surfaced roll roofing and is suitable on jobs where old roofing material has been removed.

Cementing down both the flashing (upper right) and the cut valley shingles insures a tight valley that will drain well without leaking.

Capping a Ridge

Ridge shingles are single-tab widths cut from shingle strips and applied with same exposure as used with the field shingles. Use one nail each side of the ridge. With hands, carefully pre-blend each ridge shingle. In some areas, suppliers offer pre-cut ridge and hip shingles.

Aluminum foil-faced sealing tape can be a real time-saver in re-roofing for flashing around plumbing and chimney roof projections. At left, the foil-faced sealer, which comes in rolls of varying widths, is pressed into place around the base of a plumbing pipe. At right, a 4-in. strip of the sealing material is pressed into position as base flashing around a stone chimney. Called "Flashband," the material bonds to normal building materials. It is useful for other roof flashings also including such locations as sidewall junctures, antenna bases, skylights and ventilators. Made by Evode Inc.

Built-up gravel surfaced roofs require renewal work by experts. The application of fresh hot asphalt and roofing felt layers involves the use of specialized equipment and mopping skills beyond the scope of do-it-yourselfers.

Built-up Roofs

Built-up roofs are usually three to six layers thick (of 15 or 30 pound roofing felts) and they are protected from the sun by a covering of small rocks. Built-up roofs are easily renewed by recoating with asphalt and adding layers of felt paper.

Wood Shingles and Shakes

Wood shingles and shakes made from cedar and other durable wood species are highly attractive and very popular in many areas of the country. They may be laid on slopes as gentle as one in four, but they perform best on steeper slopes. This type of roofing gives an attractive roof and shadow line and can be easily applied over smooth shingle roofs.

The wood may be stained or left natural, and some shingles and shakes are offered prestained.

In new construction, wood shingles and shakes may be applied over a solid roof sheathing or with slats that allow air flow from the attic space and reduce the high temperature and high moisture problems common to many geographic areas.

Ceramic, clay and concrete tile roofing is manufactured in flat, rectangular units as well as special shapes for minimum roof pitches of 4 in. per foot. With integral color, this type roofing has an indefinite life expectancy. Tile is applied over a solid decking covered with felt and may require additional framing. Tile roofs are rated Class A when it comes to incombustibility. Slate roofing is applied in the same manner as tile, has a long life expectancy and shows the grain and texture of stone. This roofing material is among the most costly.

Re-roofing with red cedar shakes can add new character to a home. Here the shakes are being applied directly over dated composition shingles surfaced first with roofing felt. Shakes come in three lengths—16, 18 and 24 in.—for coarse exposure of 5, 5½ or 7½ in. if the roof pitch is 4 in. in 12 in. or steeper. (Photo: Red Cedar Single and Handsplit Shake Bureau.)

Before

This "before" and "after" photo combination shows the dramatic transformation of a 1914-vintage house accomplished by San Francisco architect Hood Chatham. Red cedar shingles were selected for both the new roof and sidewalls. Note how the dormer was extended with updated windows to provide a better roof line appearance. (Photos: Red Cedar Shingle and Handsplit Shake Bureau.)

After

Re-roofing with Shingles and Shakes

A re-roof .or over-roof can work wonders with an older home giving it a dramatic new look. Both wood shingles and shakes can be applied directly over the existing asphalt roof to provide new beauty, insulation and greater structural strength. Shingles are thinner than shakes, which have a bolder appearance and provide a shadow-like effect. While most shingles are finished smooth, the shakes are rough textures with pronounced vertical grain. The reddish-brown color of the wood may be left natural or stained. The accompanying photographs depict a typical over-roof job using shakes.

1. Over-roofing begins with the application of a 36-in. wide strip of 15 pound asphalt felt over the old shingles at the eave line. Then 18-in. strips of felt are applied shingle style at 10-in. intervals up the roof. Next, a starter course of shingles is applied at the eave line extending approximately 1½ in. over the eave edge.

2. The first course of shakes is then applied directly over the starter course. The tip ends of each course of shakes are tucked under the felt strips. With a 24-in. long shake laid at 10-in. exposure, the top 4 in. of the shake will be covered by felt. The shakes should be spaced about ½-in. apart to allow for possible expansion. These joints or spaces between the shakes should be broken or offset at least 1½ in. in adjacent courses.

3. Felt covers the old shingles, and each felt overlaps the top 4 in. of the shakes. Longer nails are used in over-roofing than in new construction.

4. A metal valley, at least 26 gauge galvanized iron, painted for anti-rust protection, center and edge crimped, is laid in place. When new valley metal may come in contact with old metal, a strip of lumber should be placed in each valley to separate them.

5. Shakes are cut parallel with valleys as courses are applied over the metal valley. Valley gutters should approximate 6 in. in width. Metal valley sheets should be at least 20 in. wide with a 4- to 6-in. head lap.

6. Shakes are cut parallel to the hip line. The nails visible here will later be covered and concealed.

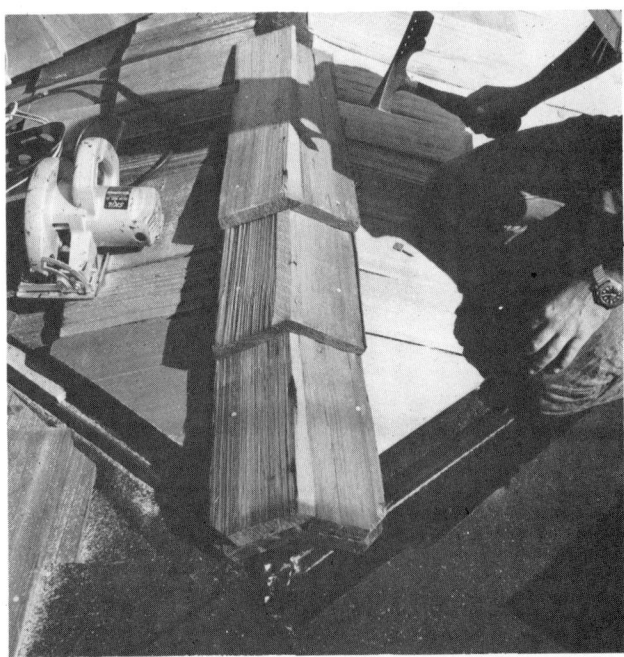

7. Factory-assembled "hip-and-ridge" units finish the hips and ridges. Hip-and-ridge units should be applied at the same exposure as field of roof, and longer nails should be used to ensure approximately ¾-in. sheathing penetration. (Photos courtesy Red Cedar Shingle & Handsplit Shake Bureau)

Aluminum roofing in the form of shake panels or "shingle-shakes" as they're sometimes called is increasingly in use on commercial buildings and some residences. Shown at left and above are the 12x36-in. panels produced by Reynolds Metals Company. The company offers a complete range of accessory trim materials including hip and ridge caps, eave or gable trim strips and valley channels. As the photo above indicates, the shingle-shakes are slightly irregularly formed in order to give a textured appearance roughly comparable to that of handsplit wood shakes.

Using Aluminum Shake Panels

Shake panels by Kaiser Aluminum are 12x60 in. in size. Panels are designed so that all four edges interlock with adjacent shakes. Photo above indicates over-and-under type of flashing flanges for roof projections. Photo at right shows completed roof with ridge and hip caps applied.

5. Decks & Patios

Where generations past spent most of their outdoor leisure time in public parks or at the beach, today's families more frequently resort to their own yards for those restful periods. The advent of backyard swimming pools, patios and decks has done as much as anything to influence the exterior of the modern home. Today there are well over a million private residential swimming pools, and this figure can be multiplied many, many times to arrive at the number of home patios and decks.

In planning and building a backyard (side or front yard) patio or deck, remember that you're going to have to live with it for many years to come. You should have well in mind your moods and needs, for the finished construction will be much more difficult (and costly) to redo than re-painting or changing wallpaper.

Decks and patios truly can be looked upon as outdoor rooms, extensions of an entire side of the home, or of more specific areas such as the master bath, the family room, the kitchen, the living room, or other family living space. The finished outdoor room can be a private haven, a party room, play room or entertainment center—depending upon your specific needs and desires.

Shorter working hours have made the deck and patio far from a passing fad. Homeowners realize full well the pleasures to be derived from sitting, standing, reading, playing and eating in the open air.

The smaller the residential lot the more important it is to use every inch of space wisely and the bigger the challenge to the deck and patio designer. Well-planned patios and decks will involve other elements as well: strategic screens, fences, dividers, planters, furnishings and accessories. And in some parts of the country the end result can be enjoyed nearly every month of the year.

Whether you decide on a patio or a sundeck, try to envision it not as a single structure, but as a part of a whole outdoor living development and, most importantly, as part of the main dwelling. The patio should suit the site in relation to scale and style, and take into consideration surroundings, property lines and privacy, existing landscaping, wind and sun exposure. To a large degree, you can control the climate via roofs and overhangs, shades and trellises.

Flooring

The patio or deck, of course, begins with your selection of the basic flooring material. Here you may choose from brick, masonry units, poured concrete finished smooth, with decorative aggregate or sculptured pattern, or a wide variety of wood deck designs supported by a weatherproof framing system.

Stack and running bond brick patterns were used for the steps and landing of this attractive terrace and planter. The terrace continues the running bond pattern in distinctive sections. (Photo: Structural Clay Products Institute)

Before

The only connection between house and yard was a narrow stairway from the kitchen. Garden grades of redwood were used to extend this deck well into the wooded yard behind this suburban home, creating 640 square feet of versatile living space out of a previously little-used sloping backyard. Predominant in the sloping yard was a drainage ditch which has been hidden by the deck. Redwood also was used to construct a convenient storage cabinet below the kitchen windows, with the top of the cabinet a handy place for food and beverage serving. (Photos: California Redwood Assn.)

After

Precast concrete patio blocks set on a bed of sand provide the outdoor patio area of this waterfront home. The three-stone-high planter was constructed with a weeping mortar joint while the patio surface simply was laid with sand brushed into joints.

Personal taste will dictate to a large extent the flooring system you choose, but a few basics should be kept in mind. First, if the surface is to be of wood, it should be of redwood or treated wood that will resist rot and insects, especially termites. Second, if the surface is concrete and will be subject to moisture (from the swimming pool or elements) it should be finished with a skid-resistant, broomed surface. Third, the finished outdoor floor should be several inches, at minimum, above surrounding terrain for ease of cleaning.

Many tract builders over the years have placed 10-foot-wide concrete pads off the rear of the home and called them patios. In the opinion of those who have purchased such homes, this space is far from desirable, usually further reduced in usage by the presence of wood columns every 8, 10 or 12 ft. to support a not-quite-big-enough overhang.

Redwood is much at home in this waterfront setting where it has been used for the dock, paving, shelter and built-in benches designed by Warren Callister. (Photo: California Redwood Assn.)

Simpson redwood forms the paving squares for this poured-in-place patio featuring attractive redwood built-ins that blend with the wood shingle structure.

SUGGESTED JOIST SPANS

JOIST SIZE		SELECT OR COMMON
2x6	16″ o.c.	5′-0″
	24″ o.c.	5′-0″
	36″ o.c.	4′-0″
2x8	16″ o.c.	9′-0″
	24″ o.c.	7′-6″
	36″ o.c.	6′-9″
2x10	16″ o.c.	13′-0″
	24″ o.c.	11′-0″
	36″ o.c.	9′-0″

(o.c. means "on center")
Deflection limited to L/240

Patios should be a minimum of 20 x 20 ft. to provide ample space for the functions that will take place out of doors. This is not to say that the patio should be perfectly square, for other desirable shapes create more interest and allow for flexible furniture arrangement.

Masonry

Brick and concrete masonry patio floors can be laid by a handy amateur and require little maintenance. Before laying the blocks or bricks in place, the area should be leveled with a slight grade for drainage, and excavated enough to allow a 2 in. layer of sand beneath the block or brick. The units are laid in the desired pattern and tamped as close together as possible. Sand is then brushed over them to fill any voids. A further suggestion would be to cement in place the perimeter material, which would help keep the inner area as you first install it.

PATTERNS

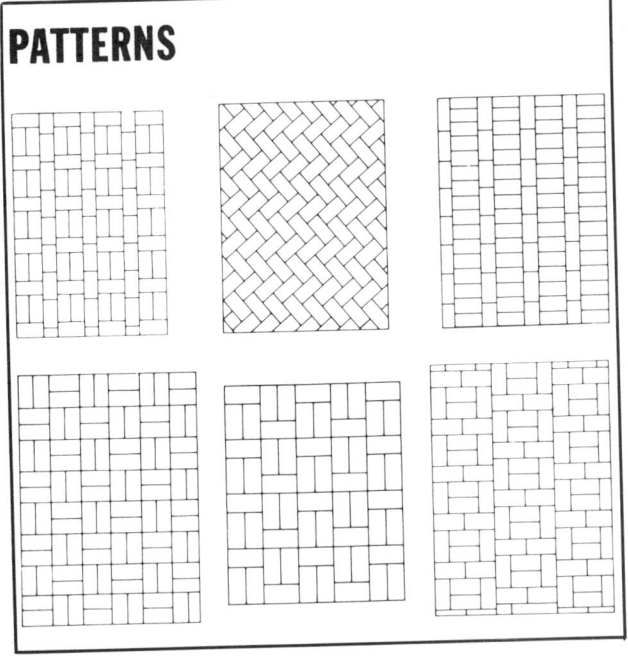

A wide range of patterns provides the homeowner with his first decision in laying a brick patio. Selecting a pattern that uses full-size bricks will speed construction. (Drawing: Pacific Clay Products)

Face brick for decking comes in three basic sizes:

Roman, which comes in red mingled, flashed red, gray and buff, is 1½ x 3½ x 11½ in. Approximately three and one-half bricks are required per square foot of surface.

Norman, which comes in red, gray and buff, is 2³/₁₆ x 3½ x 11½ in. Three and one-half bricks are needed per square foot.

Standard, which comes in buff, gray and red, has smooth and textured surfaces and measures 2³/₁₆ x 3½ x 7½ in. Approximately four and one-half bricks are required per square foot.

Still other brick varieties may be used for flat patio surfaces and walkways, including manufactured used brick or paving.

Patio floor and walkway patterns and bonds are virtually endless with the basket pattern heading the list in popularity. It should be noted that in most other patterns, including herrringbone and basket weave on angle, half bricks are required and thus the craftsman must cut the material with a heavy chisel.

Brick floors also may be laid with a finished mortar joint (instead of the brushed-in sand) and

For instructions on how to make your own used paving, and other specifics on concrete and blocks, consult Practical & Decorative Concrete, a Successful book by Robert Wilde.

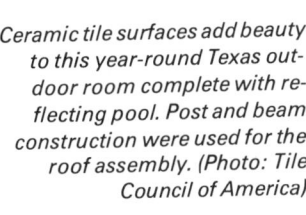

Ceramic tile surfaces add beauty to this year-round Texas outdoor room complete with reflecting pool. Post and beam construction were used for the roof assembly. (Photo: Tile Council of America)

either type of floor may be laid over a concrete slab which has been gently sloped (approximately 1 in. in every five feet) for drainage.

When using mortar, it should be mixed extra thin and poured into the crevices with an old coffee pot or gallon can and the joint then smoothed immediately with a small trowel.

Decks

Wood decks vary in construction from the cantilevered units hung from the side of the house over a hillside, to the more common just-above-ground units built with post and beam systems.

In building a post and beam deck, concrete footings should be installed on firm ground, below the frost level, and six inches above grade. Upright posts should be end-drilled to fit over steel dowels set in wet concrete. An asphalt roofing pad should be placed under the posts to stop upward transmission of surface water from the concrete to the post.

Redwood, western red cedar and newer "outdoor" wood that has been pressure treated are among the most commonly used decking materials. Depending upon the part of the deck in question, the choice of grade of the lumber should be dictated primarily by qualities of appearance, strength, and durability.

Decking brings out the best in a natural, rustic setting, even to the extent of permitting tasteful construction around large trees. Simple foam cushions can be easily moved from place to place. (Photo: California Redwoood Assn.)

Preassembled sections can be used in basketweave pattern in assembling decks. Here the units merely are set atop a well-prepared earth surface, eliminating the need for structural framing. (Photo: Western Wood Products Assn.)

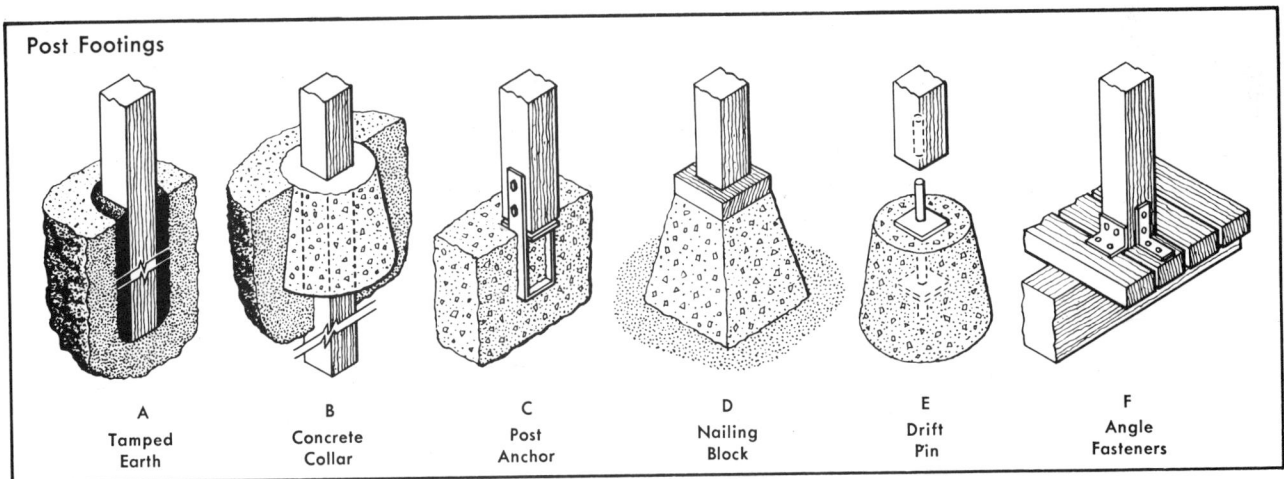

Post Footings

A	B	C	D	E	F
Tamped Earth	Concrete Collar	Post Anchor	Nailing Block	Drift Pin	Angle Fasteners

Post footings can be constructed in several approved ways, always making certain that the posts are carefully plumbed with a level. Depth varies according to frost conditions but 36 in. is usually adequate for most structures. (Drawings: California Redwood Assn.)

The upper, or architectural grades (clear all heart and clear) are outstanding in their freedom from knots and imperfections. The garden grades (select heart, select, construction heart, and construction common) which are less perfect, contain knots and other limiting characteristics.

The upper grades are available with mixed flat and vertical grains, or in special vertical grain selections. They are also available kiln dried, assuring minimum shrinkage and tight joints. The garden grades are less expensive and not ordinarily kiln dried. Garden grades are perfectly satisfactory for use in many decks, where they are in keeping with the less exacting requirements of a natural setting.

In adding a deck to your home, survey the landscaping situation and decide which problems the deck should solve. Determine the approximate location and then check your local building department to see which regulations, provisions, restrictions, or guidelines are placed upon the deck you wish to build.

Building regulations may include foundation requirements, railings, load limits, height and projection limits and other requirements. If the construction problem is a difficult one, or if the deck is more than a few feet above the ground, a building professional such as a structural engineer, architect or contractor should be consulted. They can save you much grief.

The key elements of a successfully built deck include: the top layer or decking itself, joists which support the decking, beams which carry the joists, and posts which transmit the load of the entire structure to the concrete footings. It should be noted that in extremely low-level decks, the beams may rest directly on the footings.

Buying the Lumber

California Redwood Association design engineers recommend two-in. nominal material for most decking situations. The most common sizes are 2 x 4 and 2 x 6, although wider pieces are sometimes used for special effects. Nominal 1-in.-thick material may be used where joists are placed within 16 in. on center. Where a pattern of narrow lines is desired, 2 x 4's may be used on edge, with longer spans than are possible when the decking is laid flat. Decking spans will vary according to the grade and species.

Two-inch dimension lumber is generally used for joists, again with spans determined by grade and

Basic Deck Construction

These drawings prepared by Koppers Co. detail the use of Wolmanized lumber in constructing ground level and elevated decks.

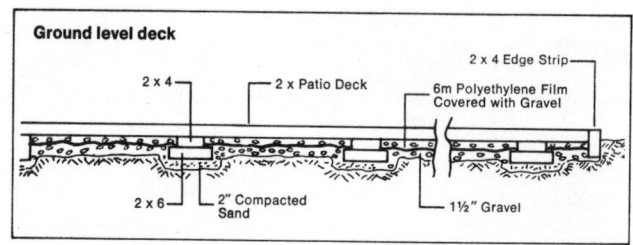

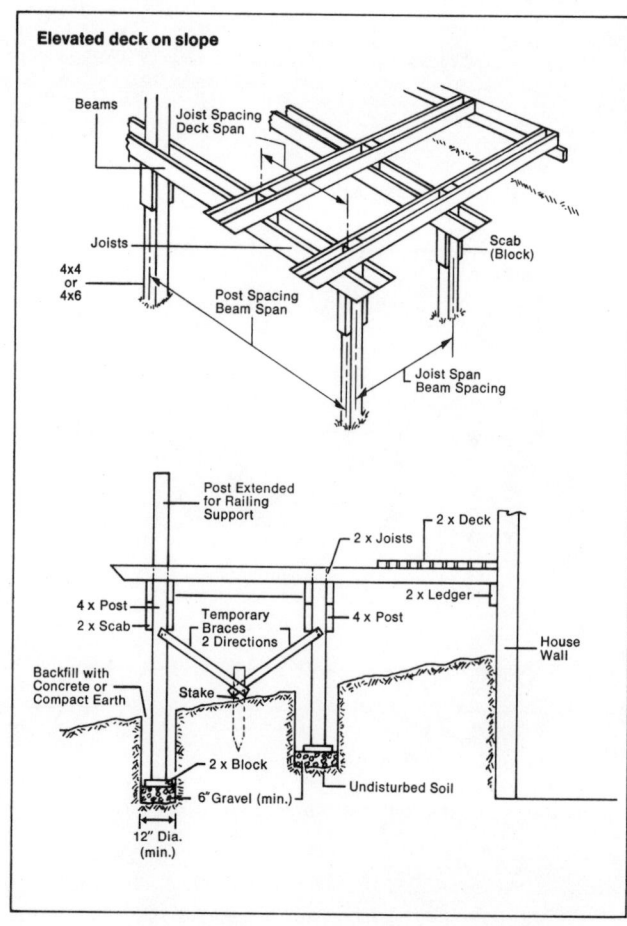

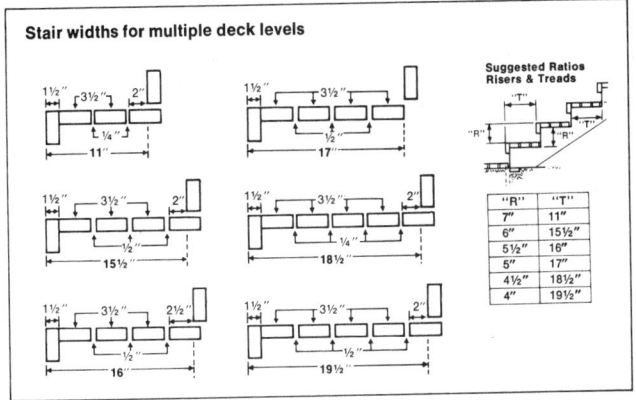

Stair construction can vary greatly according to the deck levels involved. These sketches show suggested ratios of risers and treads, typical construction details, and the two most popular methods of attaching steps to stringers.

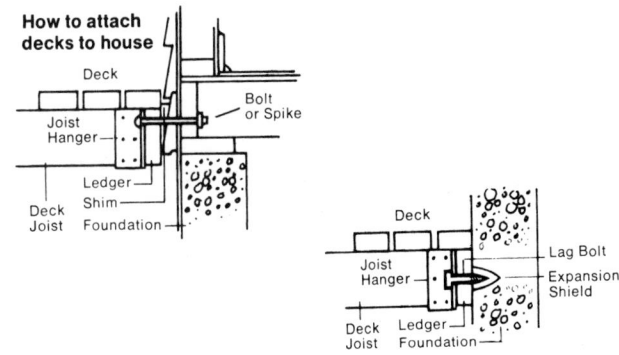

Attaching a deck to the house can be handled in various ways, including the two popular methods illustrated here that require a minimum of hardware. All hangers, bolts and nails should be galvanized. (Sketch: Koppers Co.)

specie. Beam sizes depend upon the spacing and span of the beams; however, a general rule is to utilize as large a beam as necessary to minimize the number of posts and footings. Beams of 4-in. thickness and greater are often used.

Posts bearing the weight of the deck are most frequently 4 x 4's, although larger posts may be required for steep sites or heavy loads of people, snow, planters and the like. Concrete footings frequently are fitted with metal post anchors or steel straps to secure the posts in place.

Nailing

Nailing decking to joists varies again with the decking material being used. For example, tongue-and-groove decking can be toe-nailed without face nails unless the nominal width of the decking is three times the thickness of the material.

Only noncorroding nails and fastenings should be used in order to prevent staining, and those galvanized by the electroplating method should not be used. For 2-in. decking, use 16-penny nails. Use 8-penny nails for 1-in. decking. Predrilling nail holes helps prevent splitting and achieve secure fastening.

When tongue-and-groove materials are not used for decking, a common 3½-in. nail is a handy gauge for spacing the deck boards. The deck spacing will increase slightly as the lumber dries and this will compensate for future expansion and retraction. Deck nails should be long enough to penetrate two-thirds of the length of the shank into the joist or holding member.

Before

This typical 1948 house with postage-stamp-size entry stoop offered little in the way of outdoor living before remodeling.

A redwood deck was designed as an extension of the house for a more attractive entry and a comfortable setting for outdoor relaxation. Deck, benches and fencing were constructed entirely of lower-cost garden grades of redwood characterized by rustic knots and streaks of cream-colored sapwood. The decking is 2x6 construction common; the benches 2x4's on edge; planters 2x4's and 1x6's, steps 2x4's, and fences 1x6's. Finish consisted of two coats of water repellent to protect the natural color and minimize shrinkage.

Decks for Leisure

After

The existing fixed windows were untouched in the remodeling and now provide a view of the pleasant patio and gardens beyond. (Photos: California Redwood Assn.)

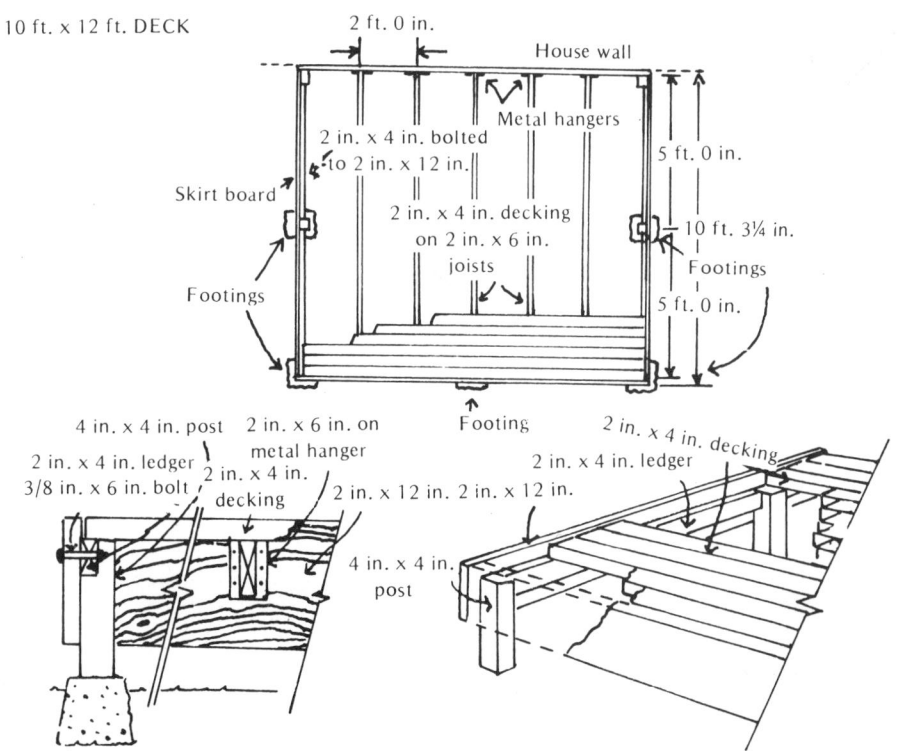

10 ft. x 12 ft. DECK

2 ft. 0 in.

House wall

Metal hangers

2 in. x 4 in. bolted
to 2 in. x 12 in.

5 ft. 0 in.

Skirt board

2 in. x 4 in. decking
on 2 in. x 6 in.
joists

10 ft. 3¼ in.

Footings

Footings

5 ft. 0 in.

Footing

4 in. x 4 in. post   2 in. x 6 in. on
metal hanger
2 in. x 4 in. ledger
3/8 in. x 6 in. bolt   2 in. x 4 in.
decking

2 in. x 12 in. 2 in. x 12 in.

4 in. x 4 in.
post

2 in. x 4 in. decking

2 in. x 4 in. ledger

4 in. x 4 in.
post

How-to illustration for building a standard 10 ft. by 12 ft. deck

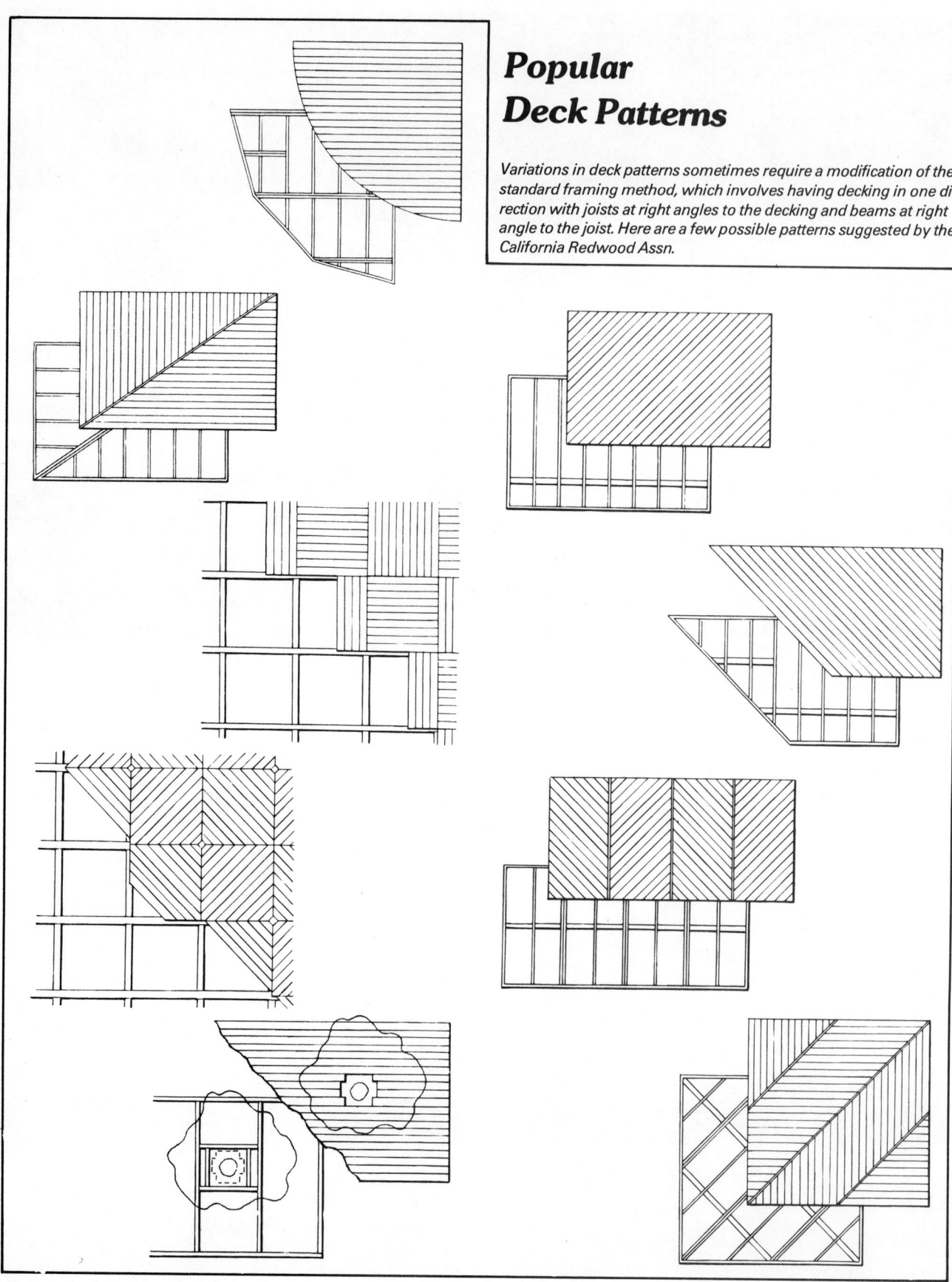

Popular Deck Patterns

Variations in deck patterns sometimes require a modification of the standard framing method, which involves having decking in one direction with joists at right angles to the decking and beams at right angle to the joist. Here are a few possible patterns suggested by the California Redwood Assn.

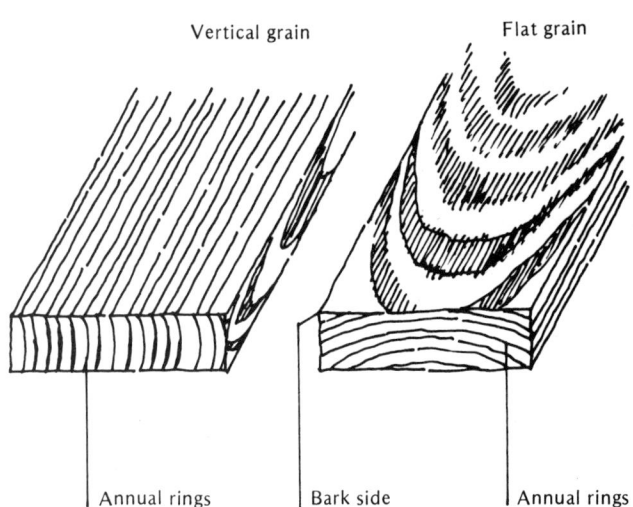

Vertical grain   Flat grain

| Annual rings | Bark side | Annual rings |

Wood grain – Vertical-grain boards make the best decking.

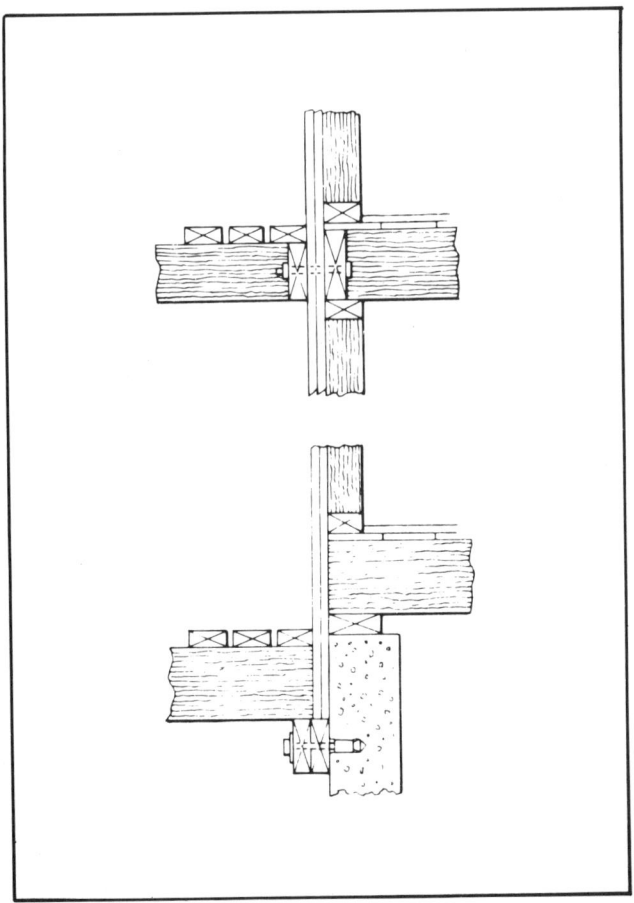

Ledgers: a) normal 2 in. ledger, b) thicker ledger positioned below floor level.

SUGGESTED BEAM SPANS					
BEAM SIZE	GRADE	WIDTH OF DECK			
		6'	8'	10'	12'
4x6	Select	Span 6'-6"	Span 6'-0"	Span 5'-0"	Span 4'-0"
	Common	4'-6"	4'-0"	3'-6"	3'-0"
4x8	Select	9'-0"	8'-0"	7'-0"	6'-0"
	Common	6'-0"	5'-0"	4'-6"	4'-0"
4x10	Select	11'-6"	10'-0"	8'-6"	7'-6"
	Common	7'-6"	6'-6"	6'-0"	5'-6"

Elevated decks should be constructed with railings for safety reasons. Many buildings codes will require railings if the deck is two or more ft. off the ground, and it's good practice to limit any opening between vertical members to six in. so children cannot fall through.

Elevated decks also require stairways and the easiest to build are those where treads rest on cleats nailed directly to the stringers. Although slightly more difficult to build, the best step supports are sawed into the stringers themselves. Variations include bolting 2 x 8's as carriages to the stringers, then making steps of 2 x 4's set on edge.

Treads should be a minimum of 11 in. wide. Risers should be no higher than 7 in., but can be as low as 4 in. When doubtful about making one step or two, build two to avoid one high step.

Even small decks can provide an entertainment area over sloping ground that otherwise has little utility. Wolmanized pressure-treated lumber was used for the deck, railing and stairs. (Photo: Koppers Co.)

Close-to-the-ground decks help to define specific relaxation areas around the home. This U-shape deck features a pond in the center which flows under the closed end of the "U." Douglas fir 2x4's were used for the decking. (Photo: Western Wood Products Assn.)

Decks and screens are a basic part of the landscape scheme, which divides this yard into outdoor rooms and use areas, some garden-oriented and others serving as extensions of interior spaces. The small deck of Douglas Fir 2x4's connects to the kitchen. Beyond lies the main outdoor living room. (Photo: Western Wood Products Assn.)

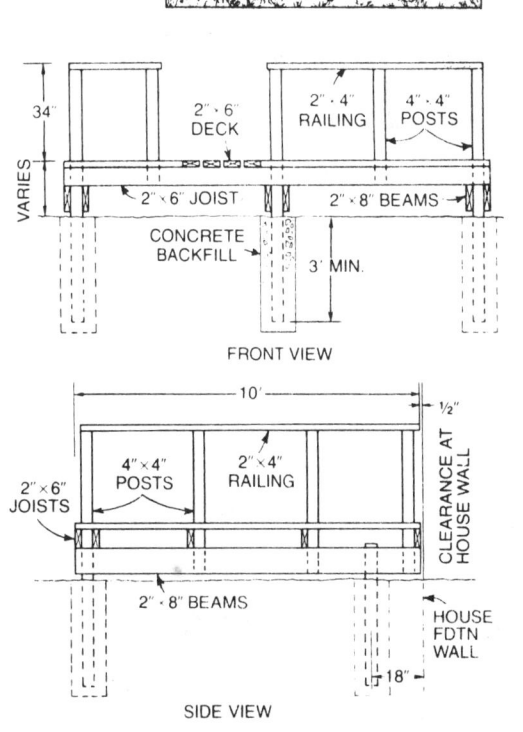

Patio Deck

MATERIALS LIST

    9 pcs 4''x4''x8' Posts and Blocks
    6 pcs 2''x8''x10' Beams
    5 pcs 2''x6''x12' Joists
    26 pcs 2''x6''x10' Decking
    3 pcs 2''x4''x10' Railing

Note: Length of 4x4's will vary depending upon height of deck above ground.

Drawings: Koppers Co., Inc.

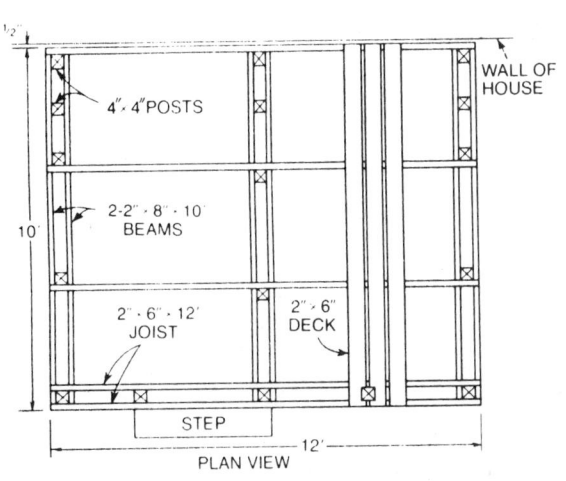

Patio Roofs

Successful patio roofs take many shapes, forms and sizes and can be constructed of a varied list of materials, most of them well known to the average homeowner. The range of possibilities runs from a festive canvas canopy hung from columns to an electrically powered roof that retracts to one end or side at the push of a button, opening the entire area to the sky and stars.

Two of the biggest factors in determining the size, shape and style patio roof for a given home are the overall architectural design of the dwelling and the orientation of the patio to the sun.

It may be well to consider a few orientation basics:

(1) south-facing patios get the warmth of the sun the entire day, regardless of season or latitude;

(2) west-oriented patios receive the full force of the late afternoon, often getting a great radiation of heat from the wall of the house—a patio roof in this area will make the space comfortable from 11 to 4 p.m. during the summer, but other screening devices will be required late in the day;

Varied roof slopes add to the modernistic design of this home patio. Translucent plastic roofing panels provide weather protection, light and a wide range of colors. (Photo: Western Wood Products Assn.)

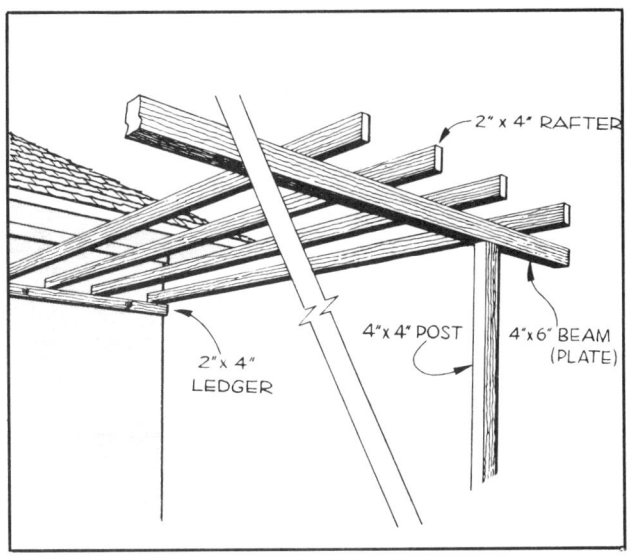

(3) the northern-exposed patio is the coolest and never receives direct sun. If this area is to the rear of a two-story home, it may well be in the shade the entire year round;

(4) eastern-facing patios benefit from the morning sun and tend to cool off in the afternoon.

Simple patio roof framework consists of a ledger (to tie the roof to the house wall), posts, beams and rafters. Such assemblies are constructed much in the way a deck is built, only the framework needn't have the weight-carrying capabilities of the deck. The framework, however, should be substantial enough to support a workman or, if surfaced with a solid roofing, carry snow loads in colder climates.

Local building codes determine the size of ledger and rafter materials required for constructing a patio roof in the typical manner, shown here. Rafters rest on the ledger secured to the house wall and on the opposite beam supported by 4x4-in. posts. Spacing of rafters varies according to finish roofing selected. (Sketch: California Redwood Assn.)

The basic design of this home incorporates the patio roof into the house roof, keeping materials uniform. The open center section is spacious, airy and bright. Flanking smaller outdoor rooms also have roof protection plus decorative filigree screening.

Constructing a Concrete Patio

In building a patio, all sod and debris must first be carefully removed from the patio area.

Forms are set to the proper grade. Sometimes the forms, of redwood here, are left in as dividers.

Sand is placed to a depth of two inches over the entire patio area using a rake to fill all voids.

Redwood forms can be covered with masking tape in order to preserve their rich color during construction.

The concrete is placed and consolidated. Note the consistency of the concrete.

Concrete is struck off with a long 2x4. Form stakes were cut off to aid strike-off.

A fine-bristle broom is used to give texture to the surface which has been struck-off with a wood float.

While one workman pours an adjoining section, another workman tamps the fresh cement securely into place.

A plastic film weighted at the edges seals in moisture for proper cement curing. (Photos: Portland Cement Assn.)

Literally dozens of materials are good choices for patio roofs, each depending upon the patio site orientation, translucency requirements, architectural styling and personal preferences. Among these materials are: canvas, fiberglass panels, plywood, lath and lumber, woven wood panels, grapestakes, cord-woven wood slats, aluminum lath, bamboo blinds, louvered screens, glass, aluminum, steel, and others.

Support posts, too, can be one of several materials including wood, steel, wrought iron or pipe. Placement should take into consideration appearance and traffic as well as structural considerations.

A combination of solid panels and pull-back fabric proved to be both an efficient and attractive solution to roofing this patio. The modern design is in keeping with furnishings, and the wide expanse of glass blends the in-doors with outdoors.

6. Garden Shelters, Firepits & Benches

Shelters

A garden shelter can be many things to many people. It can range from little more than a windbreak to a structure of Victorian design and massive scope. Careful planning will ensure that the shelter will serve the person using it, and not the other way around.

First, what do you want the shelter for? Simple expansion of your living room or family room? Privacy on a confined city lot? An entertainment center, or barbecue area? A potting shed where you can putter undisturbed? Or a place to be alone, and enjoy the fruits of your labor in the garden?

Many shelters are placed adjacent to the house itself, giving extra living space and frequent use by all members of the family. However, separate structures—free-standing in the garden—usually offer more solitude, personal privacy and elegant usage. Sometimes, two garden shelters are used to fill both needs.

Basic components of a garden center include decks, fences, trellises, roofing of some nature, screens, and appropriate supporting members—

Movable screens of redwood and translucent plastic combine with overhead sunshade, raised redwood deck, and fencing to provide a quiet garden center with some measure of weather control. (Photo: California Redwood Assn.)

Redwood A-frame shelter offers protection from the sun and wind while serving as the garden's focal point. Stylized flowers painted on the redwood fence behind add whimsical touch. (Photo: California Redwood Assn.)

A Garden Shelter

Building an overhead shelter—When an overhead shelter is attached directly to a house wall, only two or three supporting posts will be required.

posts, beams, rafters, etc. You can use all or some of these features, and combine them into a shelter that is especially tailored to you.

A garden shelter should do just that—shelter...from the elements...from the children... from noise and neighbors and other nuisances.

The location of a garden shelter will affect the use you get from it. A deck and sunshade extending from the house will serve as a second living room; a separate gazebo will be more like a private study.

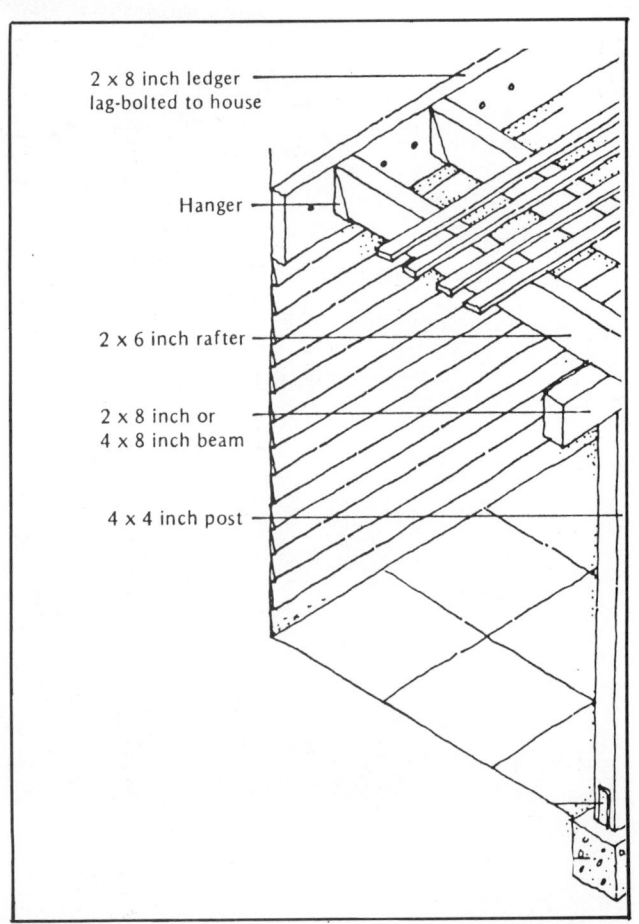

2 x 8 inch ledger
lag-bolted to house

Hanger

2 x 6 inch rafter

2 x 8 inch or
4 x 8 inch beam

4 x 4 inch post

Extensive yard remodeling at this home included an arbor room off the living room with screen of 2x2s, benches of 2x4s, posts of 4x4s, all western cedar. The graceful arch out into the swimming pool surrounds tree that shades decking of 2x4 Douglas fir. (Landscape architect: Robert Perron, ASLA. Photo: Western Wood Products Assn.)

A screen of western red cedar added off the kitchen at the front of this home offers a private area for informal meals and relaxation. The bench is built onto the screen of 1x2s supported on 4x4 posts. The walk along the house leads from the driveway to the front entrance. (Landscape architect: Barbara Fealy, ASLA. Photo: Western Wood Products Assn.)

This privacy porch-deck adds 12 x 15-foot outdoor living space at the side of the house. The privacy wall is framed with 2x4 fir, has a 2x6 cap railing, and is faced with 1/2x6 western cedar bevel siding to match the house siding. The decking is 2x4 Douglas fir on edge. Bench legs are band-sawn fir 2x12s alternated with 2x4 filled strips set into the deck. The bench seat is 2x4 fir. Window was replaced with two wood-framed glass doors for access from the house. (Designer: Tim Jones. Photo: Western Wood Products Assn.)

Five acres of oak, pine, rhododendrons and azaleas, with a creek-fed pond, impart a lasting beauty to this irregular U-shaped home nested among the trees. Architect Will Shaw selected clear-finished redwood siding on the exterior with a roof of taper-sawn redwood shakes. (Photo: California Redwood Assn.)

Few home settings offer the year-round beauty enjoyed by the residents of this home looking across Puget Sound to Vashon Island and the Kitsap Peninsula beyond. Architect Ralph Anderson selected redwood for the total exterior. (Photo: California Redwood Assn.)

Stepped screens surround the entry court of this home to block the view from the street
above. The screens were constructed from 1x4 western cedar boards on 2x4 stringers,
4x4 posts, with 2x6 flat cap. Landscape architect was John Herbst, Jr., ASLA. (Photo:
Western Wood Products Assn.)

The front entrance remodeling of this home features an engawa of 2x2 western wood
decking along two sides of the house, and a recirculating pond enclosed by a screen
topped with wisteria. (Landscape architect: John Herbst, Jr., ASLA. Photo: Western Wood
Products Assn.)

A small rose garden adds to home appearance; in this instance the perimeter is lighted with high mushroom fixtures, while central lighting is achieved with two 40-watt lamps concealed under the surface of the sun dial. (Photo: General Electric)

Low-voltage units under the overhang illuminate the planters and rock garden area of this home. In the soffit a 12-volt transformer is mounted feeding three 1383 airplane reading lamps. These deep-shielded units are on swivels and can be adjusted to feature different areas as they come to bloom. The Japanese lantern is wired for a 12-volt automotive bulb.

Safety lighting is a must at home entries. This contemporary split-level home with its gravel garden is illuminated by three prismatic wall fixtures. Each fixture uses two 50-watt A-line lamps, all controlled on a high-low switch. Decorative lighting accents are provided by a three-lamp decorative planter fixture at the corner of the garage. Additional accent lighting comes from a waterproof ground-recessed fixture under the small dogwood, equipped with 75R30/BW. (Photo: General Electric)

A "wren house" 40-watt fixture suspended from a tree branch and concealed by the lower branches provides a wide distribution of light along the path of this home. A tall mushroom unit housing a 75-watt bulb lights the steps. (Photo: General Electric)

Blue-white incandescent downlights accent the texture of the Mexican brick, while standard incandescent downlights highlight plantings in front of the playroom of this home. Lights are recessed in an overhang 8 in. from the wall. (Photo: General Electric)

Multi-purpose gazebos are part of many American home exterior settings and add immeasurably to the appearance of the property. This eight-sided gazebo is practical, too, for at the back is a shed ideal for storing bicycles as well as lawn and garden furniture. (Photo: Masonite Corp.)

A garden shelter can serve many purposes as well as greatly enhance the home exterior. This shelter, designed by John Matthias, has a two-way counter at center, built-in seating and ample storage. (Photos: California Redwood Assn.)

Choosing Your Shelter Material

Popular materials for overhead shelters—Choose your shelter material according to your nuisance: rain, a hot sun, mosquitoes.

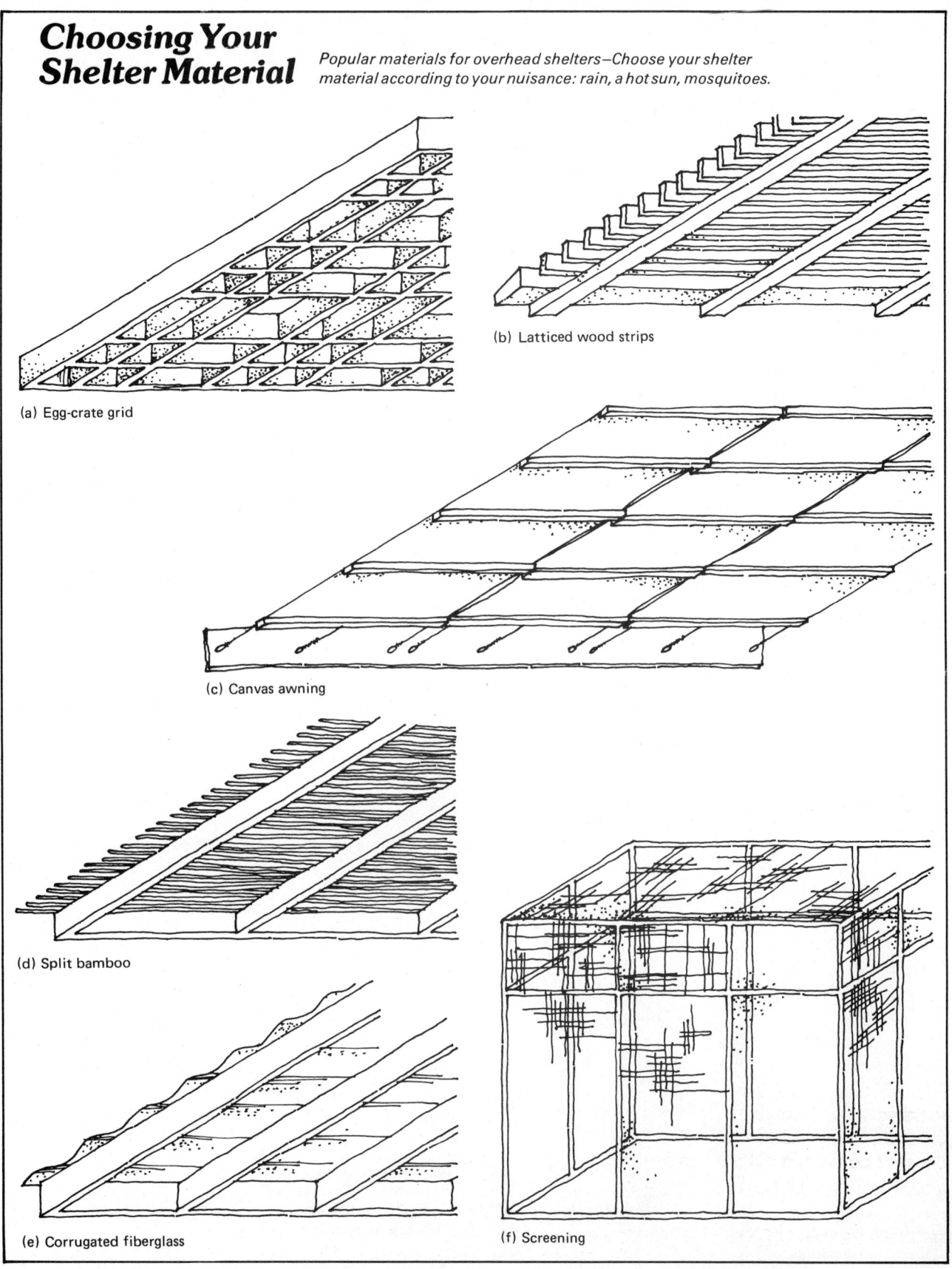

(a) Egg-crate grid

(b) Latticed wood strips

(c) Canvas awning

(d) Split bamboo

(e) Corrugated fiberglass

(f) Screening

Firepits and Barbecues

Adding a portable or built-in backyard barbecue or firepit will have a profound effect on most families, for such units serve as great stimulants to outdoor living. Literally hundreds of different portable barbecues are available from local sources.

Both portables and built-ins can be equipped to use the fuel source most to your liking—charcoal, electric, gas or even wood logs. Each fire source has its own merits, of which you are undoubtedly familiar.

Sunken and raised firepits go beyond cooking and provide a relaxed and informal setting for family and guest entertaining. Such units can be assembled over a weekend using basic materials available from local building supply dealers —cement, brick or block, and expanded or rod grillework. Wood, too, can be used to surround the masonry walls and as a cover that helps keep the pit clean and permits the area to be used for other purposes when fireless.

Like the sunken conversation pit indoors, a backyard combination deck and firepit can be a great gathering spot. This plan, designed by the Western Wood Products Assn., includes a 3-foot square (outside dimensions) firepit constructed of forty 4x4x16 concrete blocks, a bag of mortar, four pieces each 2x6x3-ft. 3½-in. mitered at both ends, eight carriage bolts ⅓ x6-in. with nuts and washers (see drawings).

Build a Deck and Firepit

Courses of 2x4-inch western wood are cut to size, laid on sleepers of treated 4x4s set on bed of 1½″-minus gravel, spaced with quarter-inch plywood.

Decking of 2x4s is toe-nailed to sleepers with 6d nails. Two sleepers are placed at right angles to each side of firepit, and one at each corner.

Each 2x4 also is faced-nailed at each corner with two 16d galvanized nails. Spacers are left in until all nailing is finished, then removed.

Finished deck courses show lap pattern. Firepit has five courses of 4x4x16 concrete blocks; surround of mitered 2x6s is attached with carriage bolts.

Materials List

Treated 4x4s
- 4 pcs 10′
- 1 pc 8′ — 1 pc 14′

2x4 decking
- 13 pcs 8′ — 8 pcs 14′
- 17 pcs 10′ — 8 pcs 16′
- 8 pcs 12′

6d and 16d galvanized nails

Cu yd gravel 1¼″-minus

Firepit
- 40 concrete blocks 4x4x16
- bag mortar
- 4 pcs 2x6 3′3⅛″ mitered both ends
- 8 carriage bolts ⅜x6″ w/nut & washer

Cut Sizes

(Same material as in list above)

Treated 4x4 sleepers:
- 2 pcs 10′ — 4 pcs 4′6½″ mitered 45°
- 2 pcs 3′
- 4 pcs 3′2½″ — 4 pcs 5⅞″

2x4 deck courses from center out:
- 2 pcs 3′, 2 pcs 3′3″
- 2 pcs 3′3¾″, 2 pcs 3′6¾″
- 2 pcs 3′7⅜″, 2 pcs 3′10⅜″
- 2 pcs 3′11″, 2 pcs 4′2″
- 2 pcs 4′2¾″, 2 pcs 4′5¾″
- 2 pcs 4′6¼″, 2 pcs 4′9¼″
- 2 pcs 4′9⅞″, 2 pcs 5′⅞″
- 2 pcs 5′1⅝″, 2 pcs 5′4⅝″
- 2 pcs 5′5⅛″, 2 pcs 5′8⅛″
- 2 pcs 5′8⅞″, 2 pcs 5′11⅞″
- 2 pcs 6′⅜″, 2 pcs 6′3⅜″
- 2 pcs 6′4″, 2 pcs 6′7¼″
- 2 pcs 6′7¾″, 2 pcs 6′10⅞″
- 2 pcs 11⅜″, 2 pcs 7′2⅜″
- 2 pcs 7′3⅛″, 2 pcs 7′6⅛″
- 2 pcs 7′6¾″, 2 pcs 7′9¾″
- 2 pcs 7′10⅜″, 2 pcs 8′1⅜″
- 2 pcs 8′2″, 2 pcs 8′5″
- 2 pcs 8′5⅝″, 2 pcs 8′8⅝″
- 2 pcs 8′9⅜″, 2 pcs 9′⅜″
- 12 pcs 9′⅜″

Note: Decking extends under benches up to bench post.
10′-0″
ENTER
Edge of Deck
Fire Pit
A
10′-0″
1′-6″
3′-0″
4′-0″
7′-0″
1′-6″
3′-0″
9′-0″
4′-2 3/4″
1′-6″
Typical Short Bench
Typical Long Bench
Bench Outline
4×4 Treated sleepers. Stake to ground & Nail 2×4 Deck to top with 1/4″ Spacing.
DECK PLAN
1′-6″
2x4 1/4″ Space
1′-3″
Treated 4x4 Set in 12″ Conc.
2x6 Bolt to Concrete
2x4 Decking
3″
4x4x16 Conc. Block
1′-8″
3′-0″
3 1/2″ Thick gravel 1 1/4″ Minus.
12″ϕ
SECTION A-A
2x4 Bench Supports
(2) 3/8 x 7 Carriage bolts
4x4 Treated post
BENCH SUPPORT

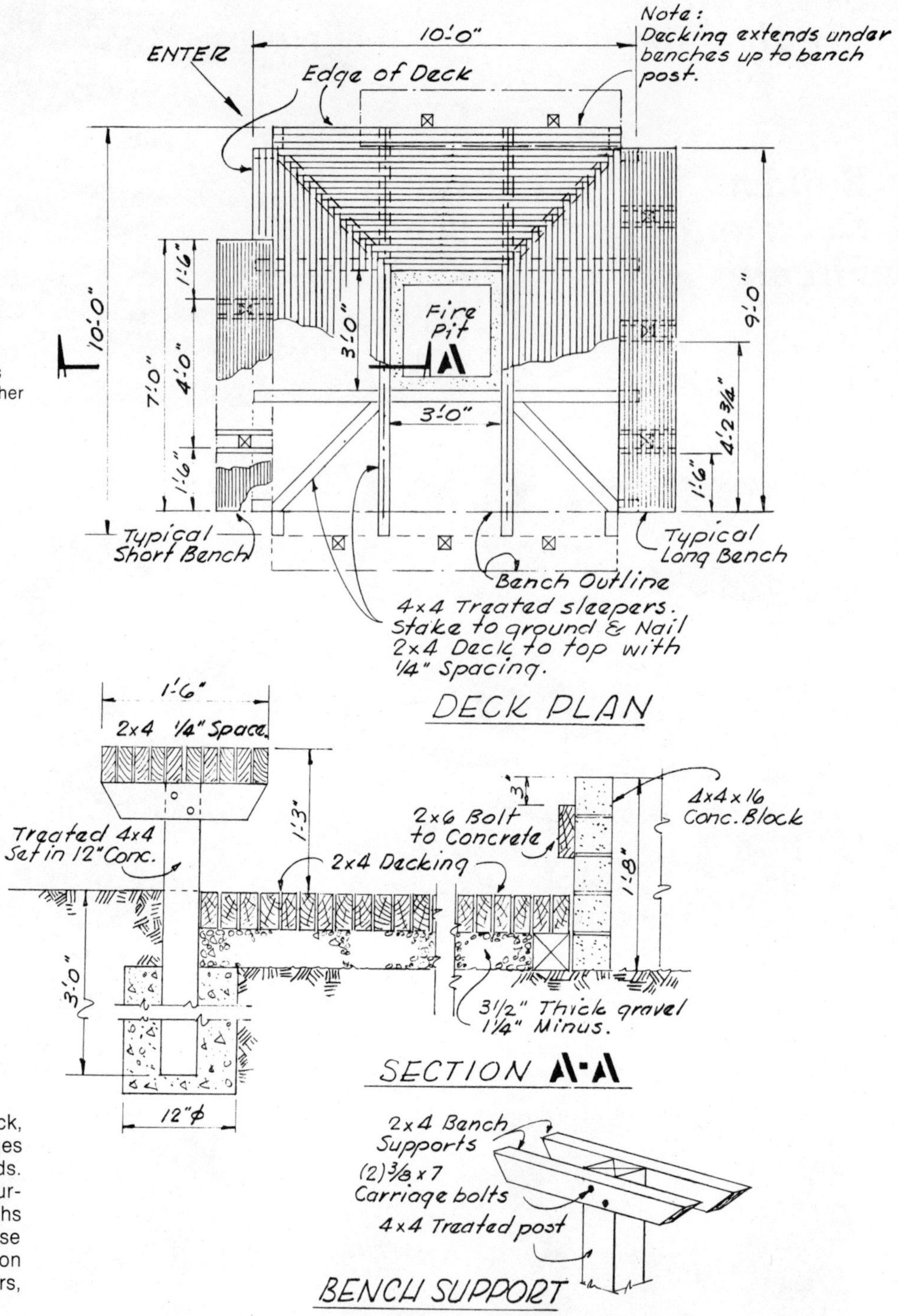

Alternate Designs

Three alternate patterns for the deck, illustrated below, offer the advantages of less cutting and fewer trim ends. Using three-foot modules, 2x4s purchased in six, nine or 12-foot lengths will eliminate wasteful trimming. These deck sections can be placed on treated skids rather than 4x4 sleepers, also cutting costs.

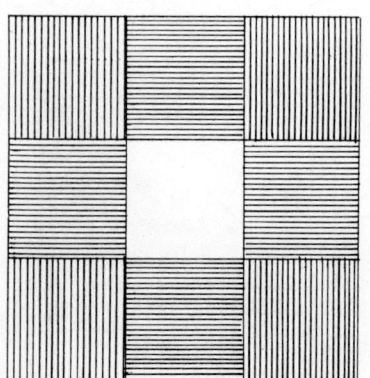

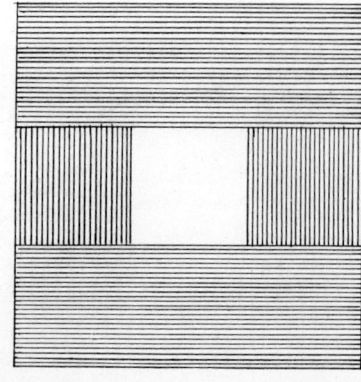

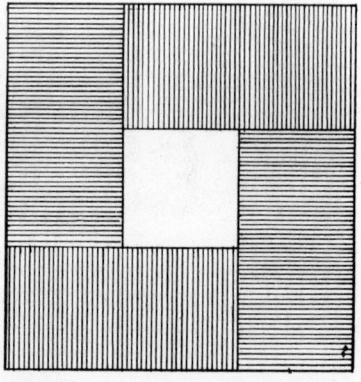

A Cover/Table for the Firepit

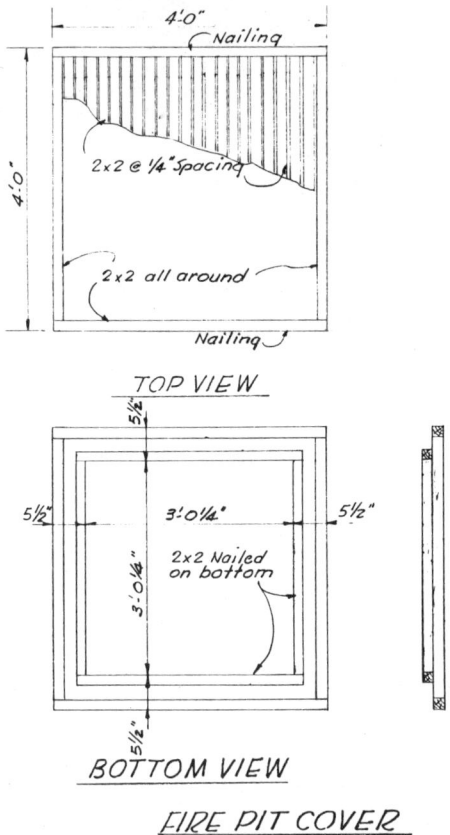

4'0" Nailing

4'0"

2x2 @ ¼" Spacing

2x2 all around

Nailing

TOP VIEW

5½"

5½" 3'0¼" 5½"

3'0¼"

2x2 Nailed on bottom

5½"

BOTTOM VIEW

FIRE PIT COVER

A removable cover for the firepit also serves as a table or extra seating. Shown bottom side up in photo, it's easily assembled of 2x2" western wood, with the inside of the smaller frame fitting outside dimensions of pit.

Materials List

2x2 16 pcs 8'
2x2 1 pc 4'

Benches for Deck or Garden

Easily built deck benches adapt well to freestanding use, enhancing garden view.

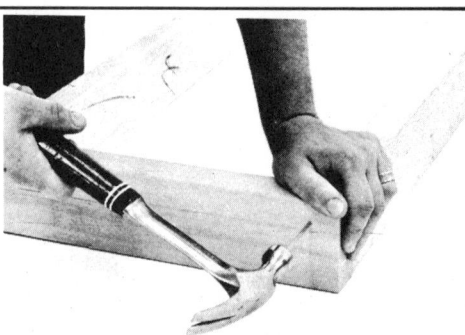

Bench seat is framed by nailing outside 2x4s to 1'6" end cap.

Two holes are drilled through braces, legs to hold bolts.

Eight 2x4s are placed in the frame, spaced with ¼-inch slats.

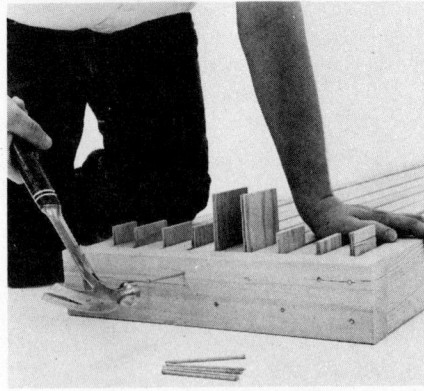

Spacers are removed after nailing 2x4s to end cap with 16d nails.

Braces cut 30 degrees on each end are nailed to 4x4 treated posts.

Two 3/8x7″ carriage bolts secure each leg to two braces of 2x4s.

Nine-foot bench requires three legs, seven-foot bench only two.

Leg braces are toe-nailed on both sides, ends to each 2x4.

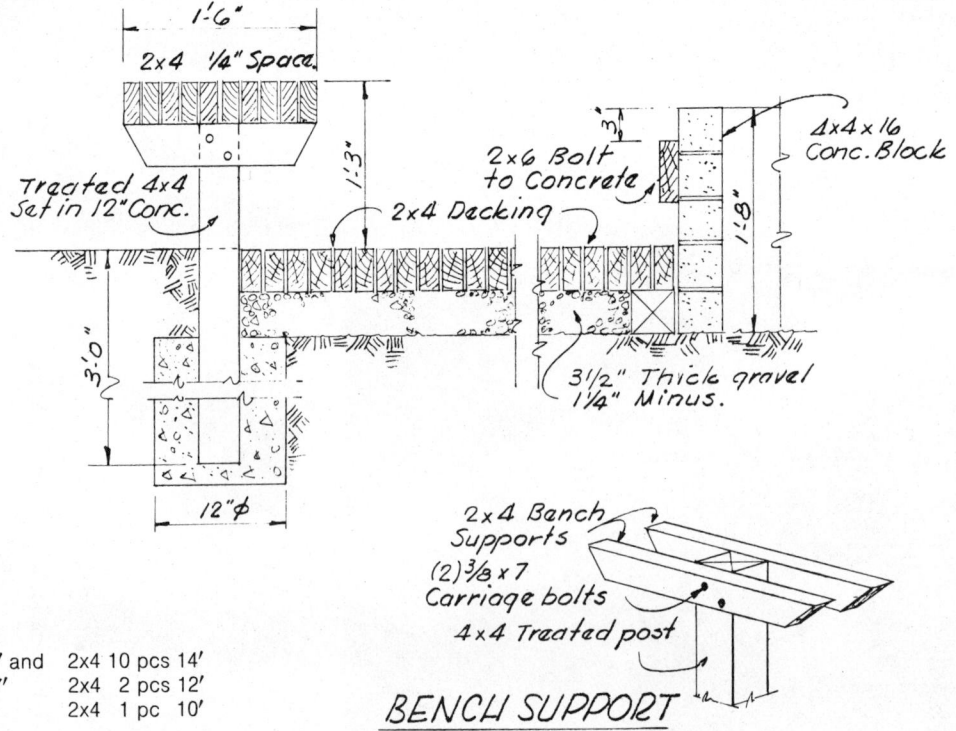

1'-6"
2x4 ¼" Space
Treated 4x4 Set in 12" Conc.
1'-3"
2x6 Bolt to Concrete
2x4 Decking
4x4x16 Conc. Block
3
1'-8"
3'-0"
12"Ø
3½" Thick gravel 1¼" Minus.

2x4 Bench Supports
(2) ⅜ x 7 Carriage bolts
4x4 Treated post

BENCH SUPPORT

Materials List

Two benches 9' and
  two benches 7'
4x4 5 pcs 8'
2x4 20 pcs 10'
20 carriage bolts 3/8x7″ w/nut & washer
6d & 16d galvanized nails

2x4 10 pcs 14'
2x4 2 pcs 12'
2x4 1 pc 10'

In planning the dimension of a firepit, keep in mind that full-length cordwood runs to four feet. Other common log lengths are 16 and 36 in.

The material you choose for constructing an outdoor barbecue, fire pit or fireplace will set the style, whether dignified and formal or rustic and informal. Be sure to make the unit high enough to afford a convenient working level, or low enough if you intend to be sitting when cooking and enjoying the log flames.

Areas of the fire pit that come in contact with heat and flames should be of fire-resistant block or firebrick to avoid damage from sudden temperature changes. Tops of fireplace walls should be capped to prevent water from seeping down through the masonry.

When winter comes, the metal grille should be warmed with a small fire, then rubbed with suet for a protective coating of grease. Clean the ashpit thoroughly, and cover the chimney and cooking area to keep out snow and dirt.

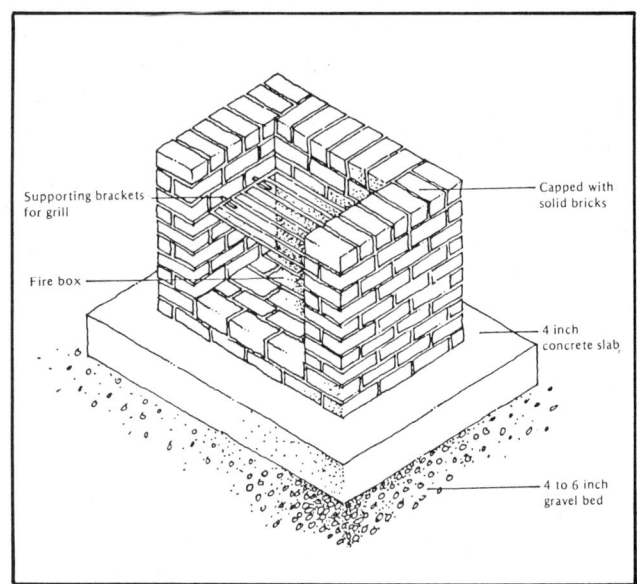

Because of its weight, a brick barbecue should be built on a slab of concrete at least four inches thick.

A gracefully curving brick charcoal grill blends in with the low garden wall to create an attractive outdoor cooking area. The wide ledge gives needed working space and provides a surface area near the heat to keep food warm.

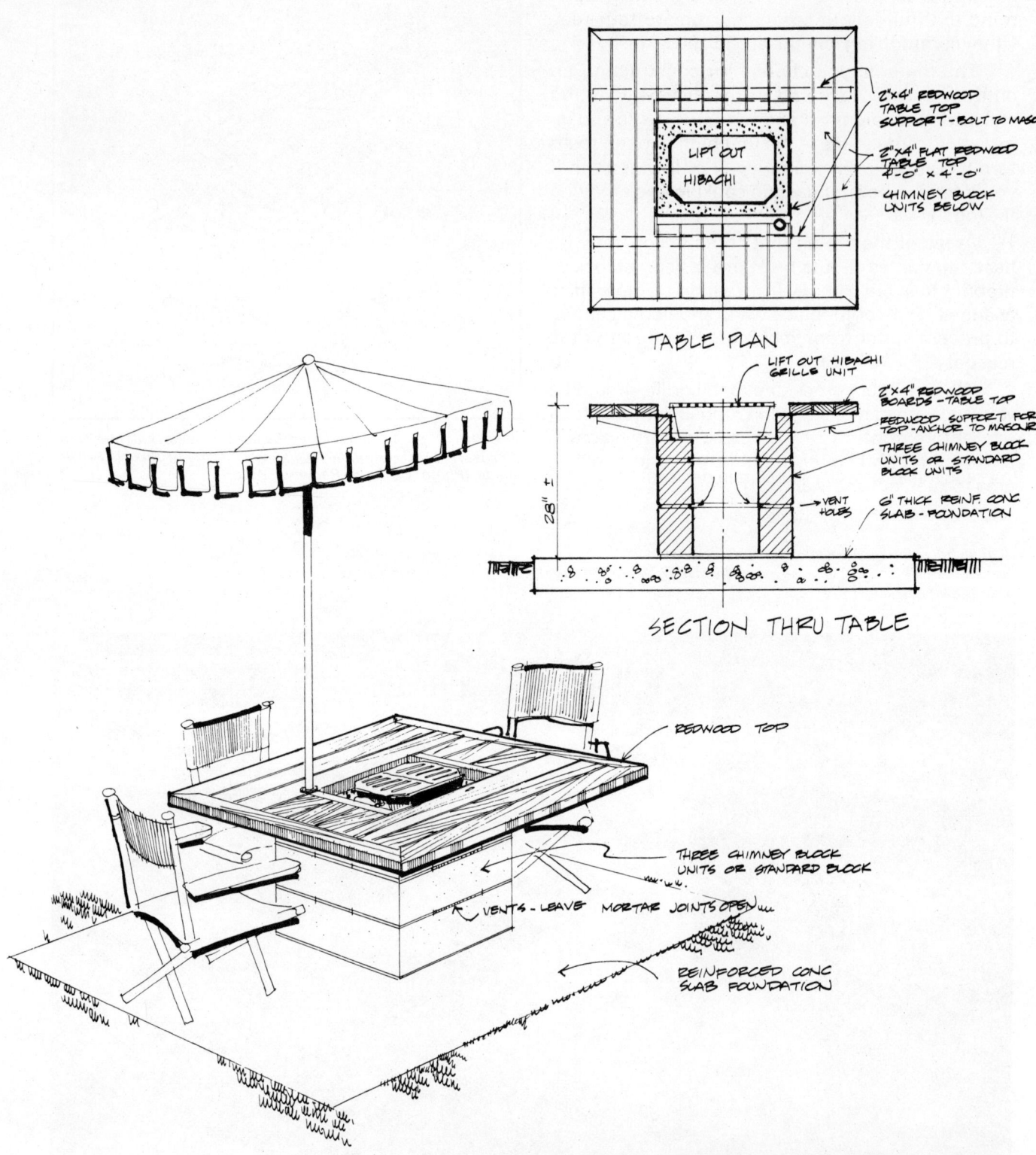

2"x4" REDWOOD TABLE TOP SUPPORT - BOLT TO MASONRY

2"x4" FLAT REDWOOD TABLE TOP 4'-0" x 4'-0"

CHIMNEY BLOCK UNITS BELOW

LIFT OUT HIBACHI

TABLE PLAN

LIFT OUT HIBACHI GRILLE UNIT

2"x4" REDWOOD BOARDS - TABLE TOP

REDWOOD SUPPORT FOR TOP - ANCHOR TO MASONRY

THREE CHIMNEY BLOCK UNITS OR STANDARD BLOCK UNITS

VENT HOLES

6" THICK REINF. CONC. SLAB - FOUNDATION

28" ±

SECTION THRU TABLE

REDWOOD TOP

THREE CHIMNEY BLOCK UNITS OR STANDARD BLOCK

VENTS - LEAVE MORTAR JOINTS OPEN

REINFORCED CONC. SLAB FOUNDATION

This low-cost backyard barbecue can be built using a Hibachi charcoal grill. Unit includes table, beach umbrella, and concrete patio floor.

Benches

There is no prescribed length or width (suggested minimum 12 in.) for a garden bench, but most designers recommend it be 15 to 18 in. high comfortable seating, and slightly lower if you intend to use mats atop the finished surface.

Benches, of course, can be portable or installed permanently, and may be built with or without a back. By definition, a bench is a long outdoor seat for two or more people, but in reality it may also serve as a platform for dining or sun bathing, game table and the like.

Wood is the most commonly used material for benches and most assemblies utilize basic 2x4's placed either flat or on edge atop a structural frame. The 2x4 also is frequently used for cross members below the seating surface and for the finish fascia. Support columns can be basic 4x4's or 2 in. thick material spaced 4 ft. on center or the entire length of the bench if a "closed" support is desired.

Free-standing benches constructed by the home craftsman can be located at will on the deck, patio or in the yard. This redwood unit has hand grips on the wings, making it easy to move to sun or shade. (Photo: California Redwood Assn.)

Western cedar 2x4's were used to construct this patio bench as part of a 2x4 wood deck. The cantilevered effect was achieved by using a series of U-shaped metal straps that are hidden between the 2x4's in the seat, back and deck. (Photo: Western Wood Products Assn.)

Build a Bench

This L-shaped bench requires: 9 pieces 2x4, each 10 ft. long; 2 pieces 2x12, each 10 ft. long; 1 piece 2x12, 6 ft. long. Use hot-dipped galvanized nails for lasting wear. (Photo: Koppers Co.)

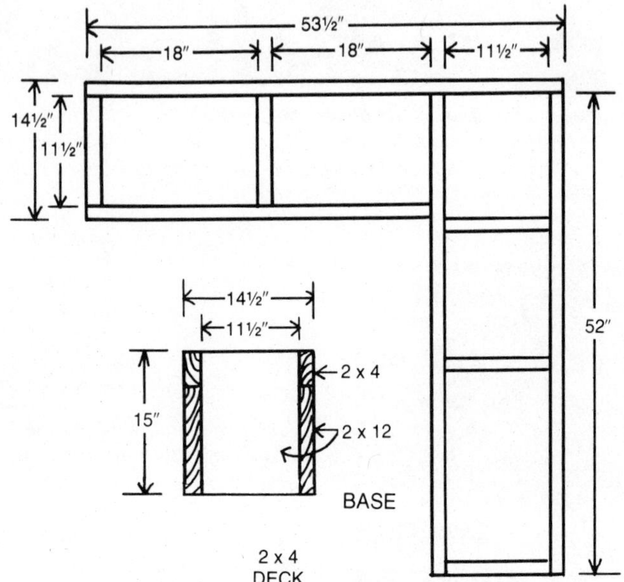

53½"

18" 18" 11½"

14½"
11½"

52"

14½"
11½"

15"

2 x 4

2 x 12

BASE

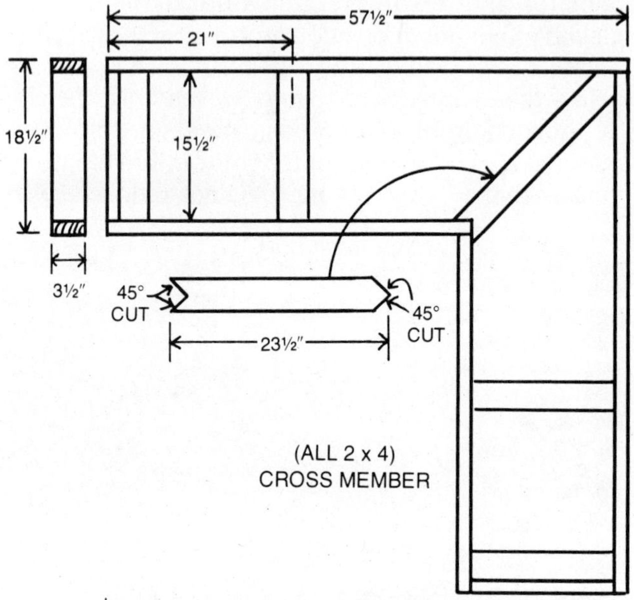

2 x 4
DECK

2 x 12

2 x 12
SPACER

2 x 4

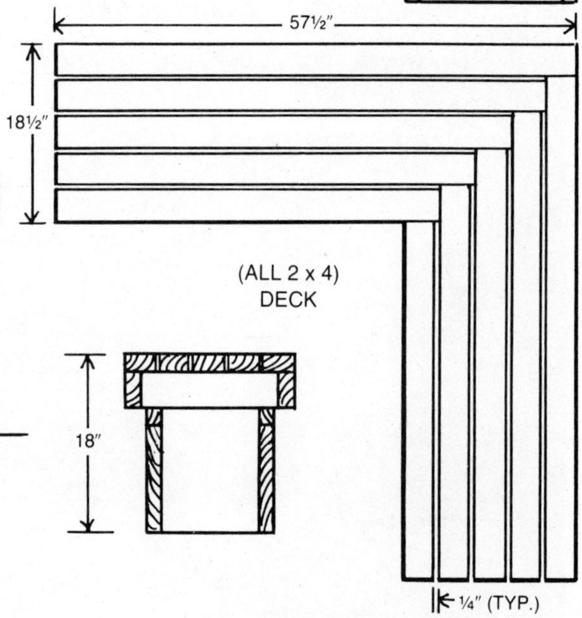

57½"

21"

18½"

15½"

3½"

45°
CUT

45°
CUT

23½"

(ALL 2 x 4)
CROSS MEMBER

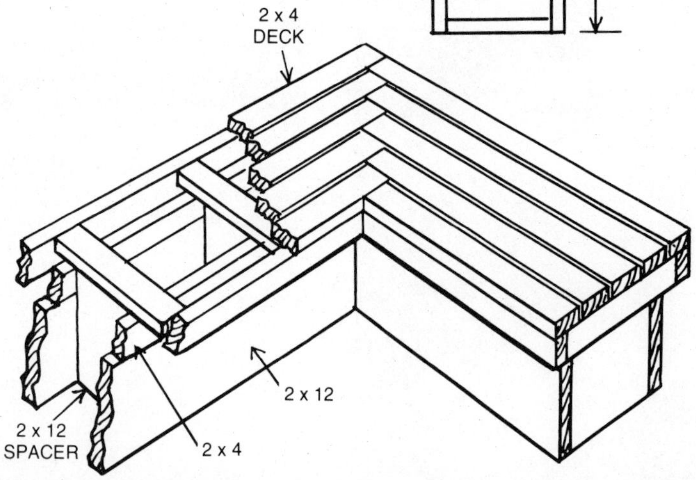

57½"

18½"

(ALL 2 x 4)
DECK

18"

¼" (TYP.)

OUTDOOR WOOD
MATERIAL LIST:
9 PCS. 2 x 4 — 10' LONG
2 PCS. 2 x 12 — 10' LONG
1 PC. 2 x 12 — 6' LONG
HOT-DIPPED GALVANIZED NAILS

Built-in seating is an added benefit of this attractive engawa (outdoor corridor or passageway) which serves as a link between indoor rooms and garden. The L-shaped seating assembly was built with 2x4's and is hung from engawa columns as well as supported by ground posts. (Photo: Western Wood Products Assn.)

All-heartwood grade garden redwood or pressure-treated wood should be used if the bench will be standing directly on the ground. If the bench is used on a deck or otherwise off the ground, either heartwood or sapwood grades of redwood are fine. Manufacturers further recommend that the bench seat surface be either vertical grain or, if flat grain, placed bark-side up. The bark side is the side that grew outermost in the tree. It can be determined by looking at the end of the piece of lumber and turning it until the growth rings arch upward.

As is true in building wood decks, all nails and fastening devices should be stainless steel, aluminum alloy or top-quality hot-dipped galvanized, not plain iron, steel or cement-coated nails that will discolor the wood surface.

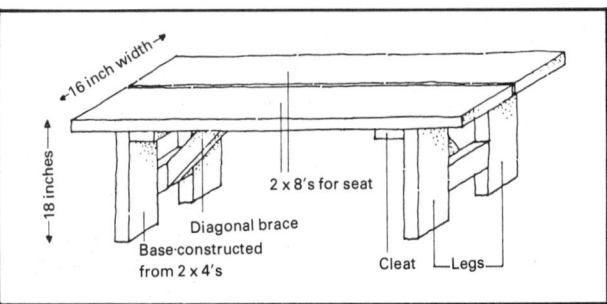

Heavy boards make a small two-seater bench more stable.

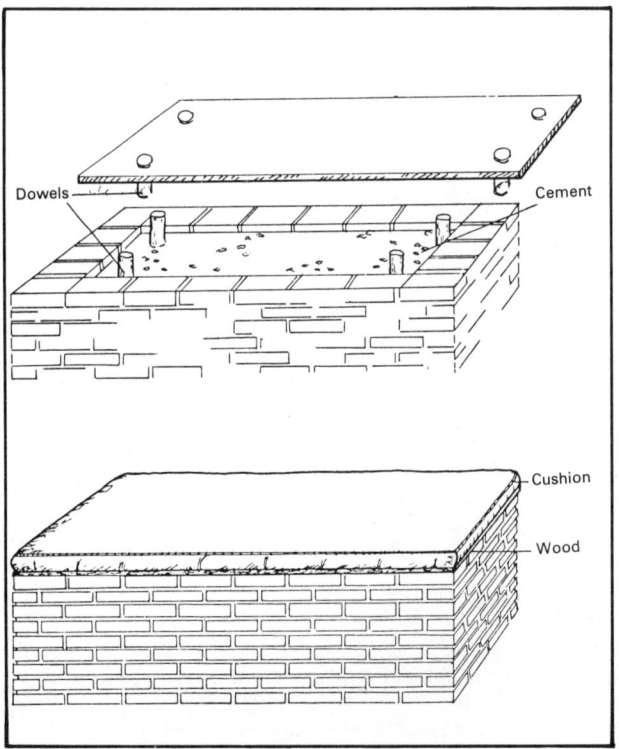

A bench of patio blocks takes a cushion for added comfort.

Redwood, a highly popular material for oudoor lighting fixtures, has been used in these three models from an extensive line by Victor Mfg. Co., Inc. The garden lamp (top) provides four-sided illumination to foilage and walkway while the wall lantern (above) produces a pleasant combination of wood, brick and plastic. The walkway lamp (right) has a 12-ft. total height with a 2-ft. embedment in concrete. Cross-arms may be used for single or double lamps.

7. Outdoor Lighting

While often taken much for granted, outdoor lighting should provide safety, security and decorative functions. Proper lighting can make a home as attractive and useful at night as it is in the bright sunlight.

In appraising successful night-time exterior home illumination, it's well to understand the basic elements involved. Among these are:

- kind of lighting—permanent, portable or both;
- types of lighting—flood, spot or other;
- place of installation for best possible "task" purpose and beauty;
- types of fixtures and bulbs including color bulbs, mercury lamps, reflectors, and wiring controls.

The popularity of outdoor residential lighting probably received its biggest boost with the introduction of the post-World War II picture windows, which builders installed by the thousands to "open" American homes to the beauty possible with decorative landscaping. This was soon followed by the sliding glass door, which virtually opened up whole walls of a home, expanding living space from indoors to out with the opening of a door.

Today, the higher value of land for residential use has placed a tremendous demand on using every available square foot for some form of modern living. No longer are grounds around a home considered merely a place for lawn and shrubs. Instead, the yard has become an integral part of the home, sometimes used as often as certain indoor rooms.

Codes and Safety

Lighting for home exteriors should be considered for walks, paths, steps, gardens, flower beds, trees, pools and fountains, sculpture, barbecuing and dining, outdoor work, sports and games, porches and terraces, and plain old-fashioned relaxation.

Noryl and Lexan plastic resins in the manufacture of this outdoor lamp fixture make the unit nearly unbreakable, and it will never rust or corrode. The Lexan resin provides a choice of clear or opalescent lens. (Manufacturer: Thomas Industries)

Adequate wiring is the first essential for full enjoyment of outdoor living after dark, as well as for safety. Underground wiring offers maximum safety and convenience, but frequently weatherproof cords are employed to satisfy temporary lighting needs. Most electrical codes will require that overhead wiring, if used, be at least 8 ft. above the ground and supported about every 15 ft. When wire is used at lower than 8 ft. heights, it must be protected by conduit.

The National Electrical Code specifies the use of USE or UF wire for direct burial underground use, and since 1975 has required "ground fault interrupter" devices on all 15-amp and 20-amp receptacle outlets installed outdoors or within 15 ft. of swimming pools. GFI protective devices constantly monitor the ground circuit, and when any small flow of current-leak (between 5 and 15 milli-amperes) is detected, the device interrupts the circuit, shutting it off. This doesn't prevent a person from getting an initial shock when coming in contact with the "leaking" outlet, but does reduce the shock and permits the person to free himself and thus avoid serious shock injury.

General Electric lighting engineers have devoted years to developing suggested lighting levels, fixture placement and specific installations for each outdoor location. Among their recommendations are the following.

Location and Activities

Entrances and Walkways

Wise selection and placement of entranceway lighting equipment depend upon these considerations: architectural suitability; minimum glare; and a light distribution for clear sight along walks and over steps, as well as quick recognition of callers by someone opening the door.

You will have a wide choice of exterior fixtures for post, wall, or ceiling mounting. In a given styling, they do not all serve equally well in their basic function of providing safe seeing. The best include some directional control of the light toward what's to be seen—the faces of callers at the doorway, the steps, the ground or walk leading to them. Etched glass, or an even more diffusing glass, is preferred over clear glass because it lessens bulb brightness.

Wattage of bulb varies with the size and transmission of its shielding glass; usually 40 to 60 watts for brackets, 60 to 75 watts for post lanterns; 75 to 120 watts in fixtures that are surface or flush mounted.

Where suitable, a pair of wall brackets, mounted 66 in. above the floor at both sides of the entranceway is preferred to one above the door. At side and rear doors, a single bracket may suffice, at the same height and on the keyhole side.

If steps are some distance from the door, additional equipment placed near them is essential. Lighted house numbers, visible from the street, are thoughtful courtesies. Numerals should be a minimum of 3 in. high with a half-inch stroke to be legible at 75 ft.

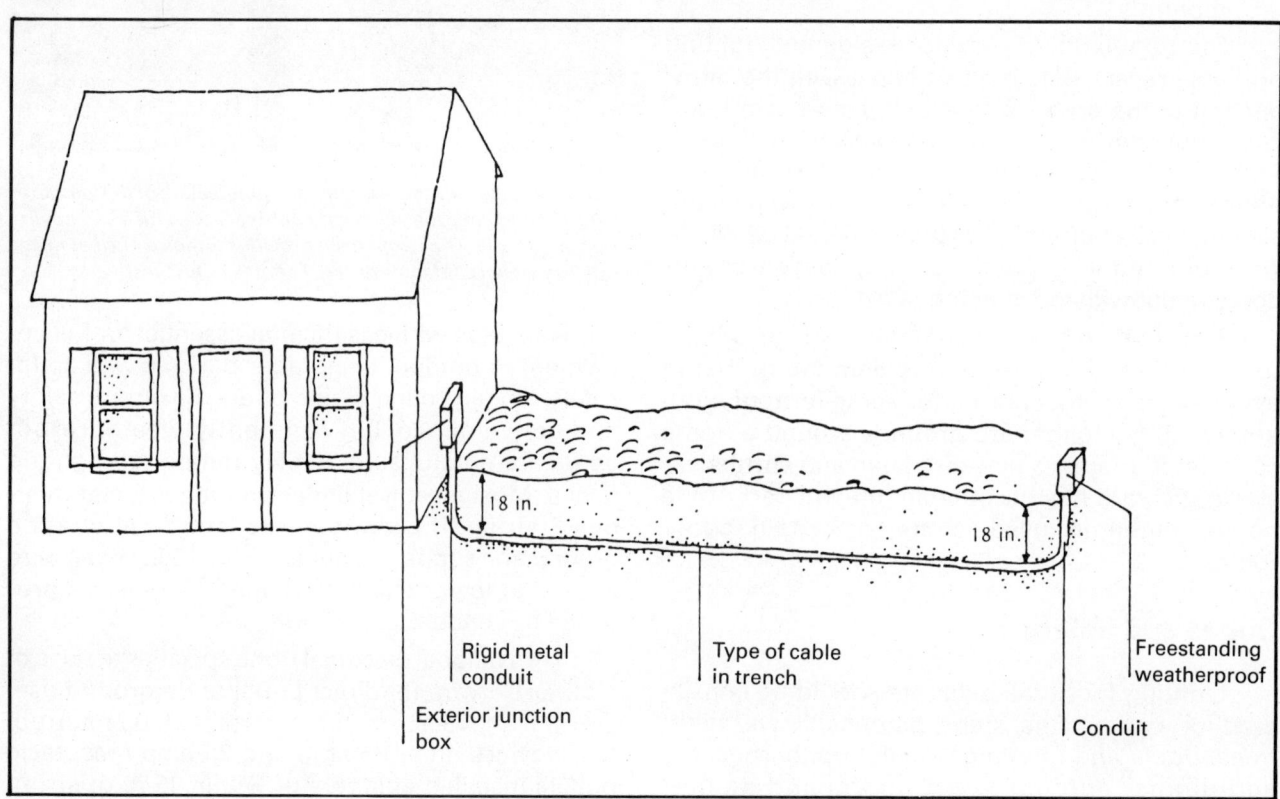

Use type UF cable for exterior 120-volt circuit.

Portable electric garden lamps fabricated from Tenite butyrate plastic provide the color, shape and simulated texture of a ginger leaf. Seen from the front, the fixtures screen out the light source. (Photo: Natur-A-Lite Co.)

As persons move away from the lighted house into and about the yard, their eyes gradually adapt to the darker surroundings. Then lower light levels (minimum ½ footcandle) are sufficient to guide steps safely, provided bright light sources are not in the line of view. Conventional post lanterns are thus not as desirable as lower units like "mushroom" units, which conceal the light source when mounted on posts.

On long broad driveways, post lanterns should be spaced about 25 ft. apart. On typical small house lots, PAR lamps attached to the house light the grounds well for safe circulation and for protection against intruders.

Steps and walks are usually lighted by one of these methods:
- mushroom-type reflectors, using 25- to 50-watt bulbs, and fixtures placed at the head of the steps and along paths, not more than 16 ft. apart;
- floodlights, 150-watt PAR bulbs, or enclosed floor lighting with 100- to 200-watt blubs, units placed 10 to 20 ft. above the area to be lighted, in tree or on building. Clamp-on shields or louvers will keep glare out of eyes;
- recessed lighting units, louvered or lens-type fixtures, for surface or recessed mounting, with 6- to 25-watt bulbs. These units should be placed on the stair riser, mounted to the side of steps, 16 to 24 inches above ground, recessed in building and not more than 8 ft. apart.

Terrace style lights designed to accommodate a small, 100A23 mercury lamp are excellent for lighting flowers and low plantings. Large scale white boulders were selected to enhance this setting. (Photo: General Electric)

Porches and Terraces

Activities on porches and terraces should be lighted to suit their varying demands on sight. Footcandle recommendations include: 5 on tables used for eating; 10 on tables used for armchair recreations like cards, games and the like; 20 to 40 at chairs for reading and sewing. Surrounding these seeing centers, and equally essential, is fill-in light of at least one-tenth the value, suited also to less sight-demanding pursuits like conversation and dancing. Lack of fill-in light can cause eye strain as the eye travels from well-lighted areas to those in darkness.

The selection and placement of lighting units to obtain these light levels depend upon structural design of the porch or terrace. Fully roofed, semi-enclosed porches may be lighted just as indoor living rooms for full usefulness. Light levels in keeping with those indoors should total 3 to 5 watts per square foot of porch area.

On more open but roofed porches and patios, indoor portables may be moved out for an evening's use, placed close within furniture groupings. Or light may be supplied from shielded or recessed downlights, or suspended units with openings placed with relation to chairs or tables. Open louver or beam overhangs allow this treatment, but when the terrace or patio is uncovered it must depend upon floodlighting equipment attached to adjacent buildings or trees.

Suggested placement of lighting fixtures for a closed porch or terrace includes: downlights over activity areas; brackets on the wall, reflecting upward light down from the terrace roof; and portable lamps for seeing tasks. Bulb selection includes 75-watt spot and flood downlights and 150-watt lamp bulbs, adequately shielded from eyes.

On the open terrace, wall brackets should have dome-type top reflectors to direct light downward toward the floor. These units should be secured on the building or other structure near the terrace. Portable lamps should be equipped with reflector tops which direct light on seeing tasks.

Cooking and Dining

Outdoor barbecuing and dining have become as popular as hamburgers and ice cream and certainly need not be confined to daylight hours. The amount of lighting required will vary according to location and proximity to fixtures installed for other lighting purposes (patio, game areas, etc.).

A pair of 150-watt PAR-38 floodlamps placed 12 to 20 ft. above ground, in a tree or on a pole or side of a building approximately 20 ft. from the cooking area, will provide ample illumination for the backyard chef.

For tables 8- to 12-ft. long, two units lamped with 60-watt bulbs, can be hung from ceiling, branches or overhang, 3 to 5 ft. above the table to provide adequate eating illumination. Lawn umbrella tables can be lighted with a 60- or 100-watt yellow lamp. The unit should be clamped to the pole with the top of the fixture located above the bottom edge of the umbrella. White or near-white umbrella lining gives the best reflection.

Outdoor Work

Suitable outdoor lighting allows you to do yard work, transplanting, and similar tasks after dark when it is cooler. Permanent lighting should be provided for areas in which chores are done regularly. Placed on the house, under an eave, or in a tree (at least 16 ft. above ground), permanent lighting should employ 150-watt PAR-38 floodlamps. Portable lighting, using the same lamps, is recommended for placement 3 to 6 ft. from the specific work area. Such placement will provide 100 footcandles.

Swimming Pools & Other Pools

Most in-ground swimming pools are built with underwater lighting for safe use at night. Beyond this, however, poolside lighting is highly desirable for both safety and added beauty.

Regular-voltage or low-voltage PAR floodlights are good choices for overall lighting, but if located around the pool cannot be closer than 5 feet, according to the National Electrical Code. For underwater lighting, 12-volt low-voltage lamps are recommended. These are available in 300- and 500-watt sizes. A ground-fault circuit interrupter insures electrical safety in either use.

For floodlighting the pool apron and surroundings, deep-shielded bullet-type fixtures are effective mounted 20 or less feet above the ground in trees, on poles or on fence tops. Rule-of-thumb for spacings between units is not more than twice the distance above ground—10 ft. apart, for example—at the top of a 5-ft.-high fence.

Safety requirements are described for underwater lighting in the National Electrical Code. Details of both wet-niche and dry-niche systems are fully explained. Dry-niche systems require that access be provided for relamping and servicing from outside the pool; the tops and lenses covering underwater lighting ports must be at least 18 in. below the normal water level to insure constant-and-uniform lens cooling. The underwater luminous density recommended by the Illuminating Engineering Society is 60 lumens per square foot of pool surface. Lamp spacings of 8 to 10 ft. are rec-

A lamp post for the yard or entryway can be constructed with this plan. (Art courtesy of Western Wood Products Assn.)

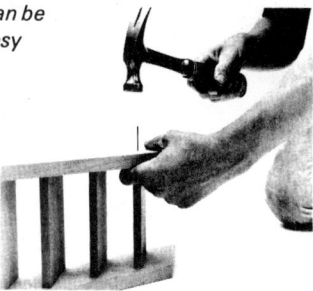

(1) Spacing lines are marked and louvers nailed to sides of four units.

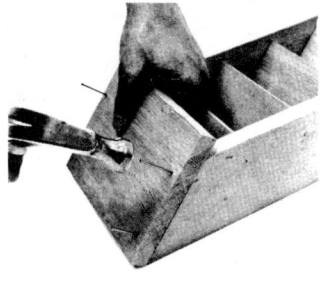

(2) Four nails are set in top pieces, then nailed to sides of louver units.

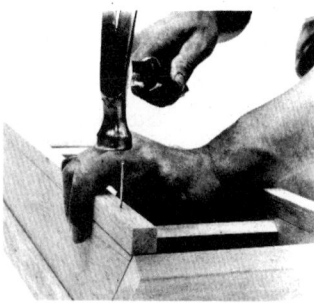

(3) Filler strips of 1x1s are nailed to inside edges of two louver units.

(4) Filler strips are used to secure units to each other, aligned carefully.

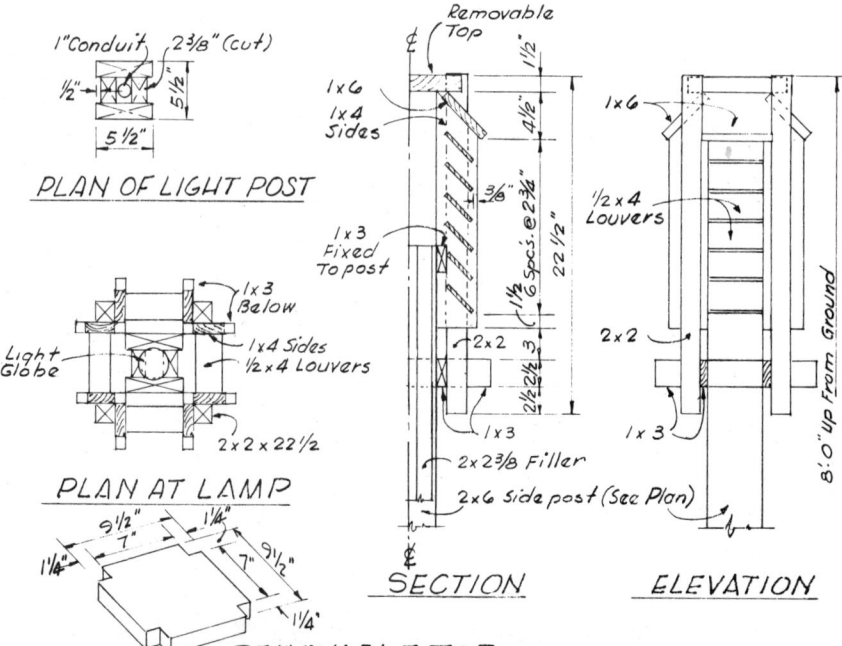

PLAN OF LIGHT POST

PLAN AT LAMP

REMOVABLE TOP
cut from 2x10

SECTION

ELEVATION

Materials List

2x6 2 pcs 8'
2x3 2 pcs 8'
2x2 1 pc 12'
1x3 1 pc 5'
½x4 2 pcs 7'
1x4 2 pcs 8'
1x1 1 pc 3'
2x10 1 pc 1'
3d & 5d nails
Wiring, fittings additional

Cut Sizes
(Same material as in list above)

2x6   2 pcs 8' post sides
2x2⅜ 2 pcs 8' post fillers
2x2   4 pcs 2'8"
1x3   2 pcs 1'4"
1x3   4 pcs 5½"
½x4   28 pcs 5½" louvers
1x4   8 pcs 22½" louver sides
1x1   4 pcs 22½"
1x6   4 pcs 7" tops of louvers
2x10 1 pc 9½" sq. top of lamp

(5) Placing fourth unit requires careful nailing to assure lamp fits over post.

(6) Lengths of 2x2s 22½″ long are toe-nailed into four corners formed by louver units.

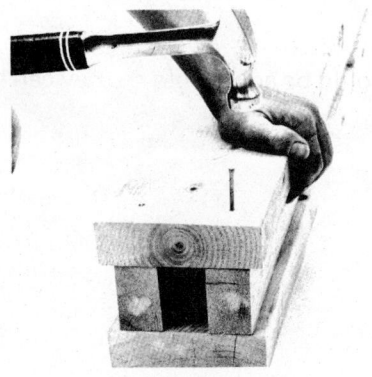

(7) Lamp post, fabricated from 2x6s and filler pieces cut to 2⅜″, holds wire conduit.

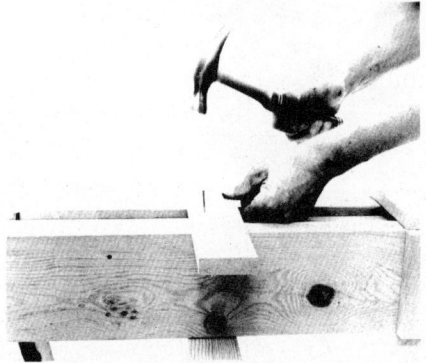

(8) Collar of 1x3s at top of post, 1x3 strips below help hold lamp assembly in place.

(9) Lamp assembly is slipped over top of post, 2x2s are toe-nailed to 1x3 strips.

(10) Removable top cut from 2x10, with corners notched, fits snugly into 2x2s.

ommended for uniformity of illumination, except that closer spacing is usually urged for added safety in deep-water areas.

Lighting sculpture and garden pools adds after-dark beauty to these exterior design elements. Floodlamps or 150-watt PAR-38 spot lights can be placed in trees, on a building, in front of or at the side of scultpure. For a shadow effect similar to daylight, aim lamps so that the light strikes sculpture from above, as sunlight does. If sculpture is wet or polished, place floodlamps so that light grazes surface; the result will be an interesting play of highlights.

Watertight sockets are required for lighting decorative pools. The sockets can be lamped with 15- or 25-watt bulbs, allowing 2 to 4 watts per sq. ft. of pool surface. Ornamental devices such as lily pads can be used to conceal lamps where natural shielding is not available. For best effect, place the fixtures under water in areas concealed by the pool ledge or plantings.

Jet pools require an underwater fixture at the base, aimed upwards and lamped with 15 to 25 watts per foot of jet height. Spray pools require an underwater unit at the base, aimed slightly below the nozzle angle. Use 4 watts per square foot of spray area.

Lighting Sports & Games

Lawn, net and target games can be enjoyed after dark with lighting that is easy to plan and install. Here again, buildings and trees are good locations for the fixtures, or telescopic poles may be used.

Lighting units should be mounted at least 16 to 20 ft. above ground to keep the light out of players' eyes. Lighting coming from several directions reduces shadows and provides a more uniform light.

For lawn games, three floodlamps should be located on poles located at each side of the center line of the game court, 16 to 20 ft. above the ground. The lamps should be adjustable so they can be aimed in different ways to fill the court with light. Identical lighting is excellent for net games.

Lighting equipment concealed among the foliage brings out the night beauty and colors of flowers. Weatherproof spot and floodlights are used to create shadows on the trees and shrubbery. Colored bulbs may be used if desired. (Photo: General Electric)

For target games, one spotlight and one flood-lamp on a telescopic pole should be located behind and to the side of the players. If the distance from the target exceeds 25 ft., use two spotlights and one floodlamp. A second pole, located behind the target with the floodlamp facing away from the players, will help in finding lost arrows or game pieces.

Gardens and Trees

Creation of a beautiful outdoor picture featuring trees, flowers, fences and other accessories, is largely a matter of individual artistry using the very controllable medium of electric light. The wattage of the light source, its brightness, its shape and color, allow tremendous latitude.

Outdoor lighting can flatten a form or provide its three dimensions. The overall design may be subdued, restful, stimulating or dramatic, depending upon your wishes.

Lighting engineers suggest you choose a focal point of interest and make this area 2 to 5 times brighter than other features you illuminate. Small areas or objects need more emphasis than large. When the brightness of large areas materially exceeds about 10 footcandles on white, a low level of overall flood lighting is needed to unify the effect.

The parts of a flower, a tree or shrub reflect different amounts of light, and these reflection capabilities should be taken into account in lighting. Those that are pale-tinted reflect most of the light (60 to 90 percent) and give the sensation of white or nearly so, because they are seen in contrast to soil, grass and foliage that reflect little light (50 to 20 percent).

For floodlighting of flowers, General Electric engineers recommend 150-watt PAR-38 flood-lamps, one lamp per 750 sq. ft. of area. An alternate is the enclosed floodlamp which should be calculated to provide two- or three-tenths watt per sq. ft. These types of fixtures and lamps should be 16 to 24 ft. above the ground and aimed at the area to be illuminated.

Open flower beds can be illuminated with mushroom-type reflectors, using 25 to 40 watt bulbs, 12 to 24 in. above the flowers. Each unit provides a 6- to 10-ft. circle of light.

The house or fence can be backlighted to silhouette flowers by using 150-watt PAR-38 flood-lamps, placed on the ground, 2 to 3 ft. from the base of the background, and 6 to 10 ft. between lighting units.

Beautiful trees often are the focal point of an illuminated outdoor setting. And, of course, the type of tree, its size, location and the effect you desire will help you to determine the lighting plan.

If you wish the tree to be a focal point, light it from two or three directions; this helps avoid a "flat" appearance. Use a spotlight on one featured area and floodlights from the other directions to emphasize shape. Lamps should be located 12 to 16 ft. above ground and 20 to 30 ft. away from the tree.

Trees may also be lighted from behind to provide attractive background viewing. This method is widely used for slender trees, with floodlamps on the ground 6 to 10 ft. apart, 3 to 6 ft. from the tree. The bulbs may be aimed at the lower or upper section for the desired effect.

A Kim "blueball" fixture is used here to light the mums, while a blue flourescent is located in the fence corner for background lighting. (Photo: General Electric)

Still another popular way of illuminating trees is to mount floodlamps either at the tree base or in the tree, above eye level. The lamps can be aimed either up into the tree or at lower foliage, to reflect light down from the foliage.

In total, lighting can be a very effective element of a successful home exterior, but is often given the least attention although it can add hours of usefulness and pleasure.

Weatherproof electrical outlets and low-voltage equipment can be mounted on an exterior wall or fence post for convenience, and then hidden from view by plantings such as this palm tree which shields arrangement from a patio setting. Note that the units have been kept 2 ft. above ground level. (Photo: General Electric)

PAR 36 spots in well-shielded fixtures usually are mounted on spikes, but here were modified by mounting on conduit to highlight the pine from two directions. The conduit attachment was selected so the lamps could be aimed down to avoid light being directed into anyone's eyes. (Photo: General Electric)

Long entry walkways can be handled in various ways to enhance the setting. Here medium-sized rocks and boulders complement the exposed concrete walkway. A partially open overhead permits interesting sun and light reflections. (Photo: Western Wood Products Assn.)

8. Walkways and Fences

Walks

Concrete has long been the basic construction material for walkways around the home, but this versatile, long-lasting material is just one of many materials you can use successfully for this purpose. Among others are: brick, redwood, loose aggregates, flagstones, tile, asphalt, adobe blocks, exposed aggregate, pebble mosaic, blocks and rounds, and other treatments.

When choosing home paving you must determine both traffic patterns and appearance, the latter also considering maintenance and durability. A good walkway should be one that is appreciated when seen but maintained simply by an occasional brooming or wash-down with the garden hose. Walkways that require frequent resurfacing should be avoided.

A bit of imagination in planning a walkway will remove the sterile approach so common in certain areas of the country, where a 4-ft.-wide straight run begins at the sidewalk perpendicular to the street and concludes at the front house steps.

Giving walkways a slight slope (away from the house) will provide necessary drainage, or drain tile can be placed in a narrow trench about a foot deep along the walkway, to more quickly disperse water.

Concrete

Concrete used for walkways is composed essentially of three materials—cement, water and aggregates. Sometimes a fourth material, an admixture, is added for a variety of specific purposes, such as acceleration or retardation of setting and hardening.

Standard portland cement is used for general concrete construction such as walkways. Local firms in many areas can provide U-haul, self-dumping trailers which permit you to pick up from 1 to 3 yards a trip. Or, you may prefer to have the entire amount you need delivered to the site by a ready-mix truck. If you live in a cold, snowy region be sure to specify air-entrained cement.

Use 2x4's for forming walkways, setting them on edge and securing them in place with regularly spaced stakes. Concrete walks normally can be placed directly on graded earth, but it's preferable to have a thin layer of sand, gravel or crushed stone between the earth and concrete.

Long or large walkways should be blocked off into smaller areas that can be completed one at a time. This will further provide the opportunity to install wood headers and create joints that help prevent concrete cracking due to expansion and contraction.

The best time to pour concrete is in the morning when it is cool before it becomes too hot. Excessive heat makes concrete set too quickly and places a great demand on the persons pouring it to complete the surface finishing.

A broom finish is perhaps the most desirable treatment for plain concrete; this surface provides better footing, especially for bare feet. With this in mind, some homeowners select exposed aggregate for its sure traction as well as added beauty.

Concrete can be colored before or after hardening. When wet, powered pigments are dusted on the surface and then worked into the mixture with a wood float. More experienced workmen mix the pigment dry with the cement and light aggregate, but this approach usually is beyond the amateur. Still another way is to let the concrete harden and then apply a pigmented wash or special paint to the surface.

A number of fast-drying epoxy materials are now available for easy concrete repair. These products are sold through building materials dealers and may be brushed or troweled over "clean" cracked or spalled areas.

Brick Walkways

Pattern variations can be almost endless when brick is used for walkways around the home. The weather-resistant units can be laid with or without mortar in straight lines or graceful curves, and should a brick be damaged at a later time, replacement is a simple matter of dropping a new unit in place.

Bricks are attractive when damp with rain, equally so when dry and baked in the sun. And with each passing year, bricks actually gain beauty naturally, without any maintenance cost whatsoever.

Few tools are required to lay a brick walkway: a spirit level, trowel, bricklayer's hammer and a bricklayer's set which is used to cut brick on an exact line. A single short rap on the set produces a weakness in the brick that enables it to be broken by one or two short blows with the hammer.

Preparation of surfaces for bricking follow the same methods detailed in Chapter 5. Layout can be accomplished with a strong string line held by several wood stakes.

Redwood Walkways

Several grades of redwood are highly suitable for constructing on-the-ground walkways, and several other grades should be avoided for this type of application. The top-of-the-line material (and most expensive) is Clear All Heart which is free of knots, and despite contact with the ground remains strong and durable. Every cell and fiber of this wood contains natural extractives which are repugnant to the appetites of decay-producing fungi and destructive insects such as termites.

Less expensive Select Heart and Construction Heart redwood, both garden grades, also are perfectly adequate for walkways but do have knots of limited sizes and other minor imperfections.

Sapwood-containing grades of redwood (Clear, Select, Construction Common, and Merchantable) are not recommended for use within six inches of the ground. These materials do not contain a sufficient amount of extractives to make them as resistant to insects and decay.

When used directly in contact with the earth, the first step in building a redwood walkway is to re-

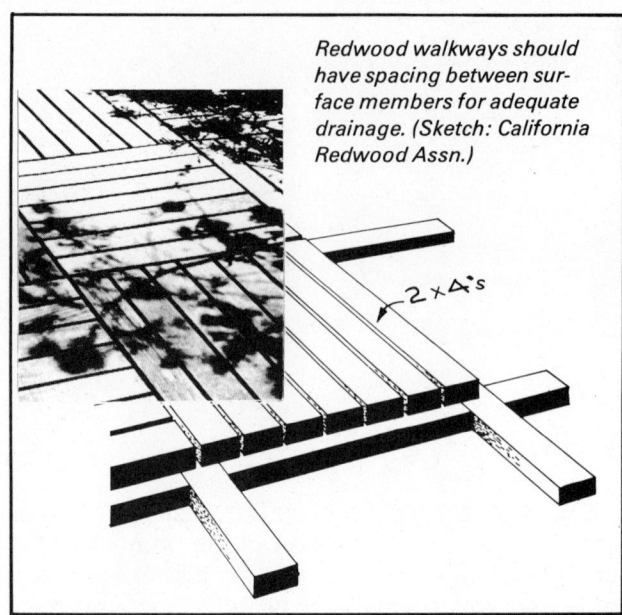

Redwood walkways should have spacing between surface members for adequate drainage. (Sketch: California Redwood Assn.)

move all vegetation from the soil and condition it with a chemical soil sterilant to prevent regrowth. On a nonpaved area, a 3-in. depth of sand or pea gravel will promote fast drainage and will help inhibit weed growth. However, a flat, tamped soil surface that drains well is a satsifactory base for laying a built-up redwood walkway.

Rough redwood or treated lumber can be used for the base of a redwood walkway, with finished lumber recommended for the top surface. Like patio paving, 2x4's may be laid flat or on edge as desired and secured with galvanized nails. If kiln-dried redwood is used, 2x4's may be spaced ⅛ to ¼ in. apart for drainage and foot comfort. If unseasoned redwood is used, shrinkage is compensated for by spacing the 2x4's 1/16 to ⅛ in. apart.

Loose Aggregate Walkways

Widely used for paving secondary areas (paths, service yards, etc.), loose aggregates such as gravel, tanbark, redrock, crushed brick and decomposed granite can add a welcome touch to the total home landscaping.

Gravel comes in a wide range of sizes and landscape gardeners will recommend you not purchase too fine or too coarse a grade. A ½-in. size generally is preferred over pea gravel as it will not be tracked into the house as easily.

Installation methods vary depending largely upon how long you intend to wish to have this type of walkway. If the need is temporary, simply lay

Patio Walkway Plan

Use two pieces 2-ft.x4-ft.x8-ft.-o-in. width thirty-six 8d galvanized nails. (Sketch: Koppers Co.)

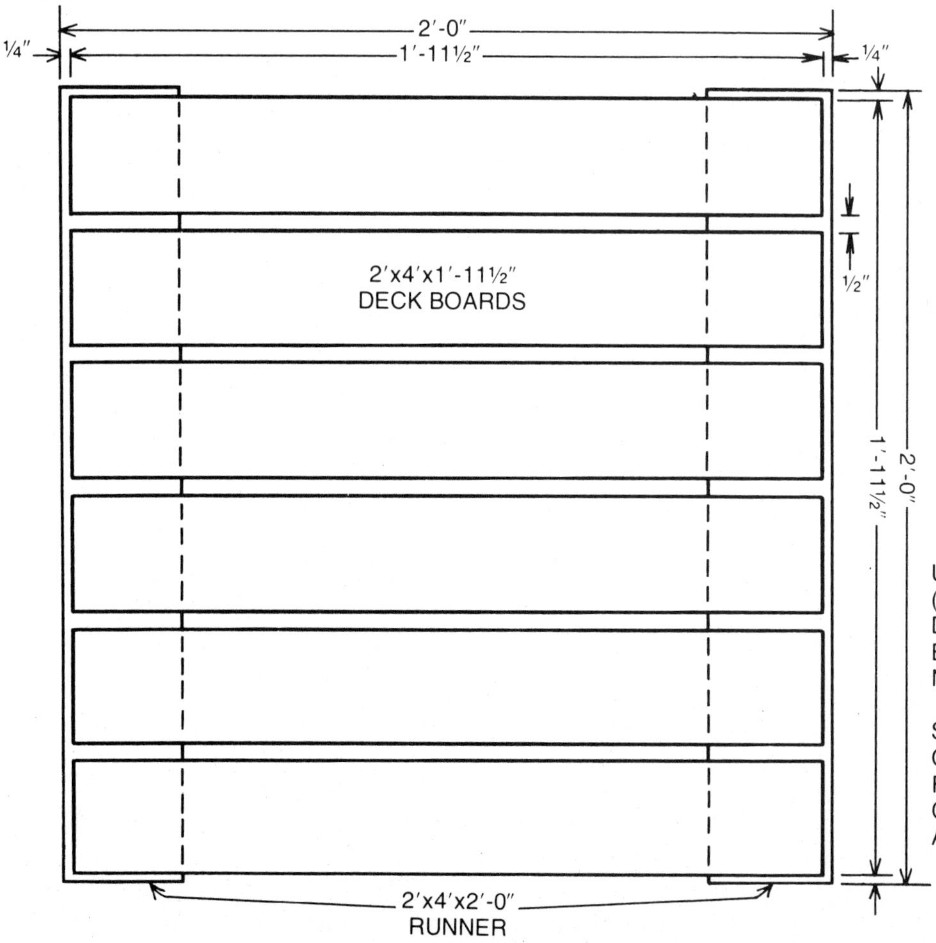

2'-0"

1'-11½"

¼" ¼"

2'x4'x1'-11½"
DECK BOARDS

½"

1'-11½"

2'-0"

USE 6 8d NAILS
(3 EACH END) TO ATTACH
DECK BOARDS TO
BOTTOM RUNNER —
NAIL FROM BOTTOM

SUGGESTED
CUTTING SCHEDULE
FROM EACH 2'x4'x8'-0"
CUT 3 pcs. 1'-11½"
AND 1 pc. 2'-0"

2'x4'x2'-0"
RUNNER

gravel about 1½ to 2 in. thick and roll it down into the earth surface. If the walkway is to be more permanent, use the gravel over a prepared base of redrock or decomposed granite. In either instance, be sure to use border strips—such as redwood or brick outline—that will keep the gravel where you want it and not allow it to be washed into the grass, patio and other non-gravel areas.

Asphalt Walkways

Asphalt, or blacktop as it is more commonly called, is serviceable for home walkways and in many areas still costs less than concrete or brick. A thickness of 1½ to 2 in. is most common for this application applied over a 4-in. thickness of ¾-in. base rock.

Asphalt is sold in two distinct types: hot-mix and cold-mix, with the latter type manufactured with a choice of three cutting stocks that determine the curing time, from rapid to medium to slow. The hot mix, used mostly by professionals, cures rapidly and is almost impossible to "work" at temperatures below 180°.

Hot mix is familiar to most motorists who have watched it being used for new stretches of roadway as well as for repair and patching projects. The material is mixed in a batch plant and trucked to the site, spread and then rolled or tamped into place. It dries quickly and then may be traveled upon. Cold mix, on the other hand, will stay workable for several days and then remains "tender" for a number of weeks, during which time footprints are easily made if the walkway is not fenced off to all traffic.

Asphalt contractors recommend homeowners attempting to lay their own blacktop walkways first prepare the surface by removing all weeds and applying a soil sterilant at the desired excavated depth. Header boards should then be installed on each side of the pathway, preferably of wood as brick may be chipped by heavy rollers used in the final smoothing process. Another suggestion offered is to apply a "pack coat" emulsion one-tenth of a gallon per square yard over the 4 in. of baserock. This provides excellent adhesion of the blacktop.

Most asphalt batching plants refrain from delivering blacktop directly to homeowners because they know the dumped material will dry hard before the owner can work it into place. Rather they suggest that the homeowner get a small vehicle to carry only as much as can be worked in a few hours and then go back for more.

Building supply dealers sell cold-mix blacktop in 1 cubic yard (and larger) sacks that have air-free plastic liners. This material is excellent for small patching jobs. The material requires no additives and is used directly from the bag.

All these pointers can be applied to resurfacing driveways as well.

Tile Walkways

Tile, like brick, can be used for walkways by installing it in sand or in mortar. This material usually is twice the price of brick or more, but used in key areas can be most effective in the overall home design. More often than not, it's installed by professionals equipped with a mason's diamond saw and other special tools.

There are several types of tile available for walkways including quarry tile and, of course, a wide range of colors, sizes and shapes.

Tile can be most easily installed over concrete etched with dilute muriatic acid wash or with a wire brush. The ceramic material also may be used on wood flooring if the walkway or steps are so constructed to handle the additional weight, approximately 20 pounds per sq. ft.

Flagstone Walkways

Flagstones, or stone slabs, can be inset in the lawn, in loose aggregate material, or cast in concrete with highly pleasing results. Each installation can reflect the designer's individual color, pattern and texture taste.

Slabs are available in rectangular or irregular shapes, usually of sandstone, slate or granite, in thicknesses ranging from ½ to 2 in. or more. A minimum 1 in. thickness is recommended for installations lacking a solid concrete base.

Pebble Mosaic Walkways

This ancient art has been used by many to create a rich accent area in the garden, at the entry gate or elsewhere around the home. The pattern selected is strictly up to the individual and the installation may be accomplished with clay mud or conventional mortar.

A base of up to 6 in. of gravel and an inch of sand is recommended when clay mud is used, similar to procedures used for centuries in Spain. Dry clay must be screened to a fine dust and then placed in a

This redwood-masonry combination fence forms a dramatic backdrop for a garden landscape. It sets an oriental mood and draws motif-support from bamboo plantings and statuary. (Photo: California Redwood Assn.)

layer to accept the stones in the desired arrangement. With the stones pressed firmly into this dust, small amounts of water are added and the mud allowed to dry.

Using a 1-part cement, 2-parts sand and water mortar, pebbles can be set in a thin bed atop an existing concrete surface. Wet the stones and press them into place by hand and then use a board to make certain the entire area is level.

Wood Blocks and Rounds

This type of outdoor walkway utilizes round discs cut straight through the trunk of a redwood, cypress or cedar tree, or blocks sawn off old railroad ties and set like brick. The wooden paving usually is set on a sand bed that has been dug out and smoothed. The wood requires a preservative treatment for longest possible life.

Fences

A fence can be as individual as a fingerprint, with as many variations as there are fence builders. Yet each fence constructed should enhance the landscape, ensure privacy, serve as a windbreak, provide a backdrop for outdoor activities, protect plants or small children, or perform some other specific function.

Aside from literally dozens of decorative masonry blocks available in most markets, today's fence can be constructed of redwood, a dozen other western woods, southern species and the common chain link materials.

In planning a new fence it is well to check with the local building department to see what restrictions may exist related to placement, height and materials used. Once you have this information, you

139

Wood baffle screens control air movement as well as providing privacy. These units direct foot traffic from the carport to the wooded rear yard. (Photo: Western Wood Products Assn.)

Contrasting redwood screens serve as privacy barriers when the owners of this home commune with nature during bath time. The private retreat also features minimum-care landscaping. (Photo: California Redwood Assn.)

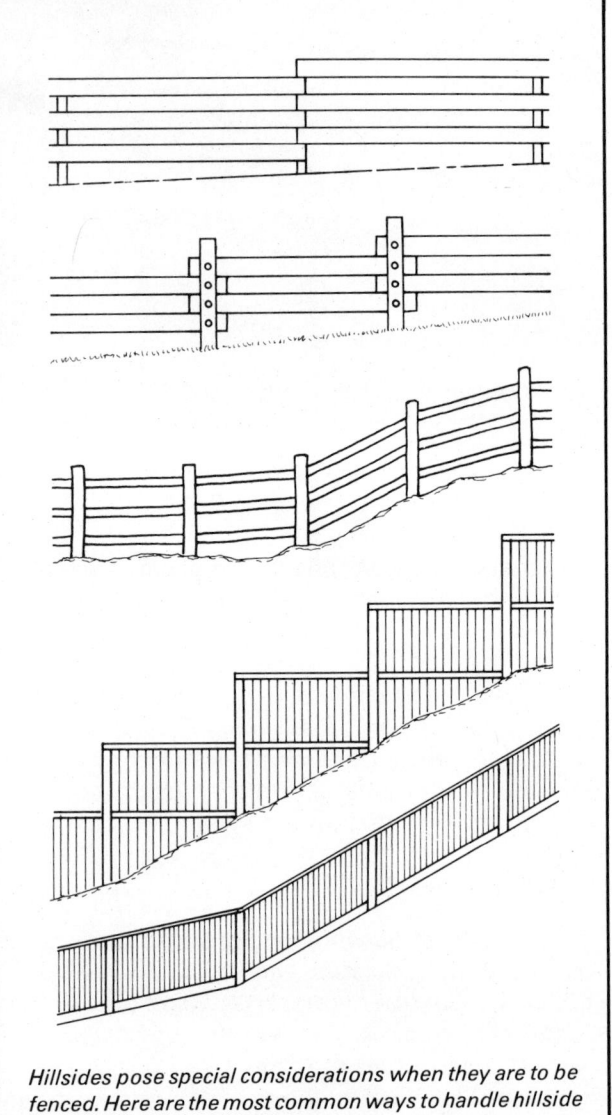

Hillsides pose special considerations when they are to be fenced. Here are the most common ways to handle hillside fencing. (Drawings: Koppers Co.)

then can determine the particular style that best meets your needs.

It's quite natural to consider the fence as a part of your investment in a home, and it will be so unless it fails to harmonize with the home's architecture, thus becoming a financial liability during resale.

Carefully consider the physical characteristics of your land. Is it steep or flat? Does it slope gradually? Is it terraced? Each of these characteristics calls for a different fence plan (see drawings showing various types).

Building a fence often is a task easily handled by the home handyman, or the job may be handled by a company specializing in this type of construction. Either way, all effort should be made to make the new structure as maintenance-free and long-lasting as possible through the selection of quality materials and use of accepted building practices. You really want to build a fence only once.

When you have your fence plan on paper, and have the necessary building permit from city hall, use stakes and a chalk line to lay out the exact course the fence will follow. True all corners with a carpenter's square.

The distance between fence posts will vary with the fence design, but a rule of thumb is that each post should be set with one-third its height under-

A stair-step fence is often the answer to hillside or other unusual terrain. Here 1x3 western pine boards have been spaced on 2x4 stringers and 4x4 posts to screen out the neighbor's gaze while still allowing light and air to filter through the hard border plants. The tallest sections ensure maximum patio privacy while the lower ones border a sunny garden. (Photo: Western Wood Products Assn.)

Choose a Fence to Suit Your Needs and Tastes

Here are the most common fence styles used to enhance today's homes. (Drawings: Koppers Co.)

Picket

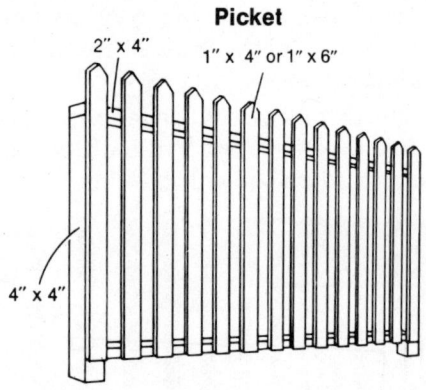

Board and Board

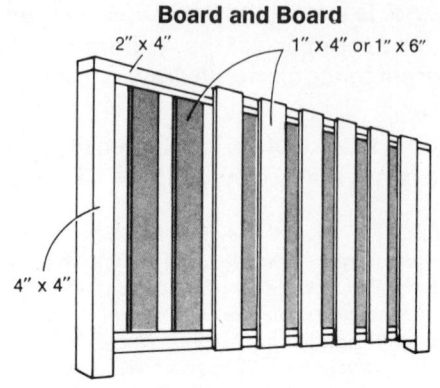

Post and Rail

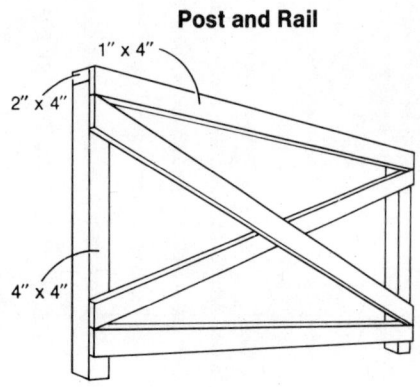

Alternate Widths

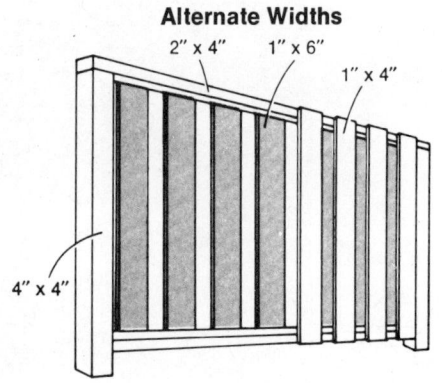

Basketweave

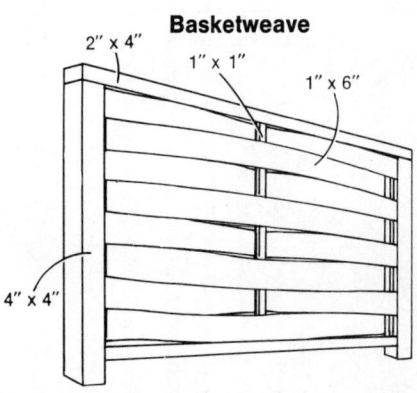

Louver

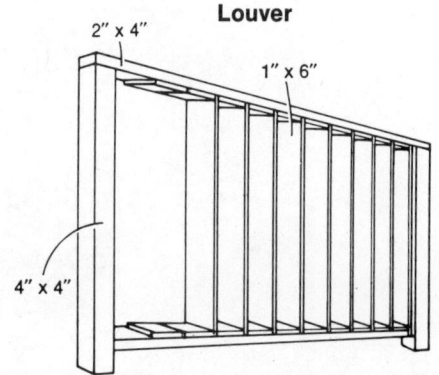

Alternate Louvers

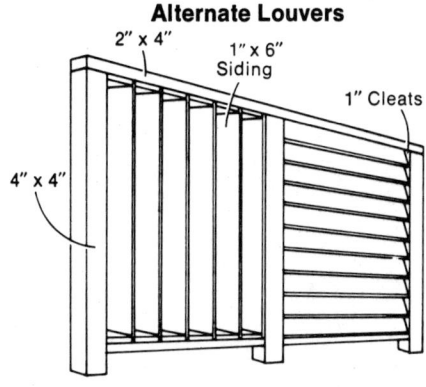

2" x 4"
1" x 6" Siding
1" Cleats
4" x 4"

Alternate Panels

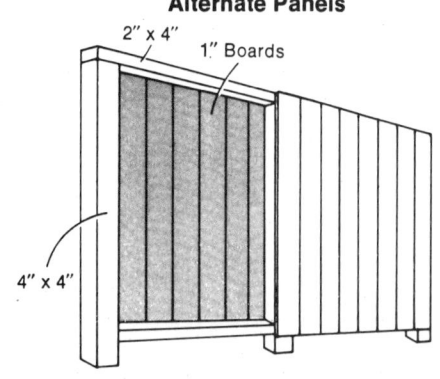

2" x 4"
1" Boards
4" x 4"

Channel Panel

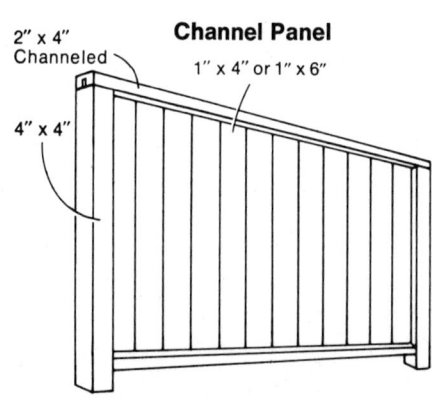

2" x 4" Channeled
1" x 4" or 1" x 6"
4" x 4"

Shaped Ends

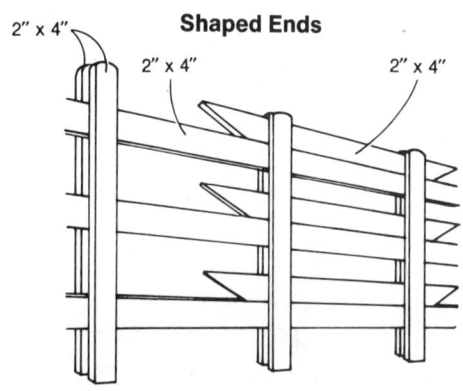

2" x 4"
2" x 4"
2" x 4"

Vertical and Horizontal Panels

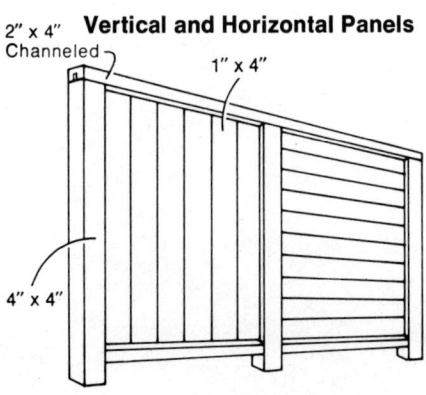

2" x 4" Channeled
1" x 4"
4" x 4"

Trellis

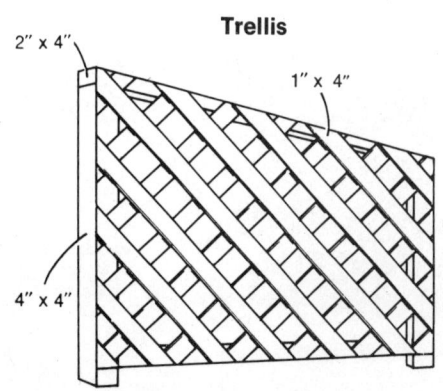

2" x 4"
1" x 4"
4" x 4"

ground. It's well to dig holes an extra 6 in. and fill in with gravel to facilitate drainage. If possible, fence posts should be peaked at the top to shed water.

Use of a level and straightedge held across the posts as they are being installed will help to achieve plumb position, which then should be secured with braceposts while the cement hardens. Koppers Co. has released data showing that pressure-treated wood in comparison with untreated wood will provide lifetime protection for wood used in ground contact applications. Their figures show that dip treatment of wood provides $1/10$ to $1/8$-in. penetration, which will give an average added life of 5 to 10 years. Brush application of the surface provides a slight penetration, giving 1 to 3 years added life to the wood.

In building wood fences, standard size posts 4x4's and boards (1x4, 1x6, 1x8) used with 2x4 rails or stringers simplify construction. Fences over 6 ft. high should has 4x6 posts and two-inch lumber.

With all posts securely in place, the next step in fence building is to add top and bottom rails, positioning the bottom rail by measuring from the top rail. Nails that are three times longer than wood thickness are recommended. Nails and other hardware should be aluminum, stainless or hot-dipped galvanized. Plain iron and steel should not be used as they will corrode, lose withdrawal resistance and cause unsightly stains.

This high fence of vertical 1x12 western pine boards, face nailed on alternate sides of 2x4 stringers, allows air circulation but blocks view of the swimming pool from the street. The solid gate features horizontal boards in an overlapping pattern. (Photo: Western Wood Products Assn.)

Fences, decks and benchs are perfect companions in American backyards. Here a partial screen helps to define the deck area while open-air-style fencing permits air passage and provides interesting shadow lines. (Photo: Western Wood Products Assn.)

Fence heights typically are referred to as "short" for 3 or 3½ ft. tall, and "high" for 5 and 6 ft. tall. Materials for both are "standard" at lumber and building materials yards.

Most fences require at least one gate, which generally is a square or rectangular frame, with a diagonal brace running from the top of the frame on the latch side down to the bottom corner opposite. Hardware should be sturdy and corrosion resistant. Gate posts should be 4x6's or 6x6's, and firmly planted. Gates should be a minimum 3 ft. wide, 1½ in. less than the space between gateposts. The bottom of the gate should clear any obstruction on the walk by ¾ in.

Gate Basics
2"x 4" Z frame
1" boards
Lag & Strap Hinge
4"x 4" posts
Hinge types
Butt
T
Lag and strap
Strap

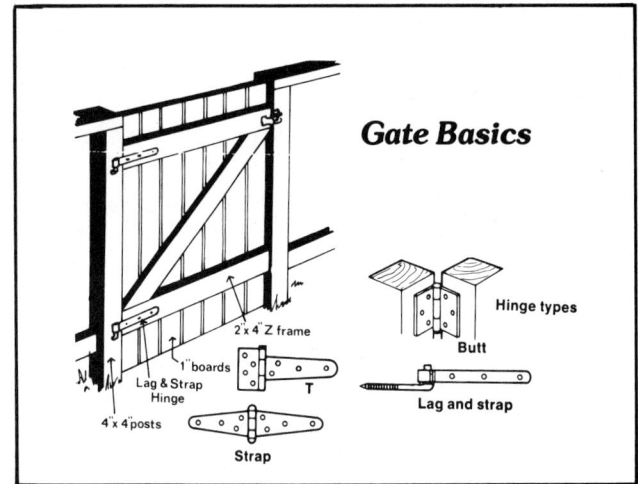

Shown here are the basics of gate building including four types of hinges that may be used successfully. Should you wish at times to completely remove the gate, use the lag-and-strap style hinge, which permits the gate to be easily lifted off without unscrewing the strap or hinge.

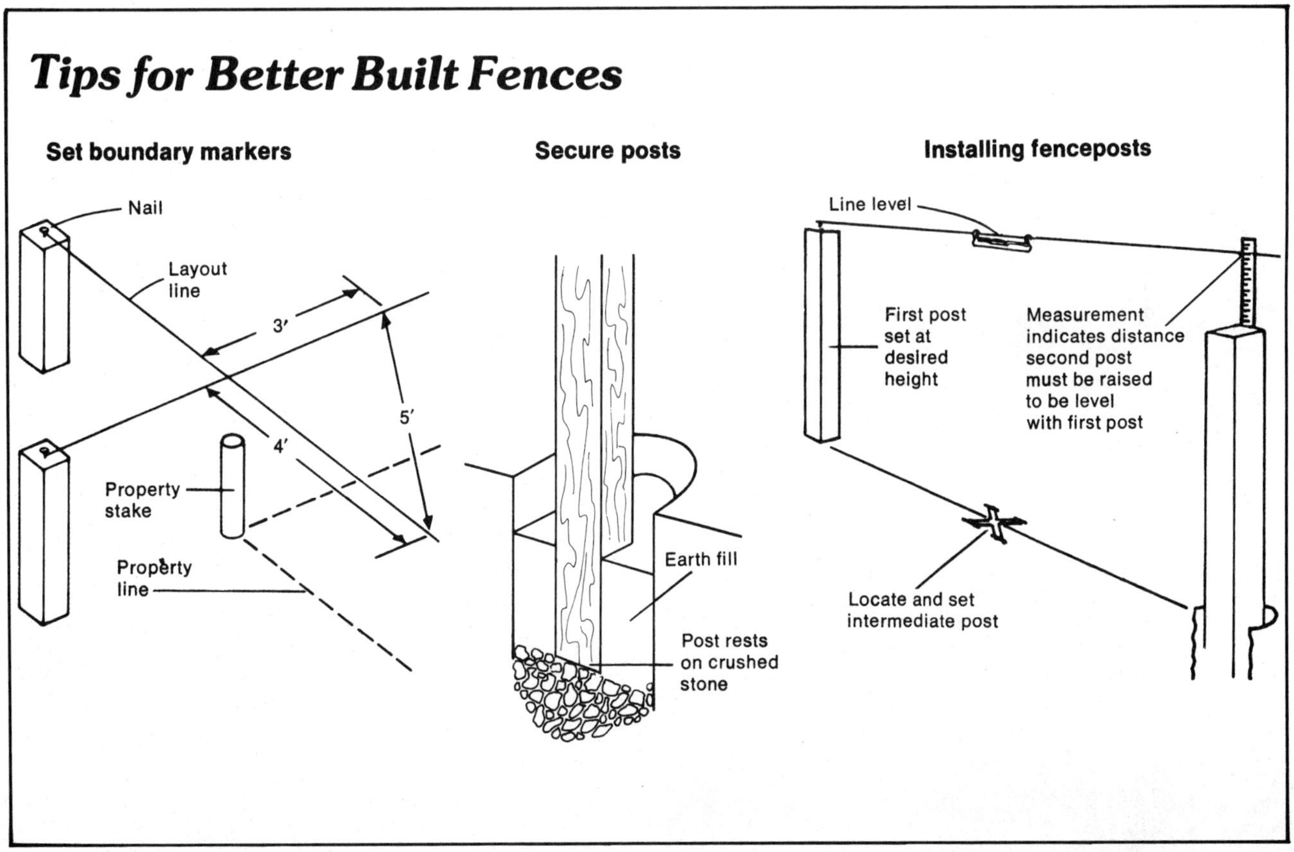

Tips for Better Built Fences
Set boundary markers
Nail
Layout line
3'
5'
4'
Property stake
Property line
Secure posts
Earth fill
Post rests on crushed stone
Installing fenceposts
Line level
First post set at desired height
Measurement indicates distance second post must be raised to be level with first post
Locate and set intermediate post

Here are a few construction details for simplifying fence building. (Drawings: Koppers Co.)

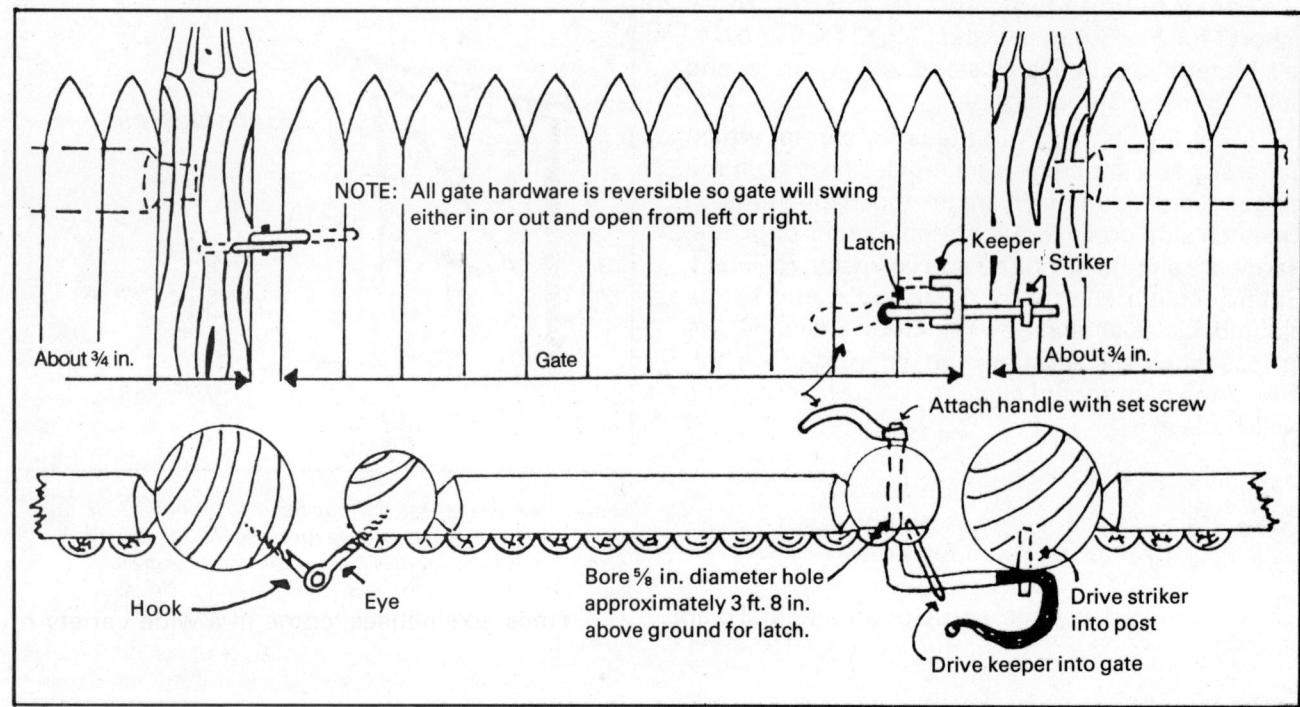

NOTE: All gate hardware is reversible so gate will swing either in or out and open from left or right.

Latch   Keeper   Striker

About ¾ in.   Gate   About ¾ in.

Attach handle with set screw

Hook   Eye

Bore ⅝ in. diameter hole approximately 3 ft. 8 in. above ground for latch.

Drive striker into post

Drive keeper into gate

Gate latch parts and how to install them.

Many home facades can be quickly and easily enhanced with the addition of a decorative screen. This one, built of 2x4 western wood, doubles as a trellis for roses. (Photo: Western Wood Products Assn.)

9. Trees and Shrubs

When landscaping a new or existing home, house orientation and location are two of the most important considerations. A highly successful design in one region of the country may be disastrous in another part of the country. What may be an attractive and healthy tree, shrub or ornamental plant on the south side of the home, may quickly die on the north side.

Basically, a house is a continual climatic regulator, with full sun and most intense radiation at the south, nearly perpetual shade at the north side, half shade to half sun to the west, and half shade with milder sun on the east.

In planning any landscaping program, your first step should be a visit to the local nursery to obtain basic information on the landscaping items that can be grown successfully in your climate. Your nurseryman can assist you in developing both an immediate and long-range plan that will enhance the outside of your home, not hinder it with misplaced, incorrect plantings.

Shade Trees

Energy conservation consciousness has prompted many homeowners to reappraise their landscaping and use the sun for more efficient living within the home. Trees and shrubs can be effectively placed to shade a home from the hot summer sun and protect it from the cold winter winds, often effecting a 20° temperature differential, or higher. A tree placed to shade the wall and roof in the afternoon will keep house temperatures more comfortable in the summer, but during the other seasons will not interfere when the warmth of the sun is desired.

Shade trees should be planted on the south and east sides of a home for the best cooling job. In colder climates, deciduous trees are recommended, as they will shed their leaves at the appropriate time and permit the winter sun to partially heat the home.

Selection

Trees, like houses, come in a wide variety of shapes the types which can be classified into large- and small-scale sizes. The larger oaks, elms, redwoods, ponderosa pines, sycamores, and others

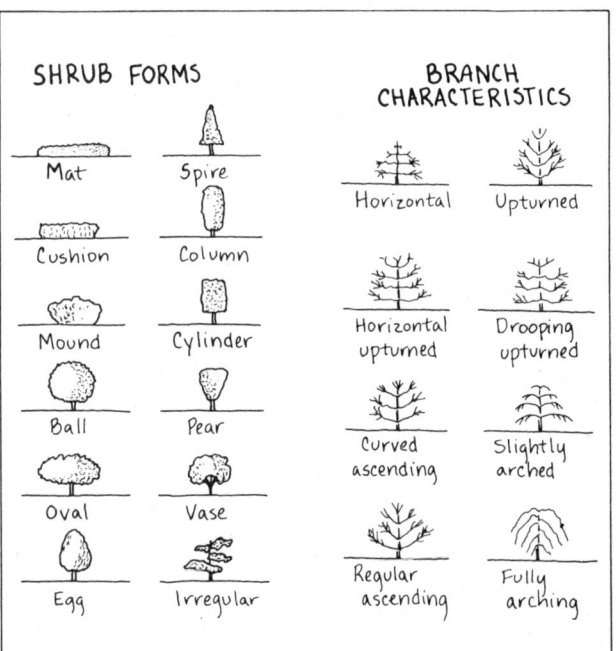

Shape and Branch Characteristics to seek in selecting landscaping shrubs. Other considerations: growth habits and degree of attention or maintenance required. HUD's Manual of Acceptable Practices suggests that initial sizes of new trees and shrubs should be sufficient for thier intended function and gives these specifics: 1½ to 2 inches caliper minimum for shade trees, a minimum of 4 to 6 feet height for evergreens, a minimum of 3 years growth for fast-growing shrubs and 5 years growth for slower ones. Often a few mature plants in a group will result in better appearance than a profushion of spread-out small ones.

Before

Tract-type homes frequently are sold without landscaping, and unfortunately many remain in this state for long periods of time. The difference is obvious in this before-and-after series, which illustrates the importance of landscaping as well as the added living area obtained with a deck or patio. (Photos: California Redwood Assn.)

After

may well be out of scale in a small lot, minimum-size home setting. It's here that the smaller-scale umbrellas, pyramidals and columnars are better suited.

Umbrella trees like weeping cherry, beech and birch are excellent for specimen plantings or for use where low-crowned trees are desired. Various crab-apple species, maples and redbud also fall into this category, with their lustrous foliage at a usual height of 20 ft. or less.

Pyramidal trees such as the Southern magnolia, American holly, white fir and Chanticleer pear grow in a way that appears "trimmed" at all times. They and other species of this type are excellent for use along streets or as components of any part of the home landscape. While the white fir is evergreen the year around, others, like the Chanticleer pear, display a different "coat" each season.

Columnars, or trees whose branches arise from the trunk at an acute angle, provide a tightly contained, narrow profile and make an excellent focal point for the yard. This tree style also is highly attractive along formal walks and drives, and may also be used to screen out utility poles. Some of the suggested species include Olmsted maple, Russian olive, Japanese maple, Sargent cherry, dogwood and Mayfield ginko.

Keep in mind that trees and shrubs in stiff rows serve a purpose only when they are planted for privacy.

Many homeowners, anxious to cut short the number of years required to produce their desired landscape plans, purchase trees grown nearly to full size. Costs range upwards from $150, but often the price is worth it. An older, stronger tree has its advantages particularly in areas of severe winds, where smaller trees are in danger of being bent over or ripped out.

The presence of a fine old tree on a home site should be treated as "money in the bank" in terms of a successful home exterior. Such trees should be carefully watered according to specific needs (shade trees with roots from one to five feet below the surface are best watered once a week with a good soaking) and fed periodically.

Pruning

All shade trees should be pruned peridocially to remove dead and injured branches. Trees should be pruned of unnecessary or unsightly branches to reduce the stress on the root system. Some of the lower limbs may be removed without lessening the shape and beauty of the tree, and the pruning of excess branches may enhance the appearance of an established tree which has not been properly pruned in the past.

Skilled pruning of especially large trees has several advantages:
(1) it can achieve the desired reduction of weight and wind resistance with minimum damage to the tree; (2) weight can be removed from weakened limbs while preserving the general outline of the tree crown; (3) the number of cuts is usually less and heal quickly, reducing the risk of decay; (4) resurgence of new growth is less vigorous and less concentrated, so you need not repeat the process as often.

Branch removal is recommended via a three-cut method. Cutting off branches with a single cut may cause damage which is avoidable. The weight of the branch as it falls must not be allowed to tear a strip of bark from the main trunk; this would seriously delay the healing of the cut. Stumps must not be left; they will not readily heal over. Water, insects and fungal spores may enter the exposed ends and rot will quickly set in.

When removing branches, make the first cut from the underside of the branch at a distance several inches or feet (depending upon thickness of the branch) from the trunk, sawing less than half way through the branch; make the second cut from the top side, several inches outward from the first cut; these two cuts will remove the branch at this further distance and permit you to make an easy, quick, clean third cut at the trunk. All "finish" cuts should be sealed with dressings incorporating a fungicide.

Shrubs

The variety of shrubs used throughout the United States seems almost endless. Some are evergreen, some treelike in size, some have seasonal blossoms, and still others bloom all year long. Broadleaved or needled evergreens are perhaps the most popular shrubs for they can be found in every part of the country.

Among the evergreen shrubs are Arborvitae, boxwood, holly, juniper, magnolia, rhododendron and yew. Nonflowing greens include dwarf huckleberry and winged euonymus.

Aside from an independent garden on the homesite, shrubs and flowers should be considered

Trees around a home exterior are most desirable; they need not be removed when constructing patios and decks. As shown here, interesting deck designs can incorporate young or old trees. In this instance the trees help shade a large glass expanse along one wall of the home. (Photo: Western Wood Products Assn.)

Seasonal flowers are easy to plant and maintain in garden redwood boxes which help establish both the decor and traffic pattern on this redwood deck. Natural landscaping along the bank helps to provide both a wind break and privacy. (Photo: California Redwood Assn.)

Desert-style plantings are easy to maintain in many areas of the country and add a uniqueness to the rustic-style home. Maintenance is low, often eliminating the need for a lawn mower completely. (Photo: Western Wood Products Assn.)

Gardens needn't be large to set a pleasant scene which may be viewed from inside the home. Here a decorative wood fence provides the backdrop for a simple planting, augmented by natural rock and sea shells. (Photo: Western Wood Products Assn.)

carefully for each purpose: foundation planting, border trim, hedge privacy or decorativeness, and ground cover.

For foundation plantings, know the maturity size of the plants and use them accordingly. For example, if the shrubs will mature to five feet, don't plant them closer than 2½-ft. from the foundation. Always think in terms of growth, not the size you are taking from a one or 5-gallon can. Azelea, Aucuba, Daphne and Pyracantha are widely used for foundation plantings.

Planting shrubs for hedges again depends upon the anticipated size and height. In general, hedge shrubs are placed one to three feet apart, the farther dimension taking preference for higher growing plants. The lower the desired height of the hedge, the closer the plants should be to one another. Among the most popular hedge shrubs are lilac, beauty bush, boxwood, yew, bridal wreath, English laurel, and privet.

Ground covers such as juniper, Irish heath, ivy, Nepeta and ajuja can add a decorative treatment to the landscape and at the same time help to prevent weeds from growing.

A general rule-of-thumb to follow in choosing shrubs is to select species that grow slowly and when established maintain their character without extensive pruning.

Vines

The old "vine-covered cottage" is still popular, and the use of vines in home landscaping certainly is far from confined to the cottage. Climbing vines need little ground space, have many uses (including screening and shading), and can provide beauty where no other plants can—on walls, fences, stanchions, trellises, or anywhere up in the air.

Some vines furnish fragrance as well as color, and here again, the secret of selection is to choose a vine that does well in your region of the country. Here are just a few selection by region:

- Central and East: Boston ivy, Bittersweet, Trumpet honeysuckle and Trumpet-vine;
- South-Southeast: Bougainvillaea, Passion-flower, Cinnamon-vine;
- Pacific Northwest: Bower actinidia, Fiveleaf akebia, Wisteria;
- California: Creeping fig, Star jasmine, Clematis, Bougainvillea;
- Texas-Southwest: Chinese trumpet-vine, Carolina-jessamine, Queens Wreath.

Planter Boxes

Planter boxes have done almost as much to stimulate the growth of home plants in recent years as soil itself. Frequently purchased at the local garden center or crafted with treated wood or redwood by the homeowner, today's planter box takes on many forms and sizes, and is much at home in the entryway as it is on the patio or deck.

Redwood heartwood grade is recommended by the California Redwood Association for building planter boxes, since this material can maintain direct contact with soil and periodic watering without decay. The material also resists shrinking, swelling, checking and cupping, and maintains a dimensional stability despite extreme variations of moisture and temperature.

Treated wood also is widely used for building planter boxes. Such ''Outdoor-brand'' or ''All-Weather'' wood also may be either stained or painted if desired.

Regardless of the design or wood selected, planter boxes should be assembled with stainless steel, aluminum alloy or top-quality, hot-dipped galvanized nails to prevent black streaks. And each planter box should have either drill holes or narrow spaces between the bottom boards for water drainage necessary to any planter.

Redwood heartwood's extractives can cause initial stains on concrete patios or walkways. To avoid this, the inside of the planter can be coated with a tar substance or lined with polyethylene film. A water repellent will discourage extractive staining, but allow two weeks before planting to let toxic agents become harmless. Another alternative suggested by the California Redwood Association is to set the new planter in a metal pan or similar container for the first two or three waterings to avoid stains.

Landscaping with boxes greatly expands the possibility of using plants in key places to enhance a setting. This three-foot-square box was constructed with 2x8 and 2x10 Douglas fir and lined with a 24-gauge metal pan to keep dirt and water within the box. (Photo: Western Wood Products Assn.)

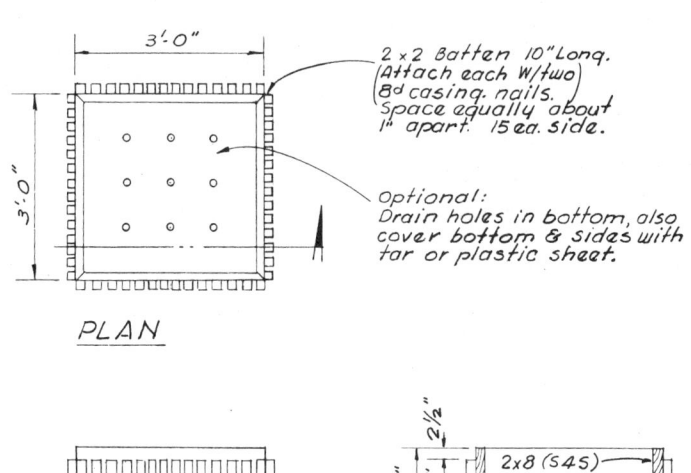

3'-0"

3'-0"

2 x 2 Batten 10" Long.
(Attach each w/two
8d casing nails.
Space equally about
1" apart. 15 ea. side.

Optional:
Drain holes in bottom, also
cover bottom & sides with
tar or plastic sheet.

PLAN

Floor of three-foot square planter is 2x6 t&g blind-nailed to 2x2 cleats.

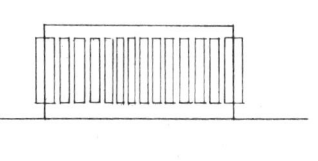

SIDE ELEV.

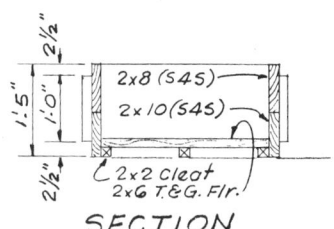

2½"

1'-5"

1'-0"

2½"

2x8 (S4S)

2x10 (S4S)

2x2 cleat
2x6 T.&G. Flr.

SECTION

Spacer guide simplifies nailing 2x2s that join 2x8, 2x10 sides of planter.

Mitered corners are joined with 8d nails; sides are nailed to floor.

After sides are joined, two 2x2s are added at each corner for finished look.

Materials List

2x10 1 pc 12'	2x2 1 pc 9'
2x8 1 pc 12'	2x2 6 pcs 10'
2x6 1 pc 12' t&g	8d & 16d galvanized nails
2x6 1 pc 8' t&g	

Western Wood species include Douglas Fir, Hem-Fir, Engelmann Spruce, Idaho White Pine, Lodgepole Pine, Sugar Pine, Ponderosa Pine, Western Larch, Western Cedar.

10. Choosing and Using Materials

Shopping for lumber and other construction materials calls for more awareness today than in all the years gone by. Prices on all building materials are higher, and that's a real incentive for careful buying.

Throughout this book are literally dozens of helpful hints and suggestions related to the application of the many building products and materials used outside the home. Aside from these considerations specifically tied to such major topics as roofing, siding, windows, doors, it's well to have a fundamental understanding of lumber, plywood, nails and other basic materials already in place, plus those you may require for upgrading the appearance of your home.

Lumber

Lumber, by far, is one of the most used exterior building materials you can expect to encounter. It's sold through local building material firms or lumber dealers in a wide range of species, grades and sizes. Each has its purpose and your dealer can be most helpful in recommending "what to buy for what" if you explain your project in sufficient detail.

Two basic keys to prevent overspending for lumber are: (1) buy the lowest grade and lowest-priced species that will do the job, and (2) buy the smallest amount possible, and that requires accurate measurement and assessment of needs.

Where lumber is to be used for framing and must bear loads in floors, roofs or the walls that carry them, it must meet varied minimums of strength. Building codes now cover almost all localities and the homeowner is expected to follow the same rules of safe construction as the professional builder.

Grade stamps on framing lumber are guides to its capabilities. They show the grade, species,

moisture content and identifying number of the producing mill. Grade names seem complex, but they can be sorted out. For wall framing, a grade called simply Stud has largely replaced Construction, Standard and Utility grades for studs.

The small portion of the old Utility category that does not qualify for Stud grade drops into Economy Stud, which is entirely adequate to frame storage, partitions, fences and the like—and is much lower in cost.

Floor joists and planks six inches and wider are graded Select Structural, #1, #2 and #3, and rafter and truss stock four inches and narrower may also carry these marks. The official span tables will show the grace and size needed for any structural use.

Another symbol on the grade stamps reads "S-*Dry*" or "S-*Grn*" to indicate whether the lumber was dry or green (unseasoned) when surfaced. Lumber S-GRN is surfaced to a larger net size to allow for shrinkage, because it dries during use.

Those familiar terms—2x4's, 2x6's, 4x4's, 1x8's—used to designate different sizes of lumber, are names rather than actual finished sizes. These "nominal" sizes are actually slightly larger than the actual dry lumber you will pull from bins at the retail yard. For example, a 2x4 is actually 1½ x 3½, and a 4x4 is 3½ x 3½.

In selecting wood for outdoor applications one must keep in mind its usage in relation to grade level, for it's widely accepted that termites are the most destructive insect enemies of wood. Untreated wood other than redwood, cedar and cypress used in the ground or closer than 6 in. above the ground, just invites decay-causing fungi, insects, marine organisms and weathering.

Redwood and Outdoor Wood

The beauty and durability of redwood are legendary and the United States Forest Products Labo-

154

ratory classes redwood heartwood among a limited number of American woods which, according to actual service records, are durable even when used under conditions that favor decay.

As early as 1776, the Franciscan missionaries on the Pacific Coast realized the natural durability of redwood and used it in the construction of buildings at Mission San José and San Francisco's Mission Dolores. After more than 150 years of service the posts and beams in these structures were found to be still sound.

What nature does for redwood, pressure-treatment with preservative chemicals does for many ordinary species of wood. These protective salts, forced deep into the wood under high pressure, provide a permanence that makes pine or other species last for decades—without impairing the natural beauty of the wood. This process for Wolmanized "Outdoor" and Osmose K-33 pressure-treated wood provides lasting protection against decay and insects.

Outdoor brand and K-33 pressure-treated wood can be embedded directly into the ground and are highly recommended for decks, fences, patios, balconies, trim, siding, sills, sleepers, pole structures and other outdoor applications.

Plywood

There is probably no building material as versatile as plywood, so called because it consists of flat panels built up of sheets of veneer called plies, united under pressure by adhesives to create panels with a bond between plies as strong as, or stronger than, the wood. Plywood is constructed with an odd number of layers, with grain of adjacent layers perpendicular.

Plywood is strong, rigid and lightweight, weighing far less than most metals, lumber or hardboard materials of equivalent strength. It has high impact resistance and does not split, chip, crack through, or crumble.

Textured plywood panels—with many different surfaces, patterns and species—are available in "exterior" type with a fully waterproof glueline for siding, fences, screens, soffits and other outdoor uses.

With each type of plywood there are several appearance grades determined by the grade of the veneer (A, B, C or D) used for the face and back of the panel. Panel grades are generally designated by type of glue (exterior and interior) and by veneer grade on the back and face. Here again, it will pay to explain specifically to your retail lumber dealer how and where you intend to use the plywood you are purchasing. He can see that you get the correct type of plywood for the application.

Nails

On any construction job or remodeling project, the cost of nails used is so small, compared with their importance, that they should always be of the best quality. Sizes (lengths) are indicated by "penny" abbreviated as "d" (as in 8d). Length of all nails will be the same in a particular penny size, regardless of head or shank configuration. Only the diameter changes. Use nonstaining siding or casing nails to prevent siding from discoloring due to nail weathering or rusting.

Common and box nails are for normal building construction, particularly framing. Smooth box nails of the same penny size will have a smaller diameter than common nails. Since the smaller diameter has less tendency to split the lumber, they are recommended for most uses. You also get more nails per pound (see chart).

Scaffold or "double-headed" nails can save you time and trouble in many applications where the fastener must later be removed—as in scaffolding, bracing, concrete forms, and temporary fastening during framing layout.

Casing and finishing nails are used where you do not want large nailheads visible, such as in exterior trim nailing and exterior siding application. To further reduce visibility, both may be driven deeper into the material with a nail-set and the holes filled with wood filler of matching color.

Nonstaining nails are necessary where exterior exposure is combined with need for good appearance; for example, in siding, fascias, soffits, exterior trim, and wood decks. Galvanizing is the most common nail coating, and offers good protection against staining. Nails also are made of metals or alloys not subject to corrosion, including aluminum, bronze, and stainless steel.

A variety of deformed-shank patterns such as screw shank, ring shank, and barbed are available. These all have greater holding power than smooth nails. Often, you may use a smaller size deformed-shank nail and still do the job satisfactorily.

Interior & Other Nails

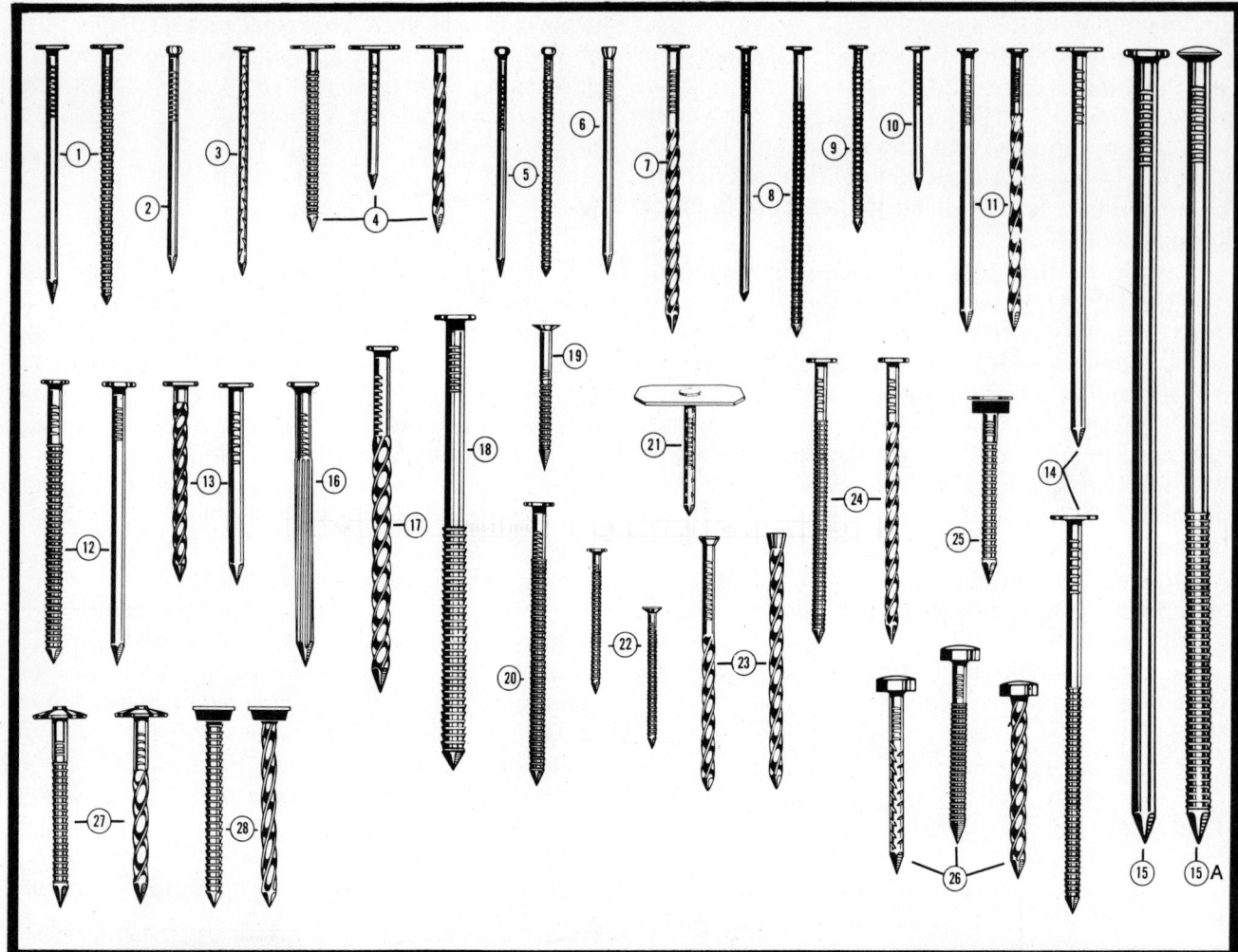

STORMGUARD® NAILS
FOR EXTERIOR APPLICATIONS
(Hot-dipped zinc-coated twice in molten zinc)

1. Wood Siding, Box (Plain & Anchor)
2. Finishing
3. Insulating, Plastic Siding
4. Asphalt Shingle (Anchor, Plain & Screw)
5. Cedar Shake (Plain & Anchor)
6. Casing
7. Cribber
8. "Split-Less" Wood Siding (Plain & Anchor)
9. Asbestos
10. Cedar Shingle
11. Hardboard Siding (Plain & Screw)
12. Common (Anchor & Plain)
13. Aluminum, Steel & Vinyl Siding (Screw & Plain)
14. Insulation Roof Deck (Plain & Anchor)
15. Gutter Spike (Plain)
15A. Gutter Spike (Anchor)

INTERIOR & OTHER NAILS

16. Masonry
17. Pole Barn, Truss Rafter (Screw)
18. Pole Barn (Anchor)
19. Drywall, GWB-54 Style
20. Underlayment, Plywood (Sub-floor, sheathing, etc.)
21. "Square-Cap" Roofing
22. Underlayment (Flat Head & Countersunk)
23. Spiral Flooring (Casing Head & Countersunk)
24. Pallet (Anchor & Screw)

Drawings: Maze Nails

METAL ROOFING NAILS

25. Rubber Washer (Stormguard, Anchor)
26. Compressed Lead Head (Barbed, Anchor & Screw)
27. Umbrella Head (Stormguard, Anchor & Screw)
28. Lead Washer (Stormguard, Anchor & Screw)

Penny-Wise Nail Lengths

2d	1″	12d	3¼″
3d	1¼″	16d	3½″
4d	1½″	20d	4″
5d	1¾″	30d	4½″
6d	2″	40d	5″
7d	2¼″	50d	5½″
8d	2½″	60d	6″
9d	2¾″	70d	7″
10d	3″	80d	8″

Roofing & Exterior Nails

FOR
EXTERIOR TRIM
GUTTER SPIKES

Ideal for both aluminum and galvanized gutters. Drive easily. Checkered heads. Come with flat or oval heads.

FLAT HEAD

PLAIN SHANK

ANCHOR-DOWN®

Stock Numbers		Length Inch	Gauge	Head	Count
Plain	Anchor				
T-362	T-362-A	6	3/16″	3/8″	24
T-364	T-364-A	7	3/16″	3/8″	17
T-365	T-365-A	8	3/16″	3/8″	15
T-366	T-366-A	8	1/4″	5/16″	8.5
T-368	T-368-A	9	1/4″	5/16″	8
T-369	T-369-A	10	1/4″	5/16″	7.5

GUTTER SPIKES OVAL HEAD

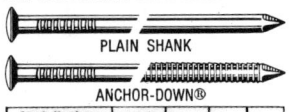

PLAIN SHANK

ANCHOR-DOWN®

Stock Numbers		Length Inch	Gauge	Head	Count
Plain	Anchor				
T-374	T-374-A	7	3/16″	3/8″	17
T-375	T-375-A	8	3/16″	3/8″	15

CASING NAILS

Designed for the secure application of window and door frames, corners and exterior molding. Eliminate need for countersinking and puttying.

PLAIN SHANK

Stock Numbers	Length Inch	Gauge	Head	Count
Plain				
T-305	2	12½	9½	212
T-307	2½	11½	8½	131
T-309	3	10	7½	85
T-3091	3½	10	7	67
T-3092	4	9	6	48

FINISHING NAILS

Designed for exterior trim applications. Brad head sets easily and insures neat, finished appearance.

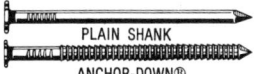

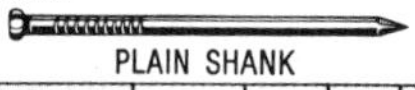

PLAIN SHANK

Stock Numbers	Length Inch	Gauge	Head	Count
Plain				
T-315	—	2	14	1/8″	310
T-317	—	2½	13	9/64″	196

COMMON NAILS

Designed for the secure application of roof dormers, louvers, steps, patio decks, etc.

PLAIN SHANK

ANCHOR-DOWN®

Stock Numbers		Length Inch	Gauge	Head	Count
Plain	Ring				
T-335	T-335-A	2	11	9/32″	137
T-337	T-337-A	2½	11	9/32″	111
T-339	T-339-A	3	10	9/32″	95
T-3391	T-3391-A	3½	9	5/16″	54
T-3392	T-3392-A	4	7	3/8″	33

FOR
ROOFING

ASPHALT SHINGLE NAILS

Designed for the secure application of asphalt shingles to solid wood sheathing, old roofing, decking and plywood. High holding anchor shanks recommended for decking and plywood applications. Large 7/16″ head provides ample hold down surface. Double-dipped in molten zinc. 11 gauge shanks.

PLAIN SHANK

ANCHOR-DOWN®

SCREW-DOWN®

Stock Numbers			Length Inch	Head	Count
Plain	Anchor	Screw			
R-100	R-100-A	R-100-S	7/8	7/16″	272
R-101	R-101-A	R-101-S	1	7/16″	250
R-102	R-102-A	R-102-S	1¼	7/16″	202
R-103	R-103-A	R-103-S	1½	7/16″	180
R-104	R-104-A	R-104-S	1¾	7/16″	156
R-105	R-105-A	R-105-S	2	7/16″	136
R-107	R-107-A	—	2½	7/16″	112

CEDAR SHINGLE NAILS

Specially designed for shingle applications. Slim shank minimizes splitting. Double-dipped in molten zinc. Meets Red Cedar Shingle Bureau specifications.

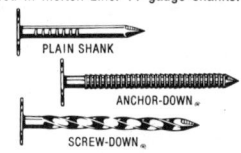

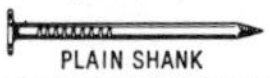

PLAIN SHANK

Stock Numbers	Length Inch	Gauge	Head	Count
Plain				
R-112	—	1¼	14	7/32″	515
R-113	—	1½	14	7/32″	392
R-114	—	1¾	14	7/32″	344
R-115	—	2	13	7/32″	232

INSULATION ROOF DECK NAILS
(And long Asphalt Shingle Nails)

Well suited to decking applications. Large head prevents pull through. Double-dipped in molten zinc.

PLAIN SHANK

ANCHOR-DOWN®

Stock Numbers		Length Inch	Gauge	Head	Count
Plain	Anchor				
R-159	R-159-A	3	10	3/8″	72
R-1591	R-1591-A	3½	10	3/8″	62
R-1592	R-1592-A	4	9	7/16″	46
R-1593	R-1593-A	4½	9	7/16″	40

UMBRELLA HEAD NAILS

Concave umbrella head caps nail hole. Threaded shanks provide greatly increased holding power. Double-dipped in molten zinc.

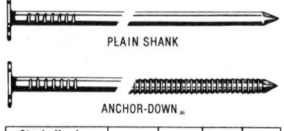

ANCHOR-DOWN®

SCREW-DOWN®

Stock Numbers		Length Inch	Gauge	Head	Count
Anchor	Screw				
R-133-A	R-133-S	1½	10	7/16″	125
R-134-A	R-134-S	1¾	10	7/16″	112
A-135-A	R-135-S	2	10	7/16″	99
R-137-A	R-137-S	2½	10	7/16″	73

RUBBER WASHER NAILS

Soft, flat washers provide fine seal and avoid sheet dimpling or denting. Checkered head enhances paint adhesion on color-matched nails. Sturdy anchor shanks hold tight. Double-dipped in molten zinc.

ANCHOR-DOWN®

Stock Numbers		Length Inch	Gauge	Head	Count
Anchor					
R-163-AF	—	1½	10	3/8″	126
R-164-AF	—	1¾	10	3/8″	111
R-165-AF	—	1	10	3/8″	100
R-167-AF	—	2½	10	3/8″	82
R-169-AF	—	3	10	3/8″	70
R-1691-AF	—	3½	10	3/8″	61
R-1692-AF	—	4	9	7/16″	45
R-1693-AF	—	4½	9	7/16″	39

LEAD WASHER NAILS

Everlasting lead washers are formed completely under the steel nail head to protect the washer when driving and to insure an excellent seal. Available with anchor shanks or screw shanks. Double-dipped in molten zinc after threading.

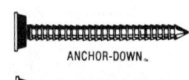

ANCHOR-DOWN®

SCREW-DOWN®

Stock Numbers		Length Inch	Gauge	Head	Count
Anchor	Screw				
R163-AL	R163-SL	1½″	10	3/8″	92
R164-AL	R164-SL	1¾″	10	3/8″	84
R165-AL	R165-SL	2″	10	3/8″	77
R167-AL	R167-SL	2½″	10	3/8″	68

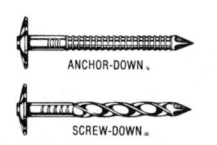

Siding Nails

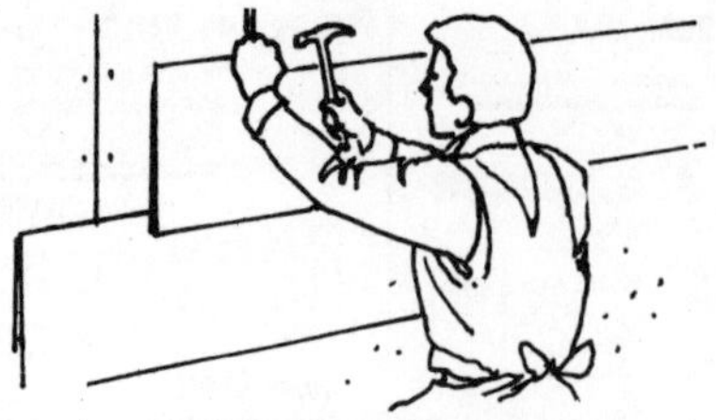

"SPLIT-LESS" WOOD SIDING NAILS

Specially designed for split-prone woods. Slim, sturdy shank and special blunt point virtually eliminate splits. Double-dipped in molten zinc. Checkered head enhances paint adhesion on color-matched nails. High count greatly reduces per nail cost. Recommended by many leading siding producers.

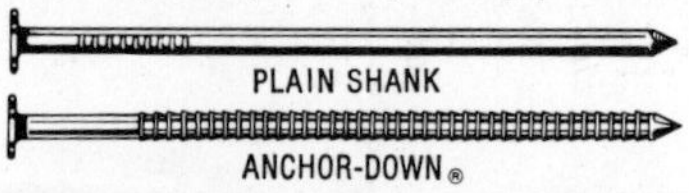
PLAIN SHANK
ANCHOR-DOWN®

Stock Numbers		Length			
Plain	Anchor	Inch	Gauge	Head	Count
S-225	S-225-A	2	14	3/16"	283
S-226	S-226-A	2 1/4	14	3/16"	248
S-227	S-227-A	2 1/2	13	7/32"	189
S-228	S-228-A	2 3/4	13	7/32"	171
S-229	S-229-A	3	13	7/32"	153
S-2291	— —	3 1/2	12	1/4"	104

WOOD SIDING BOX NAILS

Sturdy shank drives easily. Double-dipped in molten zinc. Checkered head enhances paint adhesion on color-matched nails. Type recommended by FHA for plywood sheathing.

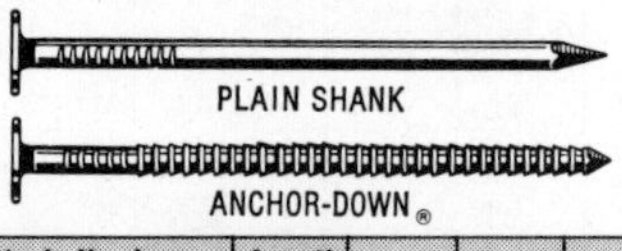
PLAIN SHANK
ANCHOR-DOWN®

Stock Numbers		Length			
Plain	Anchor	Inch	Gauge	Head	Count
S-203	S-203-A	1 1/2	14	7/32"	392
S-205	S-205-A	2	12 1/2	17/64"	194
S-206	S-206-A	2 1/4	12 1/2	17/64"	172
S-207	S-207-A	2 1/2	11 1/2	19/64"	123
S-209	S-209-A	3	11 1/2	19/64"	103

ASBESTOS SIDING NAILS

Designed for all makes of material and asbestos siding. Available in wide assortment of colors. Striated heads enhances paint adhesion. Double-dipped in molten zinc.

*For use with high density fiberboard sheathing.

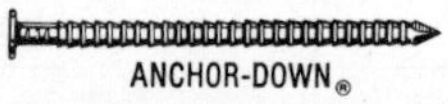
ANCHOR-DOWN®

Stock Numbers		Length			
Anchor		Inch	Gauge	Head	Count
S-211-A	— —	1	12 1/2	3/16"	387
S-212-A	— —	1 1/4	12 1/2	3/16"	324
*S-213-A	— —	1 7/16	12 1/2	3/16"	282
*S-214-A	— —	1 3/4	12 1/2	3/16"	224
*S-215-A	— —	2	12 1/2	3/16"	207
*S-217-A	— —	2 1/2	12 1/2	3/16"	169

HARDBOARD SIDING NAILS

Extra shift shank for easy driving. Self-seating head. Double-dipped in molten zinc. Recommended by leading hardboard producers.

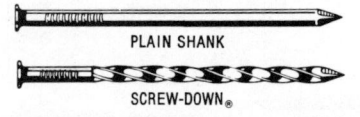

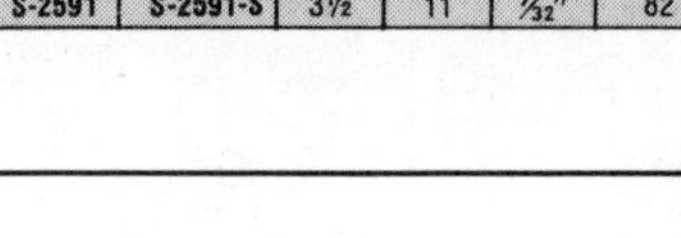
PLAIN SHANK
SCREW-DOWN®

Stock Numbers		Length			
Plain	Screw	Inch	Gauge	Head	Count
S-255	S-255-S	2	12	3/16"	181
S-257	S-257-S	2 1/2	12	3/16"	146
S-258	S-258-S	2 3/4	12	3/16"	136
S-259	S-259-S	3	11	7/32"	98
S-2591	S-2591-S	3 1/2	11	7/32"	82

NAILS FOR ALUMINUM, STEEL AND VINYL SIDING

Easy driving. Double-dipped zinc coating completely compatible with aluminum. Also ideal for application of steel, plastic and vinyl siding. Economical too—cost less per nail than aluminum.

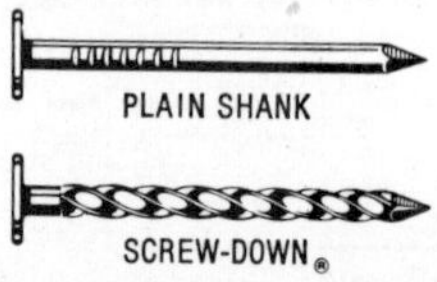
PLAIN SHANK
SCREW-DOWN®

Stock Numbers		Length			
Plain	Screw	Inch	Gauge	Head	Count
S-262	— —	1 1/4	12	5/16"	270
S-263	S-263-S	1 1/2	12	5/16"	228
S-265	S-265-S	2	12	5/16"	178
S-266	— —	2 1/4	12 1/2	17/64"	172
S-267	— —	2 1/2	11 1/2	19/64"	123
S-269	— —	3	11 1/2	19/64"	103

CEDAR SHAKE SIDING NAILS

Ideally suited to shake applications. Slim shank, blunt point, small checkered brad head. Double-dipped in molten zinc. Available painted. *HDF Nail—Type recommended over high density fiberboard sheathing.

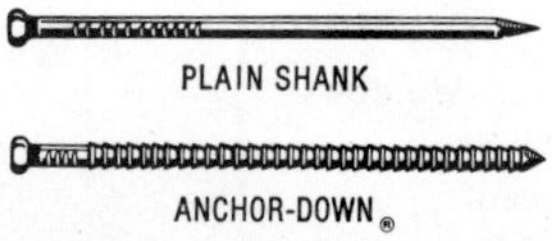
PLAIN SHANK
ANCHOR-DOWN®

Stock Numbers		Length			
Plain	Anchor	Inch	Gauge	Head	Count
S-233	S-233-A	1 1/2	14	1/8"	402
S-234	S-234-A	1 3/4	14	1/8"	346
S-235	S-235-A	2	14	1/8"	310
— —	*S-285-A	2	12 1/2	3/16"	209
S-237	S-237-A	2 1/2	13	9/64"	196

Paints & Finishes

Initial care of wood materials used for outside the home will pay long-range dividends in longer-lasting finishes and lower maintenance. Wood should never be stored for long periods of time in the sunlight or damp conditions. Finishes should be applied as soon as possible, limiting the time the raw wood is exposed to sunlight and wetting or drying. Given here are some finishing instructions for the most commonly used woods.

Redwood

Your choice of finish here can be based entirely on the appearance desired, and not primarily on any need to protect the wood.

The California Redwood Association recommends no finish or bleaches at all to maintain the natural finish of this material. Redwood left unfinished will undergo several natural color changes, depending upon climate and where the material has been used. It may turn to a soft, driftwood gray,

Exterior Paint and Other Finishes

Surface Types	FINISH TYPES	Oil or Oil-Alkyd Paint	Cement Powder Paint	Exterior Clear Finish	Aluminum Paint	Wood Stain	Roof Coating	Trim Paint	Porch & Deck Paint	Primer or Undercoater	Metal Prime	Latex House Paint	Water Repellent
Wood Surfaces													
Clapboard		X.			X					X		X.	
Natural Wood Siding & Trim				X		X							
Shutters & Other Trim		X.						X.		X		X.	
Wood Frame Windows		X.			X			X.		X		X.	
Wood Porch Floor									X				
Wood Shingle Roof						X							X
Metal Surfaces													
Aluminum Windows		X.			X			X.			X	X.	
Steel Windows		X.			X.			X.			X	X.	
Metal Roof		X.									X	X.	
Metal Siding		X.			X.			X.			X	X.	
Copper Surfaces				X									
Galvanized Surfaces		X.			X.			X.			X	X.	
Iron Surfaces		X.			X.			X.			X	X.	
Miscellaneous													
Asbestos Cement		X.								X		X	
Brick		X.	X		X					X		X	X
Cement & Cinder Block		X.	X		X					X		X	
Concrete/Masonry Porches And Floors									X			X	
Coal Tar Felt Roof							X						
Stucco	X.	X.	X		X					X		X	

• dot at right of X indicates a primer or sealer may be needed before finishing coat is applied
SOURCE: U.S. Department of Commerce

remain dark as first applied, or take on a silvery tan color.

The use of water repellents on redwood is highly recommended by CRA, if for no other reason than using the repellents allows the homeowner to change to any other finish at any time without major surface preparation. A water repellent such as Cuprinol #20, Woodlife or Pentaseal will not alter the rich, natural grain and texture of redwood. Wood so treated gradually changes from its reddish-brown color to a buckskin tan. Two coats are recommended for new wood.

Bleaches are another natural treatment possible according to the California Redwood Association. Next to leaving redwood unfinished, the bleaches come the closest to truly carefree performance. By reacting chemically with the wood, bleaches hasten redwood's natural color changes and produce a permanent driftwood gray appearance. One or two coats may be applied to new wood with brush or roller, following manufacturer's directions.

Pigmented stains also are often used to provide a finish between paint and the natural effects of a bleach or water repellent. Stains come in two basic types: light-bodied and heavy-bodied. The lighter material does not obscure the grain. Two coats of either are recommended.

Painting of redwood often requires more exacting procedures than finishing by other methods, and you are strongly urged to obtain a CRA data sheet on this subject from your local building material dealer, or by writing the Association and asking for its booklet "Painting Exterior Redwood".

Exterior redwood paints include both oil base (among these are alkyd resins and other synthetics) and the water emulsion types. Whichever kind is used, make certain it is specifically intended for use on exterior redwood.

One prime and two finish coats are recommended for finishing new redwood, and it's good practice to "follow the sun" when painting redwood so the sun's rays do not strike the surface during or immediately after painting.

Plywood

Finishing plywood can begin with a quick edge-sealing of all panels as they are in a stack. End gain surfaces pickup and lose moisture far more rapidly than side grain, thus edge-sealing will minimize possible moisture damage.

Where panels are not to be painted, such as tex-

tured siding finished with a stain, best performance is obtained by the liberal application of good water repellent preservative compatible with the finish to be applied later. Horizontal edges, particularly lower drip edges of siding, should be treated with special care because of their greater wetting exposure.

The American Plywood Association recommends the use of stains for textured plywood sidings, either high-quality oil base or latex emulsion, as these penetrate the wood surface and add formation of a continuous color film, to provide a durable breathing surface. Two coats provide greater depth of color and longer life. APA recommends use of a brush rather than roller or spray equipment.

Where masking of all substrate characteristics except texture is desired, oil or latex emulsion opaque or highly pigmented stains should be used. These stains will weather to a surface that is easily refinished without significant surface preparation.

Where paint must be used on textured plywood surfaces, or where it is applied to untextured plywood types, top quality acrylic latex exterior house paint systems are recommended by the American Plywood Association. A minimum two-coat paint system is essential for wood products, with the primer the more important always. Companion products, preferably made by the same manufacturer to be used together, are highly recommended.

Western & Other Woods

A wide variety of finishes are available to enhance the design potential of western and other wood species. Bleaches are used to gain a weathered appearance quickly. Paints and stains are used for overall effect or for accent in combination with natural wood. Water repellent treatment is used to retain the natural wood appearance.

New wood should be painted within two weeks after its installation. If weather does not permit this, it's advisable to brush a water-repellent preservative on siding, trim and into all joints for protection until you get several days of dry weather and can then paint.

The best time to paint is during dry, clear weather when temperatures are above 50° and below 95° Fahrenheit. The best hours for exterior painting are after the morning dew has evaporated.

The tendency of wood to expand and contract during changes in temperature and humidity makes it imperative that a good wood primer be applied to provide the necessary anchorage for the finish paint. Surfaces such as wood siding, porches, trim, shutters, sash, doors and window sills should be primed with an exterior primer intended for wood. Application should be by brush to thoroughly dry surfaces.

Painted wood usually does not need priming unless the old paint has cracked, blistered or peeled. Defective paint must be removed by scraping or wire brushing—prefereably down to the bare wood—and then primed. Scratches, dents, recesses and raw edges should be smoothed and then touched up with a suitable exterior primer.

All exterior surfaces, properly primed or previously painted, can be finished with either exterior oil paint or exterior latex paint, preferably applied with a brush.

Mildew, fungus, and mold growths on exterior surfaces are a problem in areas where high temperature and humidity are prevalent. In these areas it's helpful to use paint which contains agents to resist bacterial and mold growth. The manufacturer's label will state whether the paint contains such inhibitors.

Concrete

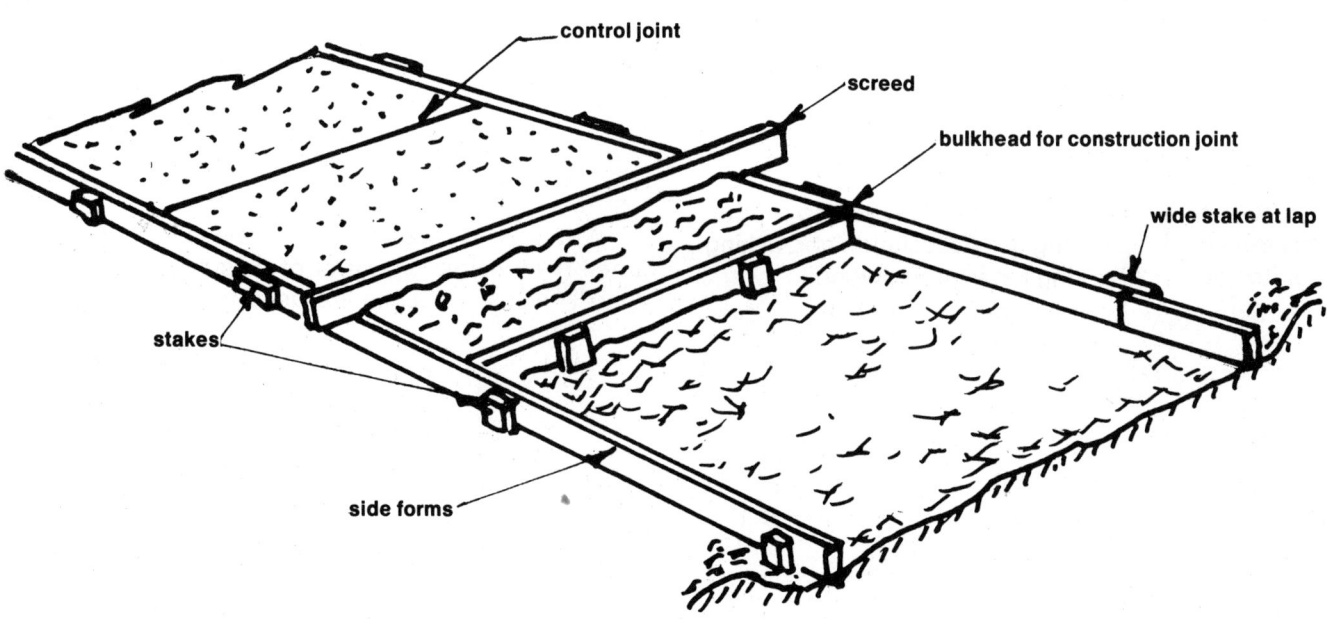

The screed or straightedge is worked back and forth to even off the concrete. The side forms should be staked securely. Use a wide stake where pieces of side forms are joined. When construction stops for the day, use a bulkhead to hold concrete; this can also function as a construction joint.

An engine-driven vibrator is shown here attached to 2-inch lumber to form a vibrating straightedge for positive control of the concrete strike-off operation. (Photo: Portland Cement Assn.)

Concrete is usually mixed in a truck on its way from the batch plant to the jobsite. The material can be placed directly from the truck, hauled in wheelbarrows or pumped through special hoses where vehicle access is impossible. (Photo: Portland Cement Assn.)

Hand trowels are used to smooth concrete steps, or the finished surface may be brushed lightly with a broom to provide a more skid-proof surface. (Photo: Portland Cement Assn.)

11. Outdoor Plans You Can Buy

The trend to outdoor living has never been greater. Reduced hours spent at one's occupation and the desire to enjoy one's entire home (most often there is more space surrounding the home than within it) has brought about countless do-it-yourself improvements outside the home.

Major manufacturers of basic building materials—wood, concrete, plastics—have employed nationally known designers and architects to create easy-to-build projects that will provide hours of pleasure, often the year-round. These projects are carefully planned to keep homeowner labor at a minimum with maximum satsifaction. The plans also are geared to readily available materials which may be obtained through local lumber and building material outlets.

Listed here are some specific plans which have been widely tested throughout the country. Still others are available from manufacturers listed in the following pages. Each firm welcomes homeowner inquiry and responds promptly to same.

BRICK PROJECTS: Illustrated instructions on using brickwork for a wide range of outdoor home improvement projects. Covers tools, materials and workmanship. Brick Institute of America.

CONCRETE PROJECTS: Eighteen home and yard projects are explained step-by-step, detailing the use of Sakrete concrete for such improvements as setting fence posts, building a patio, walkways, etc. Instructions cover working with brick, block and fieldstone. Sakrete.

ENTRANCE REMODELING: Complete instructions for step-by-step use of eleven ready-to-install door systems in traditional and modern styles. The doors feature tempered glass or may be ordered with insulating glass. General Products Co.

FENCES: Three popular types of fences—board, horizontal siding, and contemporary screen—are illustrated with construction plans, materials and tool checklist and other building data. Western Wood Products Assn., Dept. 515-P.

FENCES: Color illustrations show a wide variety of wood fences that can be constructed by the homeowner. Price 35¢. Western Wood Products Assn., Dept. 514-P.

GARDEN SHED: Plans for constructing a 4x8-ft., double-door shed for garden tools and lawn equipment using plywood panels for fast assembly. American Plywood Association.

OUTDOOR LIVING: Photos and drawings illustrate a folder detailing how to construct a planter, benches, post lamp, deck and firepit. Western Wood Products Assn., Dept. P-11.

OUTDOOR LIVING PROJECTS: Line drawings are used to illustrate complete construction plans for a sun trellis complex, entertainment gazebo, post lamp, and sun trap. Western Wood Products Assn., Dept. 539-P.

OUTDOOR PROJECTS: Detailed plans and materials lists for a wide range of projects including patios, fences, decks, overhangs, sheds, planters, furniture, and other redwood assemblies. Louisiana-Pacific.

OUTDOOR PROJECTS: Full-color plans book shows how to use pressure-treated wood for constructing such items as lamp post, benches, deck, fences, planters and other outdoor projects. Osmose.

OUTDOOR ROOMS: Plans for constructing several different outdoor rooms (including the one pictured on the cover of this book) are offered in a 12-page booklet. Among the specific plans detailed are fences, wood decks, portable deck lamp, wood sculpture, decorative screens, and step-down firepit. Western Wood Products Assn., Dept. 548-P.

OUTDOOR WOOD: Twenty-five projects that can be built with Outdoor Wood that has been pressure treated are contained in a 12-page folder. Included are retaining wall, fences, sun trellis, sun deck, 2-story gazebo, patio walkway, storage shed, play house, patio bar, and others. Koppers Co.

PATIO ROOFS: Step-by-step plans for building translucent plastic patio roofs, plus details on using plastic panels for fencing, home greenhouses and other structures. Price 25¢. Filon.

PATIO ROOFS: Four-step procedure for building a carport or patio roof with lightweight plastic panels. Reichold.

PATIOS: Color illustrations present a number of outdoor living ideas related to patio construction. Several plans relate to poolside improvements. Western Wood Products Assn., Dept. 523-P.

REDWOOD SHELTERS: Plans and basic tips for working with garden-grade redwood in the construction of redwood shelters for outdoor living. California Redwood Assn.

WOOD DECKS: Three do-it-yourself wood decks for improving home exteriors are described in detail and accompanied by complete plans for construction. A materials list is provided for each along with construction tips. Western Wood Products Assn., Dept. 513-P.

Manufacturers' Addresses

Abloy, Inc.,
6212 Oakton St.,
Morton Grove, IL 60053
(High-security locks)

Adams Rite Manufacturing Co.,
4040 South Capitol Ave.,
City of Industry, CA 91749
(Locks for sliding doors)

Alcan Building Products,
Jacobus Ave.,
South Kearny, NJ 07032

Alcoa,
1501 Alcoa Building,
Pittsburgh, PA 15219

Alside,
3773 Akron-Cleveland Rd.,
Akron, OH 44309

Andersen Corp.,
Bayport, MN 55003

American Plywood Assn.,
1119 A St.,
Tacoma, WA 98401

Automatic Doorman, Inc.,
166 Gould Ave.,
Paterson, NJ 07503

Benson Mfg. Corp.,
14700 West Commerce Dr.,
Menomonee Falls, WI 53051

Bird & Son, Inc.,
East Walpole, MA 02032

California Redwood Assn.,
617 Montgomery St.,
San Francisco, CA 94111

Certain-teed Products Corp.,
Box 860,
Valley Forge, PA 19842

Continental Customs,
Box 572,
Pleasanton, CA 94566

Eaton Security Products,
Box 25288,
Charlotte, NC 28212
(Locks)

Fichet, Inc.,
Box 767C,
Pasadena, CA 91105
(High-security locks)

Filon Div.,
Vistron Corp.,
12333 S. Van Ness Ave.,
Hawthorne, CA 90250

GAF Corp.,
140 W. 51st St.,
New York, NY 10020

General Electric Co.,
Nela Park,
Cleveland, OH 44112

Globe Amerada Glass Co.,
2001 Greenleaf Avenue,
Elk Grove Village, IL 60007
(Burglar-resistant glass)

Ilco Corporation,
35 Daniels Street,
Fitchburg, MA 01420
(Pushbutton locks)

Johns-Manville Sales Co.,
Greenwood Plaza,
Denver, CO 80217

Koppers Co., Inc.,
Koppers Building,
Pittsburgh, PA 15219

Lightcraft of California,
1600 W. Slauson Ave.,
Los Angeles, CA 90047

Louisiana-Pacific,
Box 6124,
Santa Rosa, CA 95401

M.A.G. Engineering and
Manufacturing, Inc.
13711 Alma Avenue,
Gardena, CA 90249
(Locks and lock-changing kits)

Masonite Corp.,
29 N. Wacker Dr.,
Chicago, IL 60605

Maze Nails,
400 Church St.,
Peru, IL 61354

Medeco Security Locks, Inc.,
Box 1075,
Salem, VA 24153
(Locks and cylinders)

National Forest Products Assn.,
1619 Massachusetts Ave. N.W.,
Washington, DC 20036

National Lock,
Rockford, IL 61101
(Locks)

National Paint & Coatings Assn.,
1500 Rhode Island Ave., N.W.,
Washington, DC 20005

National Woodwork
Manufacturers Assn.,
400 West Madison St.,
Chicago, IL 60606

Natur-A-Lite Co.,
3210 Vanowen Blvd.,
Burbank, CA

Osmose Wood Preserving
Co. of America, Inc.,
980 Ellicott St.,
Buffalo, NY 14209

Overhead Door Corporation,
Box 22285,
Dallas, TX 75222

Owens-Corning Fiberglas,
Fiberglas Tower,
Toledo, OH 43659

Pacific Clay Products,
2257 Green,
San Francisco, CA

Pease Co.,
Ever-Strait Div.,
7100 Dixie Highway,
Fairfield, OH 45023

Portland Cement Assn.,
Old Orchard Rd.,
Skokie, IL 60076

Red Cedar Shingle and
Handsplit Shake Bureau,
5510 White Bldg.,
Seattle, WA

Reichold Chemicals Inc.,
20800 Center Ridge Rd.,
Cleveland, OH 44116

Sakrete Inc.,
Fisher & B&O Railroad,
Cincinnati, OH 45217

Sargent & Greenleaf, Inc.,
1 Security Drive,
Nicholasville, KY 40356
(Locks)

Simpson Timber Co.,
900 Fourth Ave.,
Seattle, WA 98164

Structural Clay Products
Institute,
1750 Old Meadow Rd.,
McLean, VA 22101

Thomas Industries,
700 Oak St.,
Ft. Atkinson, WI 53538

Tile Council of America,
360 Lexington Ave.,
New York, NY 10017

3M Company,
3M Center,
St. Paul, MN 55101

U.S. Steel Corp.,
600 Grant St.,
Pittsburgh, PA 15230

Victor Mfg. Co., Inc.,
1045 Terminal Way,
San Carlos, CA 94070

Jim Walter Doors,
1500 N. Dale Mabry,
Tampa, FL 33607

Western Wood Products
Assn.,
Yeon Building,
Portland, OR 97204

Index

Other SUCCESSFUL Books

SUCCESSFUL SPACE SAVING AT HOME. The conquest of inner space in apartments, whether tiny or ample, and homes, inside and out. Storage and built-in possibilities for all living areas, with a special section of illustrated tips from the professional space planners. 8½"x11"; 128 pp; over 150 B-W and color photographs and illustrations. $12.00 Cloth. $4.95 Paper.

BOOK OF SUCCESSFUL HOME PLANS. Published in cooperation with Home Planners, Inc.; designs by Richard B. Pollman. A collection of 226 outstanding home plans, plus information on standards and clearances as outlined in HUD's *Manual of Acceptable Practices*. 8½"x11"; 192 pp; over 500 illustrations. $12.00 Cloth. $4.95 Paper.

HOW TO CUT YOU ENERGY BILLS, Derven and Nichols. A homeowner's guide designed not for just the fix-it person, but for everyone. Instructions on how to save money and fuel in all areas—lighting, appliances, insulation, caulking, and much more. If it's on your utility bill, you'll find it here. 8½"x11"; 136 pp; over 200 photographs and illustrations. $12.00 Cloth. $4.95 Paper.

FINDING & FIXING THE OLDER HOME, Schram. Tells how to check for tell-tale signs of damage when looking for homes and how to appraise and finance them. Points out the particular problems found in older homes, with instructions on how to remedy them. 8½"x11"; 160 pp; over 200 photographs and illustrations. $12.00 Cloth. $4.95 Paper.

WALL COVERINGS AND DECORATION, Banov. Describes and evaluates different types of papers, fabrics, foils and vinyls, and paneling. Chapters on art selection, principles of design and color. Complete installation instructions for all materials. 8½"x11"; 136 pp; over 150 B-W and color photographs and illustrations. $12.00 Cloth. $4.95 Paper.

BOOK OF SUCCESSFUL PAINTING, Banov. Everything about painting any surface, inside or outside. Includes surface preparation, paint selection and application, problems, and color in decorating. "Before dipping brush into paint, a few hours spent with this authoritative guide could head off disaster." —*Publishers Weekly.* 8½"x11"; 114 pp; over 150 B-W and color photographs and illustrations. $12.00 Cloth. $4.95 Paper.

BOOK OF SUCCESSFUL BATHROOMS, Schram. Complete guide to remodeling or decorating a bathroom to suit individual needs and tastes. Materials are recommended that have more than one function, need no periodic refinishing, and fit into different budgets. Complete installation instructions. 8½"x11"; 128 pp; over 200 B-W and color photographs. (Chosen by Interior Design, Woman's How-to, and Popular Science Book Clubs) $12.00 Cloth. $4.95 Paper.

TOTAL HOME PROTECTION, Miller. How to make your home burglarproof, fireproof, accidentproof, termiteproof, windproof, and lightningproof. With specific instructions and product recommendations. 8½"x11"; 124 pp; over 150 photographs and illustrations. (Chosen by McGraw-Hill's Architects Book Club) $12.00 Cloth. $4.95 Paper.

BOOK OF SUCCESSFUL SWIMMING POOLS, Derven and Nichols. Everything the present or would-be pool owner should know, from what kind of pool he can afford and site location, to construction, energy savings, accessories and maintenance and safety. 8½"x11"; over 250 B-W and color photographs and illustrations; 128 pp. $12.00 Cloth. $4.95 Paper.

HOW TO BUILD YOUR OWN HOME, Reschke. Construction methods and instructions for woodframe ranch, one-and-a-half story, two-story, and split level homes, with specific recommendations for materials and products. 8½"x11"; 336 pages; over 600 photographs, illustrations, and charts. (Main selection for McGraw-Hill's Engineers Book Club) $14.00 Cloth. $5.95 Paper.

SUCCESSFUL STUDIOS AND WORK CENTERS Davidson. How and where to set up work centers at home for the professional or amateur—for art projects, photography, sewing, woodworking, pottery and jewelry, or home office work. The author covers equipment, floor plans, basic light/plumbing/wiring requirements, and adds interviews with artists, photographers, and other professionals telling how they handled space and work problems. 8½"x11"; 144 pp; over 200 photographs and diagrams. $12.00 Cloth. $4.95 Paper.